A GUIDE TO THE

Historic Buildings

OF FREDERICKSBURG

AND GILLESPIE COUNTY

TAMX travel guides

A GUIDE TO THE

Historic Buildings

OF FREDERICKSBURG
AND GILLESPIE COUNTY

Kenneth Hafertepe

For Mark Nanley,

With best wishes,

Kenneth Hafertepe

TEXAS A&M UNIVERSITY PRESS | COLLEGE STATION

This paper meets the requirements
of ANSI/NISO Z39.48-1992
(Permanence of Paper).
Binding materials have been chosen for durability.
Manufactured in China by Everbest Printing Co.
through FCI Print Group

LIBRARY OF CONGRESS CATALOGING-IN-PUBLICATION DATA

Hafertepe, Kenneth, 1955– author.
    A guide to the historic buildings of Fredericksburg and Gillespie County /
Kenneth Hafertepe. — First edition.
        pages cm
    Includes bibliographical references and index.
    ISBN 978-1-62349-272-4 (flexbound with flaps: alk. paper) —
    ISBN 978-1-62349-273-1 (ebook)
    1. Fredericksburg (Tex.)—Buildings, structures, etc.—Guidebooks.
2. Historic buildings—Texas—Fredericksburg—Guidebooks.
3. Historic buildings—Texas—Gillespie County—Guidebooks. I. Title.
    F394.F9H34 2015
    976.4'65—dc23
                    2014037265

All illustrations by Kenneth Hafertepe unless otherwise note.

Contents

Preface

I have written this as a guide to the historic buildings of Fredericksburg and Gillespie County that are presently standing and visible from a public street or sidewalk. It is arranged geographically rather than by chronology or by building type because I want to maximize its usefulness for residents, visitors, and students of Texas architecture alike as they explore the heritage of this wonderful area.

I have attempted to include the great majority of buildings of the pioneer period, 1846 to roughly 1880, and many buildings from the Victorian era, 1880 to roughly 1914. Because I believe that more recent buildings can also be architecturally or historically significant, I have included important examples of buildings from 1914 to 1941. The buildings of the last several decades I will leave to future scholars. I have excluded a handful of buildings from inclusion because they are so poorly documented or so drastically altered.

The book starts in the very center of town, the Marktplatz and Courthouse Square, which were laid out as a single space in 1846. Here you will find discussions not only of historic buildings on these two squares but also those buildings facing them on all four sides. The next section proceeds from the Marktplatz and Courthouse Square east on Main Street, as far as the African Methodist Episcopal Church, which was on the margins of the nineteenth-century town. We then return to the center of town and go west on Main Street to Cherry Street, the original end of the town. We then consider the areas south of Main Street, then the areas north of Main Street. When a building on a north-south street is close to one of the east-west streets, I have placed it there, noting it as "Around the Corner on . . ." to save the visitor from doubling back. We will conclude with buildings in other parts of the county, starting with Highway 16 South and moving in a clockwise direction to include Cherry Spring, Doss, and Harper to the west, Crabapple and Willow Creek to the northeast, and Grape Creek, Luckenbach, Albert, and Stonewall on the southeast.

Fredericksburg was laid out not by the points of the compass, but between two creeks that run from the southeast to the northwest. As a result, the streets run in roughly the same direction. Despite this, street signs note whether a street is "north" or "south" of Main Street or "east" or "west" of the Marktplatz and Courthouse Square. To avoid confusion, I will follow the same system of orientation as the street signs.

I have made a conscious decision to exclude buildings that are not visible from the street or the sidewalk. I wish to emphasize that you, the reader, should respect the property rights of the owners of these buildings. Stay on the public right of way. *Do not trespass!* At the same time, there are some owners of buildings who need to hear that being the owner of a historic building comes with certain responsibilities. You possess a piece of Texas history; it is yours by ownership, but in a sense a historic property is something that every Texan should care about. *Treat it with respect!*

The good news is that several important buildings are now owned and maintained for your enjoyment by the Gillespie County Historical Society. You can thus visit the Kammlah house, the Fassel house, the Weber Sunday house, the Besier house, the Schandua house, and the replica of the Vereins-Kirche. You can look at these buildings up-close and personal and think about how they would have been used a century or more ago. Also in Fredericksburg is the excellent National Museum of the Pacific War, which is administered by the Texas Historical Commission.

Also open for your edification is the Lyndon B. Johnson National Park, the centerpiece of which is the LBJ Ranch. The main house has a long history, dating back to German pioneers in the 1890s. Nearby you can visit the Sauer-Beckmann Living History Farm, which features an original and quite intact log and rock house built in the years after the Civil War as well as a more modern German Texan house built during World War I, all restored and maintained by the Texas Department of Parks and Wildlife as part of the Lyndon B. Johnson State Park and Historic Site. In addition, many rural schools are being preserved by the efforts of the Friends of Gillespie County Country Schools, which has created a website, published a map with a driving tour of schools, and holds regular open houses.

Many other historic buildings in Fredericksburg retain their old use, while others have been adapted to new uses. Some of these have been prettified and/or gentrified, but a remarkable number of original buildings remain. You will be able to shop in historic structures, dine in historic structures, and even sleep in historic structures that have become bed and breakfast inns. There are several churches, both in town and in the country, that are worth seeing and that are usually open—when visiting them, please be respectful of these sacred spaces whether a service is in progress or not.

Alert readers will also notice that I refer to each house by the name of both the husband and wife whenever possible. It is more typical to use only the name of the husband, as property ownership in the nineteenth century was almost exclusively a male privilege, but I wanted to emphasize that women were a critical part of the family unit. She made sure that her husband and any children were well fed and with clean clothes, and that the children were cared for and their education begun. I know that this may sound like some idealized description of a stay-at-home mom, but without a pioneer woman by his side the pioneer man would have had a very hard time of it. And in a number of interesting situations, women who lost their husbands and did not remarry ended up taking on the decision-making role in remarkable ways.

Careful readers will notice that the dates of construction in this book may differ from those on historical markers or in earlier books. For many antiquarians the value of a building increases the older it is, and often folks have succumbed to the temptation to give a building the earliest possible date. Thus many of the oldest buildings in Fredericksburg have been dated to 1846–47, that is, a few months after German settlers arrived. However, way back in 1966 Terry Jordan pointed out in his classic book *German Seed in Texas Soil* that the settlers lived in log cabins for five or ten years before building a more permanent home of *fachwerk* or rock. Jordan's argument is supported by county tax records, but, alas, his insight did not align with traditional dates, which have usually been heeded by later writers.

The dates in this book reflect a great deal of careful research that provides a more precise dating of many properties. In many cases this is a few years; in a handful of cases, it is a couple of decades.

Regretfully, in spite of my hard work and that of many others before me, not all the construction dates of these building are certain. When I am reasonably certain of the date here assigned, I will simply give the date or dates of construction. When I feel that there is room for discussion, I will use the term "circa."

I have been coming to Fredericksburg since 1983, and I have been studying its built environment and material culture intensively since 2004. A volume on the material culture of German Texans is planned for publication in the near future; in fact, this volume was conceived when I realized that there were far more interesting historic buildings in Gillespie County than I include in a broader study of German Texans. The most intensive work for this volume was done in 2012. I could not have begun to write this book in the 1980s because my knowledge of architecture was very much focused on east coast and high style. A decade working at Historic Deerfield, a museum of New England history and art, and a membership in the Vernacular Architecture Forum taught me to take very seriously all buildings, large, small, or somewhere in between, whether or not they were designed by architects, and to seek out the cultural landscapes of everyday life.

I have continued to study the material culture of Texas in more than a dozen years of teaching in the Department of Museum Studies at Baylor University. I am interested in the many traces of German heritage that are still present in the city and the county, but I am also interested in the decisions made by pioneers and their progeny that were not German. Often these choices reflected an interest in adopting the life and styles of other Americans, but sometimes they created a distinctive blending of German and Texan, old and new. It is my hope that this volume will assist readers to appreciate the complex and still-evolving story of Fredericksburg and Gillespie County.

Map of Fredricksburg. Map by Steve McKinley.

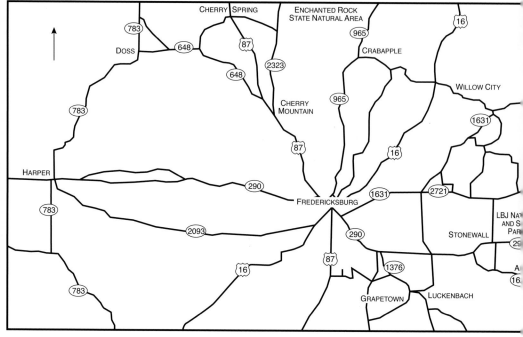

Map of Gillespie County. Map by Steve McKinley.

A GUIDE TO THE

Historic Buildings

OF FREDERICKSBURG

AND GILLESPIE COUNTY

Introduction: A Brief Overview of Fredericksburg and Gillespie County

Fredericksburg and Gillespie County were founded by German immigrants who sought a new life of economic opportunity and political freedom on what was then the western edge of American (and European) settlement in Texas. The idea of German immigration was promoted by the Adelsverein, a society of German nobility led by Archduke Adolph of Nassau that was incorporated in 1842. After failing to convince the Republic of Texas to grant the society land for colonization, the Adelsverein purchased land between the Llano and Colorado rivers, known as the Fisher-Miller Grant. Unfortunately for the settlers, this land was far inland and far from areas of European settlement, not easily reached from the coast.

The Adelsverein appointed a series of men who struggled to establish these new settlements. Most notable of these were Prince Carl of Solms-Braunfels and Baron Ottfried Hans Freiherr von Meusebach; the former was aristocratic if not imperious, strong on formalities and protocol, but weak on leadership and accounting. Baron von Meusebach dropped all his titles of nobility upon coming to Texas and became simply John O. Meusebach. In 1844 Prince Carl went to Texas and set about organizing the immigration. He was succeeded in 1845 by Meusebach, who brought order to the financial affairs of the Adelsverein and oversaw the settlement of Fredericksburg in 1846 and after. As part of this he negotiated a peace treaty with the Comanches, who apparently appreciated his bright red hair and beard and his nerves of steel.

The journey to Texas was quite arduous, requiring a long sea voyage, following by a grueling trek into the Texas interior. Most settlers of Fredericksburg landed first at Galveston, the principal port of the state, then took a smaller vessel to Indianola. Unfortunately, the Germans who landed at Indianola early in 1845 did so when the US Army had commandeered almost all wagons, carts, and food supplies for the Mexican-American War. The route from Indianola was thinly settled, running through Lavaca and Gonzales to the site of New Braunfels, located near the confluence of the Guadalupe and Comal rivers. The result was a route of starvation, disease, and death. The first settlers arrived at the site of New Braunfels on Good Friday, March 21, 1845. A little more than a year later, on May 8, 1846, Fredericksburg was founded.

The town was laid out between two streams, Town Creek on the north and Baron's Creek on the south. The two streams merged east of town, and eventually flowed into the Pedernales River. Other parts of the county are watered by Palo Alto Creek and Crabapple Creek to the north, Grape Creek to the east, and Live Oak Creek to the southwest. The area of Gillespie County originally included the southern parts of what are now Mason and Llano counties as well as parts of Burnet and Blanco counties. The current boundaries were finalized in 1883.

The town of Friedrichsburg, as it was known for most of the nineteenth century, was named by Meusebach in honor of Prince Friedrich of Prussia, whom he hoped would provide assistance to the Adelsverein. Fredericksburg, as the only settlement west of New Braunfels, became an agricultural center and an obvious choice for the seat of a newly formed county. When the time came to name the county, the German settlers wanted Piedernales or Pedernales, for the river that runs through it. However, the Texas Legislature decided to name the county for Robert Addison Gillespie, an early Texas pioneer who had died in the Battle of Monterrey during the Mexican-American War. Gillespie County built its first permanent courthouse in 1855; when a new courthouse was built in 1881–82, the old one became the post office.

The early settlers of Fredericksburg and the Hill Country came from Prussia and Nassau and Hanover, with a sprinkling from northeastern and western Germany. Often their place of birth determined their religious affiliation. More than half were Lutheran or Evangelical Lutheran—that is, followers of the Protestant reformer Martin Luther.

A large minority was Roman Catholic, and a smaller minority became Methodist. Modern-day Fredericksburg can also claim numerous other congregations, including Baptist and Episcopal as well as a Hispanic-speaking Catholic congregation.

Most of the settlers were farmers, though the land proved better suited for ranching than farming. Ranching often meant raising cattle, but flocks of sheep were also raised from a very early date. Goats are also raised in the southwestern part of the county. Many men brought other specialties, such as carpentry, cabinetmaking, blacksmithing, and baking. Some became merchants, while some became hotel keepers, brewers, barkeepers, and teachers, though the pay for the latter was poor. Opportunities for women were quite limited. In the early days the options were to marry, keep house, and raise a family or to stay unmarried. In latter days some women worked outside the home as milliners and dressmakers or as merchants, especially if their husbands had run a store in which they worked side by side.

What is Main Street today was originally San Saba Strasse; while it may seem strange for the main street to be named for a small town to the north, San Saba was also rumored to be the site of lost gold mines. Later the locals also referred to the main street as Hauptstrasse, though San Saba was still in used in the early twentieth century. The streets north and south of San Saba Strasse were named for the two largest nearby towns, Austin (seventy miles to the east) and San Antonio (sixty-five miles to the southeast). Schubert Street was named not for the composer but for Friedrich Armand Strubberg, also known as Dr. Schubbert, who briefly served as director of the colony. In the center of town was the Marktplatz (Market Square), labeled on early plans as Adolphs Platz in honor of Archduke Adolph of Nassau.

For the five years between 1848 and 1853 an army post was situated just east of town. The mission of Fort Martin Scott was to provide protection for the settlers from Lipan Apaches and Comanches. This was a fairly tall order, given that the post consisted of approximately ninety men. Nevertheless, Native Americans were pushed further to the west, and the line of forts followed them west as well. Fort Mason was similarly short-lived but led to the creation of the town of Mason. After the Civil War many men in Fredericksburg found work hauling supplies from San Antonio to the western forts. Fort Concho, near the tiny settlement of San Angela (the present-day city of San Angelo), was built with the assistance of stonemasons from Fredericksburg, and the nearby farm where Germans attempted to grow food for the troops was christened Bismarck Farm.

In the 1850s slavery was a rather abstract issue for residents of the Hill Country, but this changed dramatically with the Civil War. According to local tax records, there were only 9 enslaved workers in Gillespie County in 1852, and the number peaked at 102 in 1857. There were some individual plantations in East Texas that had more slaves than all of Gillespie County. Though that number declined quickly, there were still 25 to 30 enslaved African Americans in the county during the war years. Some Germans opposed slavery on moral grounds; for many others the question was moot, because the region received too little rain to grow cotton, and thus slavery was not economically viable.

Residents of Gillespie County voted emphatically against secession, 400 to 17. Some Gillespie County men fought for the Confederacy during the Civil War, but others who refused to serve were forced into home guard units. Some Fredericksburg men who were vocally opposed to secession were taken out by vigilantes and shot or hanged. In summer 1862, after the Confederate state government declared martial law in central Texas, sixty-one Union supporters decided to flee to Mexico. A Confederate irregular named James Duff caught up with them near the border and killed thirty-five men. To Confederates this became known as the battle of the Nueces, but to the Germans it was the Nueces Massacre. In 1892 Fredericksburg was one of the few towns in Texas to have a chapter of the Grand Army of the Republic, consisting of Germans who had fought for the Union and those who were sympathetic with the cause.

Because Fredericksburg was so far from settled communities, later development occurred in all directions. Llano, Mason, and Kerrville became county seats; so, too, did Comfort before losing the county seat to Boerne. Harper, to the west, is the second-largest town in the county; other communities include Stonewall, Albert, and Luckenbach in the eastern part of the county and Doss in the western part. Prominent streets led to these towns: Llano Street went north to Llano, Adams Street to Kerrville, US 290 to Harper and Junction, and US 87 to Mason. Around 1900 the north-south streets in the western part of town were changed to spell out "comeback," presumably to encourage visitors to come again. Not until the creation of US 87 south in the mid-1930s did Washington Street become the principal route to Comfort.

The earliest structures in the county were built using log, *fachwerk*, or rock. Log buildings were certainly the quickest to build, and many of these impermanent structures ended up lasting for years. The earliest log structures used technologies of joining wood that the German settlers learned from their Anglo-American neighbors, though the method had originally come to the United States from central Europe. The Hill Country contribution to the history of log building was to alternate logs with rows of limestone firmly mortared into place. From the German point of view, this made for not only a cozier room but also a structure that was more permanent and easier to maintain.

More characteristic of the old country was *fachwerk* construction. This system used a wooden framework, with horizontal, vertical, and diagonal posts, but filled the area in between with brick, rock, or even adobe. A nice plaster coat gave the building a more finished look, especially on the front. Not unlike half-timbering in England, it was especially popular in the central part of Germany, from which many of the settlers of Fredericksburg came. *Fachwerk* was also used by Germans settling in other states, notably in Pennsylvania and Wisconsin. As will become clear from the entries on *fachwerk* houses in this volume, most were built in the early 1850s, followed by a second group in the early 1870s, which might almost be considered a revival of the *fachwerk* house.

While some Germans replaced their original log houses with a *fachwerk* house, others decided to build entirely in stone. This was not an evolutionary step beyond *fachwerk* but a contemporaneous alternative. In the fifteen years before the Civil War, Germans built houses that were one, one-and-a-half, and two stories; in the two decades after the war it became clear that the story-and-a-half house was esteemed as the *beau ideal* of Hill Country housing. Such houses lined the main street, graced every other part of town, and were the centerpiece of many ranches. At a time when Texans from the United States were finally beginning to embrace the Victorian style that had been popular in the east for two decades or more, residents of the Hill Country rejoiced in the rock-solid simplicity of their native limestone houses.

The floor plans of early Fredericksburg houses were quite various, but they were variations on the placement of a small number of room types. The smallest houses might have one room or two rooms, one for cooking and one for living and sleeping. The former was known in German as the *kuche*, or kitchen, and the latter was the *stube*, a combination parlor and bedroom. If a third room was built, the sleeping function could be removed from the parlor, and the new room was a *kammer*, or bedchamber.

These were all traditional room types back in Germany, but the settlers of the Hill Country very rarely replicated German vernacular house types such as the *flurkuchenhaus* (direct entry into a kitchen on one side with a squarish *stube* and a smaller bedroom on the other side) or the *einhaus* (a house combined with a barn). Rather, they arranged these rooms in a new and distinctive manner. The two most typical floor plans in early Fredericksburg both had two rooms, placed either side by side or front-to-back. When the rooms were side by side, they were of a roughly equal size; sometimes there was one front door, but in many cases both rooms had a front door. When there were front and back rooms, the front room was larger and squarish and the back room smaller and rectangular. This latter arrangement seems to be an echo of the *flurkuchenhaus* plan, minus the kitchen. Neither of these plans featured a central passage, which was the norm in Anglo-Texan houses of the antebellum era. Apparently German Texans saw such passages as a waste of space. In the 1870s a few Fredericksburg residents built houses with a central passage, but they were not widely copied.

It was not until the 1880s that the styles of the American mainstream began to affect residents of Gillespie County. The key agents of change were the English-born San Antonio architect Alfred Giles and a new generation of builders who had been born in Texas. Giles made a name for himself designing a number of elegant Victorian houses for German Texans on King William Street in San Antonio. The first Giles commission in Fredericksburg was for a new county courthouse; he was hired by William Wahrmund, county judge and one of the old pioneers. Then Giles was hired by William Bierschwale, the son of an old pioneer, to design a house worthy of King William Street in San Antonio. This house had more rooms (with more specialized functions) and a sophisticated floor plan that used a two-story gallery and a studied asymmetry to insure good air circulation. Finally, Giles returned to design the Bank of Fredericksburg for Temple D. Smith, a recent arrival to the Hill Country who had been born in Virginia. This was the most notable essay in the Richardsonian Romanesque style to be built in the Hill Country.

Although the records of Gillespie County are almost entirely in English, the use of German was widespread through the nineteenth century. The US Post Office officially changed the name from Friedrichsburg to Fredericksburg on February 6, 1894, but the local newspaper, the *Fredericksburger Wochenblatt*, was still in German. And when a historical volume was published on the fiftieth anniversary of the founding of the town, the text was entirely in German. So, too, were the advertisements: twelve local ads were entirely in German, though Charles Schwarz blended German and English in the ad for his store. Of San Antonio ads, eight were in German, two were in English, and one blended the languages, as did both ads from Kerrville.

As county seat and an agricultural center, Fredericksburg was the location of a mill to process flour and cornmeal. This faced the Marktplatz on the north, an unusually central location for such a business. Felix and Frank van der Stucken, William Wahrmund, and Frederick Wrede began work on the mill in 1859, just as Carl Hilmar Guenther was abandoning his water-powered mill on Live Oak Creek and moving to San Antonio. Although it was near the meandering Town Creek, from the start it was steam powered, a more reliable source of power. By 1896 it was run by a 40-horsepower engine.

A significant improvement in transportation came when the San Antonio and Aransas Pass Railway arrived at Kerrville in 1887. Goods would then be hauled by wagon the twenty-four miles to Fredericksburg. This made possible local purchase of lumber (and even prefabricated window sashes, doors, and blinds) from Frank J. Beitel in Kerrville or Ed. Steves & Sons of San Antonio. It also allowed Oscar Krauskopf and C. L. Ransleben to import (and sometimes make) windmills, plows, wagons, and buggies. The railroad also made easier the founding of local lumber yards, notably those of Heinrich Kuene-mann and Franz Stein. Improvements in drills and saws made possible the quarrying of local red granite, first by Frank Teich of San Antonio and then Nagel Brothers Monumental Works locally. The local red granite was used as a building material and for gravestones, as were the concrete blocks and monuments produced by the Basse Brothers Cement Yard from 1910. The railroad finally arrived in Fredericksburg in 1913 but went out of business in 1942, killed by the popularity of trucks and automobiles.

The Bierschwale house was the only one in Fredericksburg designed by Giles, but along with a similar house for Dr. Albert Keidel, it set the pace for Fredericksburg houses for the next two decades. These houses opened the gates for houses with L- or T-shaped plans and lacy Victorian porches, which were built in one- and two-story versions between 1885 and 1915. Even the pioneer hotelier Charles Nimitz decided to upgrade his old building with a fanciful, ship-shaped Victorian superstructure. In spite of the late conversion to Victorian fashion, residents of the Hill Country still wanted to build with native limestone, which was cheap, durable, and, yes, beautiful too, though a few folks experimented with board-and-batten construction, in which the walls were created by vertical boards butted against one another, with the joints being covered by strips of wood called battens.

The years between 1885 and 1915 also saw a dramatic improvement in Hill Country churches. The pioneer generation worshipped in the Vereins-Kirche and in rock churches for Lutheran, Catholic, and Methodist congregations, but when the old octagonal building was abandoned, Holy Ghost Lutheran hired a San Antonio architect, James Wahrenberger, to design a handsome Gothic Revival building. This inspired many other congregations to upgrade their buildings, whether by remodeling, as was the case at Zion Lutheran, or by erecting an entirely new building, as at St. Mary's Catholic Church. In the latter case another professional architect from San Antonio was hired, Leo M. J. Dielmann, who was beginning a career in which he specialized in Catholic churches.

In the late nineteenth century and in the first half of the twentieth century, rural schools were built throughout Gillespie County. Many areas trace their schools back to the 1870s or earlier, but it was in 1889 that the commissioners of Gillespie County divided the county into school districts. These schools received a small amount of state and local support, usually enough to erect a school and pay a teacher. In some cases a house was built for the teacher, which was known as a "teacherage." The earliest rural school buildings were often log buildings; between 1880 and 1910 more permanent rock structures were built. Between 1910 and 1940 a new generation of schools was built using either board-and-batten or the locally manufactured concrete blocks known as Basse blocks. After World War II almost all of these rural schools were consolidated into the school districts in Harper, Fredericksburg, and Stonewall.

Another agent of change was industrially produced materials. This is seen especially in the commercial buildings that line Main Street. Progressive businessmen did not need to be concerned that their store would seem old-fashioned when they could order a cast-iron front for the exterior and a pressed-tin ceiling for the interior. Around the turn of the century Hill Country residents began to cover their old shingled roofs with thoroughly modern tin. Between 1900 and 1920 a number of houses, schools, and churches were covered with embossed metal siding, often shaped to resemble stone. At this same time a number of homes were built of red brick, much of it from the D'Hanis Brick Company west of San Antonio, and often clad in a late version of the Queen Anne style or the Arts and Crafts style, often referred to as bungalows. Other houses were built of Basse blocks; such houses were promoted nationally by Sears, Roebuck and Company in their *Modern Homes* catalogues of 1908 and 1911. In Fredericksburg such houses sometimes were of the type known nationally as foursquares, essentially a two-story version of a bungalow. And the walls of many Hill Country houses were enlivened by wallpapers in a variety of colors and patterns.

Younger citizens of Fredericksburg were also becoming exposed to new ways of doing things by attending college out of town. Albert Keidel, Lee Kiehne, Lyne Klingelhoefer, and Chester Nagel all attended the University of Texas in Austin, while Edward Stein, whose father Franz ran the local lumber mill and built houses, attended the Armour Institute of Technology in Chicago for three years and then worked as a draftsman in the office of San Antonio architect Leo

Dielmann. By the 1920s and 1930s citizens of Fredericksburg were building Spanish Colonial houses, Colonial Revival and Tudor Revival schools, and Art Deco banks and courthouses as if they were living in Austin or Dallas or San Antonio.

The enthusiasm for progress certainly contributed to the demolition of the Vereins-Kirche, which sat in the middle of San Saba Street until 1896. In the 1920s and 1930s, old rock houses that were unfortunate enough to be located on corners were likely to be targeted for demolition so that the newfangled automobiles could gas up at a convenient filling station. On the other hand, the seemingly hereditary frugality of Germans seems to have led to the consistent care and continued use of old buildings over many decades. Moreover, the automobile enabled young architects from out of town, notably Samuel Gideon (Austin), David R. Williams (Dallas), and O'Neil Ford (San Antonio), to come and marvel at the rugged simplicity and beauty of the old rock houses, which they thought were suitable models for a modern architecture for Texas.

In 1934, in the midst of the Great Depression, five old buildings of Fredericksburg were documented by workers for a New Deal program called the Historic American Buildings Survey (HABS). Out-of-work architects were paid to draw floor plans, elevations, and cutaway sections of buildings, photographing them and, if possible, noting historical documentation. When a historical marker or a book states that the plans of a building are in the collections of the Library of Congress, this does not mean the original plans drawn by the builder or architect, but plans drawn when the buildings was already quite old. While not as revealing as original plans might be, the HABS drawings (and accompanying photographs) are a treasure trove of information about the Tatsch house, the Pfeil house, the Krieger-Henke-Staudt house, old St. Mary's Catholic Church, and the old courthouse. In addition, the Kiehne house, the Kammlah house, and the now-demolished Dietz house were photographed without the production of measured drawings.

The danger that new development posed to Hill Country heritage was one key reason for the founding of the Gillespie County Historical Society. The first project of this organization was the recreation of the Vereins-Kirche, placed safely away from Main Street in the center of

INTRODUCTION

the northern half of the Marktplatz. The cornerstone was laid on January 6, 1934, and dedicated May 11–12, 1935. The new building housed both a museum and the local library. Twenty years later, in 1955, the society purchased the old Kammlah property on West Main Street and made the house its museum.

Over time the society has acquired adjacent buildings and land on West Main Street and also on West San Antonio Street and has moved in several structures to form what is now the Pioneer Museum. In 1963 the Schandua house, a well-preserved small house on East Austin Street, was given to the society. Happily, it was restored on its original site rather than moved (sometimes buildings must be moved to save them from destruction, but the historical context is lost in the process). The Fassel-Roeder house, next door to the Kammlah house, was purchased in 1967 and preserved on its original site, and in 1972 the Weber Sunday House was moved to the museum grounds and restored. The most recent effort has been to move the Dambach-Besier house from East Main Street to the Pioneer Museum complex in 2005. Also on the grounds of the museum is the White Oak School, which was built in the 1920s and moved from the southwestern part of the county into town in 1990. (Another school that is well preserved and open to the public is the Junction School, which is part of the Lyndon B. Johnson National Park in Stonewall.)

Though the society has achieved many preservation successes, historic preservation must be a community-wide goal. The remarkable transition to a tourism-based economy has ensured that preservation issues are rarely far beneath the surface. One troubling trend has been the relocation of historic buildings from other places, particularly log houses from Pennsylvania and Kentucky. While these buildings are certainly quaint and were historic in the context of their original location, once moved to another state in another region they do nothing but confuse the historical record. Another disturbing development is the remodeling of historic buildings in ways that do not respect the original configurations of rooms, which are an important piece of historical evidence helping us to see how the settlers lived and worked. A more positive aspect of the conversion of Fredericksburg to a tourist-based economy is that bed-and-breakfasts inns have a function very similar to the original residential function, requiring fewer modifications. The Fredericksburg experience shows that historic preservation and development can sometimes be at odds, but often work hand in hand.

Ironically, two of the most striking features of Hill Country architecture are very poorly understood in this day and age: the *fachwerk* house and the Sunday house. In many magazine articles, tourist guides, and real estate brochures, many an old rock house is called by one of these two terms. Somehow many people have lost sight of the fact that a log house or a rock house, no matter how old it is, is not *fachwerk*. The *fachwerk* house must have a wooden frame, and the space between the members must be infilled. The difference can be difficult to detect, given that both *fachwerk* and rock houses often received a coat of plaster and whitewash.

Similarly, very few of the old houses of Fredericksburg are Sunday houses. Most Sunday houses were built between 1880 and 1920, especially around the turn of the century, when families living on their farm or ranch wished to have a place in town where they could spend Saturday night and combine church on Sunday with shopping and socializing the rest of the time. Such houses were small, lightly constructed, and with few amenities. The Sunday house was made obsolete by the internal combustion engine, which allowed a family to get to town for church, shopping, or socializing and back home again without staying in town for the night. Any house that was built to be a year-round residence was, by definition, not a Sunday house, though older houses could be used as such at a later time. And such houses are clearly different from houses built as Sunday houses in greater size and permanence. Unless an entry in this book specifies that a house is constructed using *fachwerk* or is a Sunday house, the reader should assume that it is neither.

In recent decades the tourist horizon of the Hill Country has expanded dramatically. A first step in this direction was the purchase in 1963 by the State of Texas of the old Nimitz Hotel, which opened in 1967 as a museum honoring Chester W. Nimitz, admiral of the Pacific Fleet in World War II. The building was restored to its turn of-the-century appearance in 1983. Over the decades this has grown into a much larger institution, renamed the National Museum of the Pacific War in 1999. In 1966–67 the Victorian courthouse, which had been replaced in 1939, was restored and adapted as the new home of the Pioneer Memorial Library. Almost as important was the creation of state and national parks dedicated to President Lyndon B. Johnson, eleven miles east of town. LBJ was born in Blanco County, just east of Gillespie County, and acquired a large ranch on the eastern edge of Gillespie County while a member of the US Senate. Already present on the property when LBJ bought it was a rock house built by German Texans in the 1890s and enlarged by later, Anglo-Texan owners. Lyndon and Lady Bird oversaw additional campaigns of enlargement and improvement, including a swimming pool and an airstrip. Now under the care of the National Park Service, the house is slowly being restored to its appearance during the years of the Johnson presidency.

In 1971 John Russell "Hondo" Crouch and friends purchased the tiny hamlet of Luckenbach, Texas, which consisted of little more than a general store and a dance hall. Hondo became the mayor and "clown prince" of Luckenbach, whittling, making up tall tales, singing songs, and declaring that "Everybody's somebody in Luckenbach." Progressive country musician Jerry Jeff Walker recorded his album *Viva Terlingua* in its beautiful old dance hall, and Luckenbach was soon being celebrated by Nashville songwriters who had never visited and by younger Texas musicians for whom it became a sort of rustic musical mecca.

And in 1984 the State of Texas acquired the land around Enchanted Rock in northern Gillespie and southern Llano counties. The rock formation was revered by Native Americans for centuries, and the German Texan painter Hermann Lungkwitz painted it numerous times; it is now a state natural area, eighteen miles north of town. Even more recently wine making has become an important enterprise in Gillespie County. Early settlers like Meusebach experimented with growing grapes, though beer was a far more accessible (and thus popular) drink until recently; nevertheless, the early settlers would probably be glad to see the fruit of the vine so carefully crafted.

Both Fredericksburg and Gillespie County remained lightly populated well into the twentieth century. Fredericksburg did not decide to incorporate as a town until 1928; two years later the county had just over 10,000 residents, 2,416 of whom lived in town. The population of the county remained level from 1930 to 1960, though the population of Fredericksburg nearly doubled to 4,629. But in the last fifty years the population of both city and county has more than doubled, with Fredericksburg passing 10,000 and Gillespie County nearly 25,000. Like other Hill Country communities, Fredericksburg has been recognized as a good place to visit, to live in, and to retire in.

Fredericksburg and Gillespie County have witnessed a lot of history over more than 150 years, and more is to come. It is hoped that this guide will help residents and visitors to appreciate the region's remarkable past, and perhaps to plan for an even more remarkable future.

PART 1

All around the Marktplatz and Courthouse Square

1 Vereins-Kirche Replica
100 West Main Street, Marktplatz
1934–35

Circa 1890. Courtesy of the Gillespie County Historical Society.

The construction of this building was an act of demolition contrition. It was an attempt to replicate a building that had been built some ninety years before, which was then torn down fifty years later. It must be noted that a building that has been demolished is gone and cannot be brought back, but this is a good effort to remind people what was once nearby and is a constant reminder of what has been lost.

The Marktplatz originally consisted of two blocks—the one on which this building sits and the block just across Main Street as the octagonal Vereins-Kirche sat in the middle of Main Street. The Vereins-Kirche (literally "Society Church") was

initially the property of the Adelsverein, the society of nobles who promoted German immigration to Texas. The original cornerstone, which
was laid on May 9, 1847, can still be seen on the replica. In the earliest
days the structure was used by Lutherans, Evangelical Lutherans,
and Roman Catholics for their Sunday services and by the town for
a school. The octagonal shape related to centrally planned churches,
which had been in use for centuries in Europe.

The Catholics were the first to build their own church, followed by
the Lutherans and then the Methodists. The building was still used
for Evangelical Lutheran services and as a schoolhouse. Originally the
building had two doors, one on the east and the other on the west; one
old joke was that pedestrians and cattle could walk right through the
building rather than go around it. When a new courthouse [2] was
completed in 1882, the Vereins-Kirche was repaired and a new door
was put in the south wall, facing the courthouse. When the remaining
congregation of Evangelical Lutherans decided to split in 1887, a law-
suit over ownership ensued. By the time it was settled, both congregations—what are now Holy Ghost Church [77] and Bethany Lutheran
Church, originally at 107 East Austin and now at 110 West Austin
Street—had built their own buildings. The old Vereins-Kirche no
longer had a purpose and, in fact, was probably seen as a traffic hazard,
owing to its position in the middle of an increasingly busy Main Street.
In 1896, when Fredericksburg celebrated the fiftieth anniversary of its
founding, the walls of the structure were removed so that it could be
used as a pavilion during the festival, then demolished.

At least some citizens of Fredericksburg regretted the demolition,
and when the Gillespie County Historical Society was formed in 1934,
its first project was to reconstruct the Vereins-Kirche in the center of
what was formerly the northern block of the Marktplatz, still facing
the 1882 courthouse but safely away from traffic (the southern block
is now known as the courthouse square). At this time Texans were
planning numerous celebrations of the upcoming 100th anniversary
of Texas independence in 1936, and many new museums were in the
works in Austin, San Jacinto, Huntsville, Alpine, Canyon, and El Paso,
among others. Most of these were built with federal funds, thanks to
President Franklin Roosevelt's New Deal. The Civil Works Administration, an early New Deal agency, aided in the construction. The

architect for the Vereins-Kirche replica was Lee Kiehne, a twenty-four-year-old great-grandson of early pioneers Friedrich and Maria Kiehne.

For three decades the replica was used both as the public library, which occupied the front third of the interior, and the Gillespie County Historical society, which occupied the rest. The historical society expanded its scope in 1955 with the acquisition of the Kammlah house, a few blocks west on Main Street [46], but continued to use this building as well. With the adaptation of the 1882 courthouse as a library in 1966, the building was given over entirely to the display of historical exhibits.

2 Pioneer Memorial Library (formerly Gillespie County Courthouse)
115 West Main Street
1881–82

Although today visitors are struck by its quaintness and Victorian charm, the Gillespie County Courthouse was a thoroughly modern statement upon its completion in June 1882. The county commissioners hired a San Antonio architect, Alfred Giles, to design their new building. Giles had been trained in his native England but designed buildings for many leading citizens of San Antonio, including

well-to-do Germans like the Steves family and the Groos family, as well as for the US Army at Fort Sam Houston.

The new courthouse for Fredericksburg was built of local limestone from nearby quarries, but the stones were arranged according to national and international fashion. The rusticated stone walls were from the Dietz quarry two and a half miles northeast of town, while the finer work such as quoins, sills, lintels, arches, and paving stones came from the Deckert quarry ten miles east of town. Projecting pavilions framed a one-story portico, windows had segmental heads on the ground floor and round heads on the second, quoins reinforced every corner, and the building had a tin roof with iron cresting, all characteristic of Victorian eclecticism. Imported cast iron was used not only to adorn the roof but also to bound the courthouse lawn. The cast-iron fencing was ordered from the Rogers Fence Company of Springfield, Ohio; the same company provided a cast-iron fence for the house of Dr. Albert Keidel on Main Street [24].

Inside a central hallway ran from north to south, and another hall ran to the west, which also incorporated two stairs rising to the second floor. On the east side of the first floor the office of the county judge occupied the northeast corner, and the county clerk occupied the southeast corner. To the south of the stair hall was the office of the county tax collector, and to the north was the office of the county treasurer. Upstairs was one large courtroom, with a jury room at the southwest corner, and a grand jury room at the northwest corner. This was the first of three Giles-designed buildings in Fredericksburg: in 1889 he designed the William and Lina Bierschwale house [136] and in 1898 the Bank of Fredericksburg [16].

An even newer fashion put this building in the shade when a new courthouse in the Art Deco style [3] was completed in 1939. Fortunately, a new use was found for the building in 1966–67 as the home of the Pioneer Memorial Library. The idea was first suggested by Eugene and Margaret McDermott of Dallas, and their foundation funded the adaptive use. Dr. Philip O'B. Montgomery Jr. and wife Ruth Ann, who had purchased the old Crenwelge house [147] in 1965, first introduced the McDermotts to Fredericksburg and served on the restoration committee. Milton M. Moseley and his wife Johnnie of Fort Worth served as restoration architect and decorator, respectively; the Moseleys also owned and restored the Ochs house one block west on Main Street [37] and later owned the A. L. Patton Building [41].

---

3 Gillespie County Courthouse
101 West Main Street
1939

Just as the 1882 courthouse represented mainstream Victorian taste, the 1939 structure reflected the influence of a number of courthouses built in a style variously known as Moderne or Art Deco. The architect was Edward Stein, who had designed the Fredericksburg National Bank building [15] three years earlier. The base and the steps are of red granite, a material closely associated with the Texas Hill Country; the main body of the building is buff-colored brick, certainly chosen for economy; atop this is a simple stone cornice. Previously red granite had been used only for cornerstones in Fredericksburg; here it forms the pedestal on which the entire building sits. Also noteworthy is the use of aluminum for the window frames and for the spandrels between the first- and second-floor windows. Devotees of the Art Deco style took pride in the use of modern materials. The blocky form and the emphasis on the central bay were both characteristic of Art Deco in Texas public buildings. Just inside the front door is the main staircase, which evokes the Art Deco style with simple materials, terrazzo steps, and a curving iron railing with wooden handrests. This building and

---

the Post Office building [4] at the other end of the block were built with the aid of funds from the New Deal.

4 Old United States Post Office
125 West Main Street
1940

A new US Post Office building for Fredericksburg was erected in 1940 as a New Deal attempt to escape the Great Depression through public works. It was designed in Washington, DC, in the office of Louis A. Simon, the supervising architect of the US Treasury. With its buff-colored brick walls and hipped roof, the building's only touches of distinction are the red granite steps at the entry and the Art Deco–style eagle over the door, whose wing arc upward in a striking manner. Inside was a 1942 mural, *Loading Cattle*, by Otis Dozier, a noted regionalist painter and member of the Dallas Nine, done for the Works Progress Administration, another New Deal program. The painting can still be seen in the newer post office at the western end of town (1150 North US 87). This is the site of the 1855 Gillespie County

Courthouse, a two-story rock building erected by master builder Jacob Arhelger and then demolished in 1939 to make way for the present building. The old courthouse was documented by the Historic American Buildings Survey in 1934. The 1940 building now serves as the offices of the Gillespie County Attorney.

South Side of the Courthouse Square

5 Johannes and Juliane Ruegner House
105 West San Antonio Street
Circa 1870, 1873–74

A house was on this site from at least 1853, when Daniel Weyershausen sold the lot and house to the stonemason Johannes (John) Ruegner. Though it has long been thought that this is the original house, the earliest one must have been either *fachwerk* or log. Johannes built the first county jail (with his friend and fellow stonemason John J. Walch) in 1852 and worked on the grammar school in 1872. Ruegner also built the rock wall that separates the town cemetery, Der Stadt Friedhof [140], from Town Creek. The Ruegner family lived on this property

for many years; Johannes built the front rooms of this rock house around 1870, when he was aided by his sixteen-year-old son, Henry, an apprentice stonemason, and Jacob Leyendecker, a laborer. Ruegner reported a value of $1,500 to the census taker in 1870. Direct entry was into the larger west room, which was a parlor, and the smaller room on the east was a bedroom. Presumably the earlier log house continued in use as the kitchen until the two rear rooms were added. Daughter Bertha married G. A. (Adolph) Pfeil in 1879, and Johannes and son Henry may have had something to do with their house at the opposite end of this block [8]. Bertha's twin sister Emma married Carl Durst and lived at Cherry Mountain, where they eventually built their own rock house [see 170]. Johannes died in 1888, and Juliane in 1891. In 1899 their children sold the house to Alphonse Walter, a recent arrival from Switzerland, who in 1905 built a jewelry store at 124 East Main Street, which soon became the Central Drug Store [17].

6 Nagel Brothers Monumental Works (Nagel Memorials)
113 West San Antonio Street
1904

This company has been in continuous business at this site since 1904. The opening of Nagel Brothers Monumental Works coincided with the popularity of red granite grave markers. Such markers were only

possible after the development of new stonecutting machines that could cut granite, and the decision was made to build the Texas State Capitol with red granite, which necessitated a railroad line from Austin to quarries in Burnet County. Though other marble yards in Texas also produced red granite markers, it is reasonable to assume that the great majority of those in Fredericksburg were made by the four Nagel brothers, Rudolph, William, Emil, and Otto. Their complex consisted of a small board-and-batten building, which still serves as the office, and two iron-clad buildings where the gravestones were carved. In 1915 the firm had a 16-horsepower gasoline engine and an air compressor to help them work the stones. Though the Nagel company was bringing new technology to the Hill Country, the complex originally was not heated and did not have electric lights. In 1907 one of the brothers, Emil, bought a lot on West Creek Street, backing up to their business, where he built a house [100].

---

7 Gillespie County Jail
117 West San Antonio Street
1885

The stone walls and medieval battlements of the county jail, built in 1885, give the building a stern, even forbidding appearance—a tradition in American jail architecture that dates back to the Eastern State Penitentiary in Philadelphia, built 1822–29. The first Gillespie County Jail was built by stonemasons Johannes Ruegner and J. J. Walch in 1852. The house of Ruegner was just down the street [5], while that of Walch was on East Austin [121]. Ludwig Schmidt built the second jail in 1859, and Louis Doebbler built the third in 1874. These were all on different sites near the old courthouse on the west side of the Marktplatz. When a new courthouse [2], designed by San Antonio architect Alfred Giles, was built in 1882, it became clear that a new jail in a new location was needed, though a fire in January 1885, in which a prisoner lost his life, may have hastened the decision. C. F. Priess and Bro. built the present jail between April and December 1885, on a site just across San Antonio Street from the Marktplatz and the new courthouse. Charles Priess also built a store on East Main Street, with rooms above

---

to house his family [26]. The plans called for four rooms downstairs—one as a lockup and three for the jailer—and steel cells above.

8 Adolph and Bertha Pfeil House (previously known as the Meinhardt-Pfeil House)
125 West San Antonio Street
Circa 1879–80

This house has been called the Meinhardt-Pfeil house; the original owners of this lot were Albert Meinhardt and his wife Dorothea, but they lived on their farm outside of town, and it is highly unlikely that

the family ever lived in the present house. Their daughter, also named Dorothea, married G. A. (Adolph) Pfeil in 1874, but this ended in divorce. Adolph Pfeil bought the corner lot from his ex-mother-in-law and ex-wife on March 7, 1879, and he married Bertha Ruegner, daughter of John and Juliane Ruegner, in October of that same year. The Ruegner family lived at the opposite end of the block [5]. Presumably the house was built at that time, under the watchful eye of John Ruegner, a stonemason, and Bertha's older brother, Henry, who had apprenticed with their father. In the 1880 census thirty-one-year-old Adolph was working as a blacksmith, and twenty-one-year-old Bertha was keeping house.

Supposedly the west front room was used as a blacksmith shop, but nothing about its size or shape, not even the double doors front and back, provide evidence to confirm this supposition. There was direct entry into both large rooms. The kitchen was on the west and had doors on the front and back sides (the well was directly behind the back door) and two windows on the west, though one was filled in by 1934 but later reopened. On the east was a parlor, which had doors front and back and two windows on the east wall. In between the kitchen and parlor was a narrow room, used as a bedroom, which had a staircase against the front and west walls. Upstairs were two large bedrooms for the Pfeil children. Flues ran up the middle of the east and west walls, and another in the stone wall between the kitchen and the bedroom, showing that cast-iron stoves were used for cooking and heating. The six-over-six double-hung sash windows used throughout the first floor and the handsome doors with diamond-shaped panels were not popular in Fredericksburg until after the Civil War.

Later the Pfeil family moved to the Palo Alto community, where Adolph ran a cotton gin, but they kept this house as well. The rock room in back, said to have been a smokehouse, and the space between the room and the main house, probably a woodshed, were added between 1915 and 1924, as was a garage facing Crockett Street. These back rooms were the first to have a standing-seam tin roof, though the original shingle roof of the main house was replaced by a tin one before 1934.

Adolph Pfeil died 1926, but Bertha continued to live in the house. She allowed the house to be documented by the Historic American Buildings Survey in the 1934 and apparently provided a little information to architects Bartlett Cocke, who took photographs, and Homer H. Lansberry, who made measured drawings. At that time the house did not have a front porch. Bertha Pfeil died in October 1939, and the house was purchased by Benedict and Appollonia Hagel in 1945. They refurbished the house, and a porch with four squat box columns was added under their ownership. Mr. Hagel died in 1946, but Mrs. Hagel continued to live there until her death in 1977. Later owners redid the front porch, giving it turned columns and frilly Victorian ornamentation, which is quite handsome, though it confuses the historical record of the house.

To the east are two houses associated with Dr. Lindsey K. Tainter and his wife Helen. They were both natives of Iowa; he studied at the St. Louis Medical College in St. Louis, graduating in 1886. They were in Fredericksburg by 1899 and built a two-story house with Victorian ornamentation, which they sold to another doctor, A. B. Williamson, some two decades later. Around 1917 they built the two-story house with Arts and Crafts features, designed and built by Ed Stein, who had recently returned from working in San Antonio with the architect Leo M. J. Dielmann. In 1940 it was purchased by Stein's son-in-law, Henry Joseph, who worked with him at the Fredericksburg National Bank [15].

Originally the porch stretched across the entire front; the right part was enclosed in 1940, becoming part of the parlor.

West Side of the Marktplatz—North Crockett Street

9 Friedrich and Caroline Weihmiller House (Krueger-Weihmiller House)
112 North Crockett Street
1872

The Krueger-Weihmiller house is yet another classic story-and-a-half rock house, but with an earlier room to one side. The older part of the house is the one room on the north, built sometime before 1865 by Franz Krueger, a druggist. Krueger died in 1865, and the house was sold in 1867 to Friedrich Weihmiller, a native of Wurtemburg and a blacksmith, for $410. In February 1867 Weihmiller married Caroline Steffensen Kirchner, the young widow of the farmer Henry Kirchner. In the tragic days of the Civil War Henry Kirchner had been lynched on the night of March 9, 1864, for refusing to support the Confederacy.

Caroline, a native of Denmark, was left with three young children, and marrying the village blacksmith saved them all from a life of poverty. Weihmiller did a good bit of work for the hotel keeper Charles Nimitz and also made parts for wagons produced by Wilhelm Arhelger, who lived and worked on the other side of the Marktplatz.

Friedrich and Caroline completed their rock house in 1872, the year in which its valuation for tax purposes peaked at $1,500. After the new house was built, the older room was used as Friedrich's blacksmith shop. The porch has its original chamfered columns, though they have warped with age. Originally there was a railing enclosing the porch, evidenced by the mortise holes in the posts. The casing of the front door includes raised panels, not unlike the original front door of the Brockmann House on East Austin Street [122]. The floor plan is very typical of postwar Fredericksburg, with a squarish front room, the *stube*, which served as a combined parlor and bedroom. It was typical of most *stubes* in the 1870s, with the exception that the right side wall had a door into the old house. Behind the *stube* was a smaller room, probably the kitchen. Unlike many early houses, the stairs to the half story is not external but rises from the northeast corner of the kitchen.

By 1900 their daughters Annie and Minnie had moved to San Antonio, where they worked as seamstresses, and by 1910 Caroline Weihmiller was living with them. The family retained the old house in Fredericksburg as a rental property. In 1938 Annie and Minnie sold the house to Hugo Basse, from whom it descended to his daughter, then his grandson. It has served many functions, including the local office first for Lone Star Beer and then for Falstaff Beer.

When seen from the south, the house has the classic profile of what would be called in New England a "saltbox" house. Viewed from the north, the single room on the north gives the house a sort of ramshackle appearance. Over the years there have been few attempts to change it and few attempts to restore it. Perhaps this antique quality led the Dallas architect David R. Williams to photograph the house in the late 1920s. Williams admired the rugged simplicity of such houses and hoped that they might serve as models for modern Texas houses. A drawing of the house—from the north—was used for a woodcut to illustrate his article "Toward a Southwestern Architecture," in the *Southwest Review* in April 1931.

10 Felix and Christine van der Stucken House
114 West Austin Street

The 100 block of West Austin Street, which faces the north side of the Marktplatz, was shaped by the van der Stucken family, though their most prominent structure is long gone. Felix and Frank van der Stucken were not German but came from Antwerp, Belgium, arriving in Fredericksburg in the early 1850s. However, they married German girls, the sisters Christine and Sophie Schoenewolf, and became involved with local men in developing a steam mill in the center of this block. Frank and Sophie went back to Belgium in 1865, but Felix and Christine settled on this lot, and Felix became a merchant and the operator of a mill just to the east of the house.

The oldest part of this house complex may be the *fachwerk* structure to the rear. Next came a single rock room, then another behind it; this was the classic *stube*-kitchen configuration. Just west of this

one-story house a two-story section was soon built. This was built with a floor plan unusual for the Hill Country: a side passage with a staircase opening into two rooms. The front room became Felix and Christine's parlor, the back Felix's office. The side passage, which had been common in the eastern United States for decades, allowed a connection with the two rooms in the one-story section. The home had its own windmill and water tank and a barn.

The van der Stucken and Son Roller Mill, which originally occupied the lot to the east, consisted of a two-and-a-half-story wood-frame grain elevator and an equally tall rock mill, which by 1896 had a 70-horsepower steam engine. Felix and Christine's son Alfred and his wife Cornelia built their own home [11] at the other end of the block starting in 1891. After the mill closed, the land was purchased in 1948 by Bethany Lutheran Church, which had outgrown its original building two blocks away. Church members razed the mill and built a new church and rectory in 1954. It was quite unusual to have a mill sited on a town square, and its demolition gave the area a more genteel, dignified ambience. Ironically, this newest church building is the first church on or around the Marktplatz, except for the old Vereins-Kirche.

11 Alfred and Cornelia van der Stucken House
102 West Austin Street
1891, circa 1910–12

The date stone over the front door announces that construction of this house was begun in 1891. Alfred was the son of Felix and Christine van der Stucken, and in 1895 Alfred purchased a half-interest in the van der Stucken and Son Roller Mill, which was one hundred feet west of his house. He renamed it the Reliance Roller Mill. In 1889 Alfred had married Cornelia Lungkwitz, the daughter of Adolf Lungkwitz, a tin-smith, silversmith, and goldsmith, and his wife Elise, who lived a few blocks east on Main Street [25]. At first Alfred and Cornelia's house was one story and built of rock. By 1910 they had five children between the ages of sixteen and five, plus a live-in servant, Ella Saenger, twen-ty-one. A second story was added between 1910 and 1912, built not of stone but of concrete blocks, manufactured locally by the Basse Brothers Cement Yard. Even the posts of the porch were made of Basse blocks, and the rock of the ground floor was given a wash of concrete so that it would match the upper floor.

The floor plan was a fashionable Victorian "T"—but with only three rooms at first, it must have been the traditional *stube*, *kuche*, and

kammer. Things got more spacious with the addition of a second story. At first the only staircase was on the back porch, but after a family illness Franz Stein was hired to build an internal staircase rising out of the dining room. The stone and concrete exterior is softened considerably by the frilly Victorian scrollwork on the two-story porches. The yard is delineated by a cast-iron fence made by the Stewart Iron Works of Cincinnati. The family sold the house in 1912 and moved to San Antonio.

East Side of the Marktplatz—North Adams Street

12 F. W. Arhelger Wheelwright Shop
109 North Adams Street
1898

This is the last remnant of a complex of buildings owned by the Arhelger family, a locally prominent family of craftsmen. Wilhelm Arhelger, who came with his parents to Fredericksburg as a young boy, married Katharine Gruene in 1865. They built a story-and-a-half rock house to the south of the present building, and Friedrich had his wheelwright shop next door. Their son, Friedrich Wilhelm, continued the family

tradition of making wheels and the wagons that were attached to them. F. W. married Mathilde Weber in 1890, and they built a two-story frame house north of where he would build this shop in 1898. The Arhelger shop is constructed of limestone side walls, quite traditional for Fredericksburg buildings both residential and commercial, but had an up-to-date shop front with large glass windows. Adapting the building for the manufacture and sale of wagons was the concrete ramp at the front door. Inside was one open space, allowing ample room for manufacture, repair, and display. F. W. sold this shop in 1918, and in that same year bought the old Weyrich house on East Main Street [35].

East Side of the Courthouse Square—South Adams Street

13 August and Sedonie Sembritzky House
100 block of South Adams Street (now attached to the building at 102 East San Antonio Street)
1905

August Sembritzky and his wife, Sedonie, contracted with Frank Stein to build this house in 1905. Sedonie was a daughter of Conrad

Wehmeyer, the pioneer baker; she was also the widow of Edward Maier, who had died from burns received in a steam boiler explosion. By 1905 her daughter Meta Celestine Maier had married Louis Kott, who operated a farm equipment company on East Main [20]. The two lots on Adams Street, acquired from Sedonie's stepsons, faced the old southern half of the Marktplatz, just south of the present courthouse. This two-story rock house with a hipped roof cost $2,550. The west and north front are plastered, but the stonework is visible on the south and east fronts. The Sunday house of Sedonie's sister, Alwine Wehmeyer Weber, may be seen at the Pioneer Museum Complex [48].

PART 2

Main Street, East of the Marktplatz and Courthouse Square

14 Maier Building
101 East Main Street
1874, 1924

This two-story building was built of roughly carved limestone in 1874. The owner was the local merchant and entrepreneur Edward Meier, younger brother of Anton Maier, who had been in business on the lots facing the Marktplatz since 1860. In this store he carried the first sewing machines to be sold in Fredericksburg. Also in 1874 he built a steam-powered cotton gin two doors down, where 119 East Main stands today. Unfortunately, that is where Maier's life ended, as he died when the steam boiler exploded in 1884. The building was inherited by his son, Richard. A circa 1890 photograph shows the building standing alone, with no wrap-around porch but with two double doors in front and one on the side. It was being used as a bank in 1896 and as a saloon in 1902. Its first floor was remodeled in 1924, with the addition of large plate-glass windows and a cornerstone of Bear Mountain red granite, courtesy of Nagel Brothers Monumental Works [6].

The commercial building next door at 115 East Main was built in 1916 by Florent J. Maier, the son of Edward and Adele Maier. A Dallas architect, J. E. Bridgman, provided plans, and local builders Weber Brothers built it. Alas, Maier went out of business three years later.

15 Fredericksburg National Bank
119 East Main Street
1936

The Great Depression led to the closing of all banks in Fredericksburg, and in 1932 a new bank, the Fredericksburg National Bank, was
formed. In 1933 Edward Stein, a local architect and builder, became
its president, a post he held until 1969. Three years later he designed
this bank building in a local version of the Art Deco style. It is a rare
bit of private construction in the depths of the Great Depression. Stein
had been an architect and builder in Fredericksburg for more than
two decades and was responsible for many houses in town [such as
33, 134, and 164]. He was the architect for the 1926 remodeling of
the Nimitz Hotel [32] and also designed the new Gillespie County
Courthouse [3] in 1939. Like the courthouse, the bank building has a
base of granite, a buff-colored body, and a stone cornice. The entrance
is framed with red granite; the terrazzo floor continues inside. The
main block is double-height; it contains the main banking room, with
the tellers stationed between the customers and the bank vault at the
rear. A lower wing at the right allowed for more office space, including
an office for the bank president that looked out onto Main Street. The

lower wing also allowed the main banking room to be lit by a group of western glass block windows, which would be called clerestory windows were they in a church. In addition to the double front doors, there was a pair of iron gates that were barred shut at night. The night depository is still visible to the right of the main entrance.

16 Bank of Fredericksburg
120 East Main Street
1898

This is one of the most notable Romanesque-style buildings in the Hill Country. The Bank of Fredericksburg was designed in 1898, not for a German Texan client but for Temple D. Smith, a Virginia native and banker who came to Fredericksburg in 1886. The architect, Alfred Giles of San Antonio, had previously designed the 1882 Gillespie County Courthouse [2] and the 1889 William and Lina Bierschwale

house at 110 North Bowie Street [136]. On the bank building almost all of the Romanesque ornament is in the upper story, notably around the central window and the cornice. The tower with its red tile roof makes the building a landmark from both the east and the west. This was both a business and residence; above the banking house was Smith's residence, which, as the San Antonio *Daily Express* noted at the time, was "arranged and fitted up with every convenience of a modern city house." The construction of the building has been attributed to local stonemason William Klingelhoefer, son of the pioneers J. J. and Elisabeth Klingelhoefer.

17 Central Drug Store
124 East Main Street
1905

This commercial block was built as the A. Walter Jewelry Store in 1905, an indication that residents of Fredericksburg could now afford

at least some of the finer things in life and that local stores could be specialized as well as general. Alphonse Walter was a native of Switzerland who came to Texas in the 1890s. In 1905 he contracted with local builder Frank Stein to erect a two-and-a-half-story stone and concrete building. One the ground floor rough-cut blocks of red granite and creamy limestone emulate the High Victorian taste popular elsewhere thirty years before.

In 1909 Walter moved to another location and sold the building to two pharmacists, Robert G. Striegler (who one year earlier had built a house at 310 East Main [29]) and L. C. Gibson. They used the downstairs for their business; part of the upstairs was used by the telephone exchange. A 1912 photo shows that the porch was added later; originally the main façade was shaded by a canvas awning. The granite slabs at the base of the building have holes to receive the awning poles. The upper part of the central slab of red granite has "AW" inscribed on it—the only remaining sign of its original owner.

---

18 Louis Priess Store and House
141 East Main Street
Circa 1888–89, 1923

In the latter decades of the nineteenth century, German Texan merchants often erected buildings that had a store on the ground floor and a residence above. Louis Priess purchased the lot in 1888 and built this structure shortly thereafter. The builder may have been his brother, Charles, a stonemason and builder who had built his own store and residence, also on East Main Street [26], and the Gillespie County Jail [7] just a few years before.

Originally the two-story rock building had essentially identical first and second floors, with four sets of French doors on each floor. The original character of the façade can still be seen on the second floor. The ground-floor doors opened onto the sidewalk, those on the upper floor onto a cast-iron balcony. On the ground floor one could purchase dry goods, boots, shoes, hats, groceries, hardware, wooden ware, and crockery—that is, general merchandise of all sorts.

Louis and Anna Priess lived in the rooms above with their six

---

children. George R. Stucke bought the building in 1923 and turned it into a bakery. He remodeled the front of the ground floor, removing the stone wall and inserting more modern plate-glass windows. The cornerstone on the right side was brutalized at this time but still defiantly states, "UIS PRIESS."

19 Schandua Building
203 and 205 East Main Street
1897, circa 1902–3

John Schandua, who with his wife Bertha (née Klein) and their five children lived in a small house on East Austin Street [123], inherited this lot on Main Street and built the western half of the building in 1897–98. A general store was on the ground floor, but the top floor was designed to serve as a Masonic hall. The men who founded the local Masonic lodge in 1896 agreed to loan Schandua the money to erect the structure if he would provide them with a meeting space. This was a delicate situation, as Schandua, a Roman Catholic, could not join the

Masons without expecting to be excommunicated. Whether a coincidence or consequence, the pastor of St. Mary's Church founded a local chapter of the St. Joseph's Society in 1899 and erected St. Joseph's Hall [82] in 1900. John Schandua died of a heart attack in 1900.

His widow, Bertha, after a year of mourning, married John's brother Henry in November 1901. Henry took over the hardware store, and within a year or two they built the eastern half of this building, which more than doubled its size. The eastern half became the hardware store; their home was above. An unusual feature is the door in the middle of the façade—it opens into a staircase leading to an upper stair hall. Beyond were five rooms for the family. The Masons used the hall only for a few years; later the Woodmen of the World occupied the space. The eastern part of the first floor served as a hardware store, and the western half was originally a saddlery. The building continued to be used as a hardware store until 1972, when it was purchased by Houston lawyer George A. Hill III and his wife Gloria. They restored the building to the designs of Preston Bolton, a Houston architect. The first floor continues as a commercial space, and the upstairs has been converted to a bed-and-breakfast operation.

20 Louis Kott Building
241 and 245 East Main Street
1926

Louis Kott was an enterprising young man. He grew up on the family farm outside of town and was trained as a blacksmith. He worked making horseshoes for the thoroughbreds at Morris Ranch, southwest of town, and in 1900 opened a shop in town selling windmills; he also drilled water wells. In 1902 he married Meta Celestine Maier, a daughter of Edward and Sedonie Wehmeyer Maier. He subsequently did some farming and in 1912 became the first Ford automobile dealer in town. He sold the Ford business in 1925 and opened the Fredericksburg Implement Company with two partners. They built this structure the next year. The front consists of Mesker Brothers cast iron and large plate-glass windows, which allowed passersby to admire the products on display. Red granites stones which read "Louis Kott" and "1926" flank the main entrance. The side walls are built of concrete blocks made locally by the Basse Brothers cement company, which are rusticated on the front and smooth on the side. Other cast iron made by the St. Louis firm Mesker Brothers can be seen at 221 and 229 East Main and across the street at the Keidel Drug Store [23]. Kott was one of the investors in the Hotel Nimitz Company, which purchased and remodeled the hotel in 1926 [32].

21 White Elephant Saloon
246 East Main Street
1888

This tiny building provided a lot of architectural bang for the buck. It was built in 1888 by John W. Kleck as the White Elephant Saloon. The name of the saloon was prominently displayed at the top of a bracketed front porch, and Kleck's name was found just above the elephant.

The side walls were limestone rubble, but the stonework on the front was more highly finished, framing the three sets of French doors. The cornice is supported by four brackets, but interrupted in the center to create a pediment that houses the saloon's trademark elephant and hides a pitched roof behind. A Victorian crest of cast iron adds a frilly touch at the top. In front of the porch was a rail to which patrons could tie their horses. The building may have been built by A. W. Petmecky and his fellow stonemason known only as Thompson; at any rate, the pair of stonemasons borrowed a wooden elephant from a merry-go-round and made a pressing of it in sand; they then poured in concrete to create the precast pachyderm that graces this building.

22 Basse-Henke House
247 East Main Street
1868–70

Charlotte Basse, the widow of Lutheran minister and merchant Henry Basse, built this house between 1868 and 1870, probably for her son, Carl Basse. In 1873 she sold it to Henry and Dorothea Henke. Henry was a butcher, and his shop was originally just to the west of the

house. The house originally had two rooms—the front door opened directly into the *stube*, the larger western room, while the eastern room served as Henry and Dorothea's bedroom. The half story above served as sleeping quarters for their sons. By 1885 two more bedrooms were added to the rear, and later still a dining room and kitchen were attached. Henry and Dorothea's oldest daughter, Anna, married Chester Nimitz, a son of Charles and Sophie Nimitz, owners of the Nimitz Hotel [32]. Chester and Anna's son, Chester W. Nimitz, was born in the east rear bedroom. The fact that the younger Nimitz became admiral of the Pacific Fleet during World War II filled the citizens of his hometown with pride and virtually guaranteed preservation of the house.

23 Keidel Drug Store
248 East Main Street
1909

Late in his life Dr. Albert Keidel built this structure to enhance the medical careers of his four sons. The first floor was a drug store for his son Kurt, who had taken a degree in pharmacy at the University

of Texas Medical Branch in Galveston and then worked at Robert G. Striegler's drug store. On the second floor were a doctor's office for Dr. Victor Keidel and dental offices for Dr. Felix Keidel and Dr. Werner Keidel. The side walls of the building are rock, but the main façade is of cast iron and was imported, having been made by a well-known firm, Mesker Brothers of St. Louis. It was thus notable as acceptance of modern technology—at least as modern as 1887, when the Mesker Brothers patented this particular front—and also of mainstream American taste in commercial buildings. Other Mesker Brothers storefronts can be seen across the street at 221 and 229 East Main and at the Hoerster-Blum Building uptown [42].

---

24 Albert and Mathilde Keidel House
252 East Main Street
1888–90

This is one of the earliest Victorian-style houses in Fredericksburg, and also one of the best preserved. Like the William and Lina Bierschwale house [136] and the A. W. Moursund house [138], the Keidel house reflects the influence of the Victorian houses that had recently been built in the King William district in San Antonio for the Steves, Altgelt, Groos, and other German families.

When Dr. Albert Keidel and his wife Mathilde bought the property in 1881, there was already a substantial story-and-a-half rock house on the lot. The walls of this house were incorporated into the western half of the much more ambitious and fashionable Victorian house. Distinctive stonework includes quoins at all corners and lintels and sills on all windows and doors. The date stone at the lower right side of the projecting western block states "1889." The woodwork includes a dentil course and paired brackets at the cornice of the main roof and the porch. The fence that bounds the front yard was made by the Rogers Fence Company of Springfield, Ohio (patented 1881) and most likely dates to the dramatic enlargement of the house. This same company provided a cast-iron fence for the 1882 Gillespie County Courthouse [2]. In the front gate a cast-iron plate announces "Dr. A. KEIDEL," as does the lintel over the transom on the front door. The door is original

and features raised paneling with a pair of tall round-arched panels
at the top and shorter rectangular panels below, which would not be
out of place in San Antonio houses and may have been made there. A
transom and side lights illuminate the entry hall inside. There is also
a second door on the front porch leading directly into the front parlor,
perhaps a vestige of the German Texan custom of having direct entry
into the *stube*.

A formal entry hall was still something of a novelty for Fredericksburg in 1888. The newel posts and balusters utilize mahogany as well
as a lighter-color wood. The latter has very linear floral decoration, remi-
niscent of the Eastlake style. Like the front door, the staircase may well
have been brought from San Antonio. The front room on the left was
the parlor; behind this was a dining room, another specialized room use
that was still quite novel in the Hill County. The large room on the right
was originally used as Dr. Keidel's office, with a separate one-story porch
and entrance on the east side. Upstairs are three bedrooms.

Mathilde Keidel passed away in 1902, and Albert in 1914. Each of their sons inherited a one-fourth interest; by 1920 Kurt had purchased the interests of his brothers and eventually lived in the old house. In 1936 Kurt removed the wall between the two rooms on the west to create one large living room. At this point his father's office became the dining room. A den and a breakfast room were added at the rear, as was a terrace. Albert and Mathilde Keidel clearly wished to live in a fashionable and modern house, and three of their sons felt the same way: Kurt and Felix built homes in the Queen Anne style [113 and 114], their brother Victor in the Spanish Colonial style [33].

25 Adolf Lungkwitz Shop and House
254 East Main Street
1867–68

Adolf Lungkwitz was a tinsmith, silversmith, and goldsmith who came to Texas with his family in 1851. The family members included his brother, Hermann Lungkwitz, who was to become one of the most noteworthy landscape painters in nineteenth-century Texas. Adolf married Elise Heuser in 1855, and the couple made their home on Garten Street (South Lincoln Street) where the Rausch house now stands [71]. They started with one room and added several over the next decade, but in 1867 they began to build a combined shop and residence on a more prominent site on Main Street. The shop was in front, a single story, behind which was a two-story residence. The double doors are flanked with six-over-six windows, and over the doors is a transom, said to have been made by Lungkwitz, which incorporated arrows into its design. The residence had three rooms downstairs and one large bedroom upstairs for their five children. The Lungkwitz family retained the building until 1920. Adolf and Elise's daughter Cornelia married Alfred van der Stucken and lived in a house facing the Marktplatz [11] while daughter Antonie married Charles H. Nimitz Jr. and worked beside him at the Nimitz Hotel [32].

26 Charles Priess Store and House (later the Keidel Memorial
Hospital)
258 East Main Street
1882–83, 1937–38

This austere rock structure was built as a store and home by Charles F.
Priess, who acquired the lot in 1878; the building was completed July
24, 1883. Priess was a stonemason who later built the Gillespie County
Jail on San Antonio Street [7] and the store and residence of his
brother Louis one block west on East Main Street [18]. The rusticated
quoins, heavy stone lintels over the windows and doors, and paneled casing of the front door anticipate the building for Louis Priess.
Charles Priess died in 1900, and the family rented out the ground floor
to other businesses.

Dr. Victor Keidel purchased the building in 1919, sold it in 1923, then bought it back in 1937. (He had previously practiced on the second floor of the Keidel Drug Store [23].) He adapted the Preiss building to serve as the Keidel Memorial Hospital, which was known locally as the Keidel Clinic, adding a wing to the west, set back from the street, designed by Edward Stein, who was assisted by Victor Keidel's son, Albert. All of the windows in the old building were replaced with metal casement windows, which are opened by turning a handle; in order to fit these mass-produced windows into preexisting stone openings, stationary panes of glass were added at the top and bottom. Above the door a balcony was added with cast-iron trim featuring bunches of grapes. The entry to a basement-level space, in recent years used as a restaurant, had a simpler cast-iron railing with globes at each main post. At the rear Stein added a concrete upper-level gallery that shelters all entrances on the back side. The balcony and the staircases to the basement and upper floor are all enlivened with cast-iron railings.

The west wing has many hints of the Art Deco style. Stein created a new main entrance in the west wing, which also had a cast-iron porch. Above this the façade curved forward with a window made of glass blocks The most impressive interior space was just inside this door: this small lobby is dominated by a staircase with cast-iron railing

and terrazzo steps, lit by the tall round-arched window at the landing. The staircase runs along the east wall; at the bottom a fluted quarter column curves at the corner, and the lowest step curves out at the side; a matching quarter column is engaged to the western side of the opening. Dr. Keidel practiced here until his death in 1952; his son-in-law, Dr. J. Hardin Perry, continued the practice. In recent years the building has been adapted back to its original commercial use.

27 Otto Kolmeier Store
302 East Main Street
1910

The corner lot on which the Kolmeier store sits had long been the site of a hardware store. Originally there was a one-story rock building, replaced in 1910 with this two-story commercial block. There were large plate-glass windows in front, and the side walls were built of concrete blocks. Atop the main façade is a pressed tin cornice. The entrance is at the corner, a feature that had become popular in the United States in recent decades. Otto and his wife Dorothea built a

house for themselves just behind the store starting in 1901 [28]. Otto described himself as a tinner in the 1900 census, as owner of a tin shop in 1910, and as a retail merchant in hardware in 1920. The date of 1896 above the cornice probably reflects when Otto went into business. Kolmeier was one of the investors in the Hotel Nimitz Company, which purchased and remodeled the hotel in 1926 [32].

Around the Corner on North Lincoln Street

28 Otto and Dorothea Kolmeier House
101 North Lincoln Street
1901

Otto and Dorothea Kolmeier built this house in 1901, as he proudly proclaimed in the lintel over the front door. This is another house built by the children of German immigrants. Otto's parents, Wilhelm and Suzanna Kolmeier, were born in Lippe Detmold and Prussia, respectively, but all of their children were born in Texas. Dorothea, the daughter of George Wilhelm and Sophie Crenwelge, was born and reared in their two-story rock house at 415 West Main Street [56].

Otto and Dorothea were married in 1898 at the home of her parents, and they began this house three years later. The rusticated quoins that articulate each corner play off the smooth plaster of the wall. The house is quite typical of Victorian-era Fredericksburg, with its T-shaped plan, bracketed cornice, and ornamental porch. The porch was originally one story and went only from the sidewalk to the front door; by 1910 it had been expanded across the front and to a full two stories. The Otto Kolmeier Store [27], built in 1910, is just to the south fronting on Main Street. Otto and Dorothea's son Walter built a bungalow on North Llano Street in 1925 [158].

---

29 Robert and Selma Striegler House
310 East Main Street
1908

The Victorian era came late to Fredericksburg and stayed late as well. This house is one of the last examples of a two-story Victorian house type that had been popularized in the late 1880s by the houses of Albert Keidel [24], William Bierschwale [136], and A. W. Moursund [138]. Robert Striegler was a Fredericksburg native who went off to study at Sam Houston Normal School (now a state university) and the University of Texas in Austin; he then studied pharmacy at the University of Chicago. His wife Selma was also a local, being a daughter of William Weyrich, one of the sons of Carl and Margarethe [see 35].

The house was built by local contractors, the Weber Brothers, who had recently enlarged the Kraus Building in 1906 [59]. The Striegler house was built of local limestone, with heavily rusticated quoins. The living room and dining room were to the left of the entrance hall, and the kitchen to the right. There were porches of two full stories on both the front and rear of the kitchen. As with both the Keidel and Bierschwale houses, on the front porch there is a side door leading into the front room. The house also has a red granite cornerstone—presumably made by Nagel Brothers Monumental Works—with the date 1908 on the front and the initials RGS on the side. The house is fronted with a cast-iron fence made by the Stewart Iron Works in Cincinnati, as did the slightly earlier van der Stucken house on West Austin Street [11]

and the Gold house on Travis Street [149]. The living room and dining room were separated by a framed partition rather than solid rock—this allowed for double pocket doors. All other doors and windows, both external and interior, have transoms that open and are ornamented with frames with bull's eye corner block. In this regard the Weber Brothers were taking advantage of the fact that such parts were now being mass-produced and did not have to be made in town; it was thus another sign of Fredericksburg shifting from the local and traditional to the national and modern. Not too far behind the house was a one-story rock building with a water tower on the roof—a reminder that in 1908 Fredericksburg did not have a water system.

30 George and Eliza Wahrmund Shop and Residence
312 East Main Street
1881–82, 1889

Like the White Elephant Saloon [21] up the street, this is a small building that makes a big impact. In 1880 George Wahrmund was a wheelwright, and his wife Eliza was a milliner and dressmaker; they were both twenty-six and had a three-year-old daughter, Louise. The building served as Eliza Wahrmund's shop and also their residence. They bought this property in 1876; the earliest part of the structure, built around 1881–82, may be the one-story dwelling with a separate porch, which later formed a rear wing. On the front part of the building, only the first floor is rock; the mansard roof above was so tall as to be considered a full second story. There were two front doors: presumably one commercial and one residential. In the old photograph shown here, the shingles create a pattern of connected diamonds; this suggests that they were two shades of slate, but paint may well have been used to create this "polychromatic" look, which was very fashionable in the Second Empire style. Its similarity to the roof of the Nimitz Hotel [32], added between 1888 and 1896, suggests that this roof dates to the same time.

In 1896 the building was a grocery store and ice cream parlor. In 1924 it became a bakery. At this point the original front porch was removed; the pressed tin ceiling inside may date from this time as well. The building continued as a bakery for more than three decades, then fell into disrepair, but in 1975 it was adapted as a savings and loan. The work was carried out by local restorer Tyrus Cox and Austin architect Roy White. They were able to use the old photo of the house to recreate the Victorian front porch. It was adapted again to serve as a restaurant in 1989.

Another millinery and dressmaking establishment was in the same block, but on the opposite side of the street. The Weyrich Building,

Courtesy of Institute of Texan Cultures, University of Texas at San Antonio, 068–0718.

at 337 East Main Street, was the shop of Emilie Weyrich and the
home to Emilie, husband William, and their children. The western
part of the building was erected around 1875–76, and the eastern
part was added a decade later. The Weyrich family sold the place
in 1907, and later owners remodeled the front with fieldstone and
plate glass. Their daughter Selma married the druggist Robert G.
Striegler, and together they built the late Victorian house at 310
East Main [29].

31 Maier-Stoffer House
315 East Main Street
1855–56

This is one of the earliest story-and-a-half rock houses in the Hill
Country; it was begun in 1855 and completed in 1856. Anton Maier
was an early Fredericksburg merchant who served as district clerk
and then county judge during the Civil War.

The lot had been granted to Christian Doebner; by October of
1855 Doebner had the rock walls up and a roof on. However, in that
month Doebner leased the house to Anton Maier for one or possibly
two years. On that same day Doebner granted Johann Priess the
power of attorney to represent him in legal matters. This suggests

that Doebner was about to move, and he did move to Galveston, where he was listed as a carpenter on the 1860 census.

The contract stated that Maier would finish the house. This consisted of four windows and window frames, a paneled front door and plain back door, two additional doors, a plank floor in the middle room, and plastering and white washing, all for the sum of ninety-six dollars. The house was originally plastered inside and out. Though it was a small house, the front part was divided into three rooms. Maier promised to have a plank floor made for the middle room; this may mean that the middle room was the best room, or *stube*, and that the side rooms had dirt floors, or it may mean that plank floors in the side rooms had already been installed. There was also a garret accessed by a ladder or simple stair in the southeast corner. The contract does not mention the back room, but the stonework does not suggest that it was a later addition, and Doebner may have already completed the windows in the back section.

In 1866 Maier sold the house to Johann Kallenberg, who then sold it to Friedrich Stoffers, whose family owned it until 1938. Stoffers was a saddler, an important profession in a town where nearly all travel was on horseback. In 1870 he valued his real estate at $1,900, a figure consistent with a story-and-a-half rock house in the center of town. After 1938 it was used as a produce business and a package store, during which the windows on both sides of the front door were

dramatically enlarged; they have now been restored to something like their original appearance.

32 Nimitz Hotel
340 East Main Street, National Museum of the Pacific War
Late 1850s, 1890s, 1926, 1980–83

Consider a few of the things this building has seen: years as a frontier hostelry, a dramatic makeover in the late Victorian era, an even more dramatic makeover in the 1920s, a dramatic restoration in the early 1980s, and a dramatic repurposing in the last two decades to become the front door of an important national museum. Charles and Sophie Nimitz purchased this property in 1855, when a small hotel already sat on the lot, and proceeded to build the western part of the present complex. The hotel had a nicely furnished parlor and dining room, a large ballroom, and ten guest rooms. Nimitz also brewed his own beer, as did the Menger Hotel in San Antonio. Nimitz remodeled the hotel between 1888 and 1896; this resulted in a new lobby for the ballroom and, above this, additional guest rooms. The upper level of the addition was reached by a veranda that wrapped around the building; it had a mansard roof with numerous dormer windows. The veranda was supported on stilt-like posts, giving it an extremely picturesque, Victorian appearance. Many have seen a likeness to a Mississippi riverboat.

After the death of Charles Nimitz, the hotel was sold in 1926 to a group of local investors who represented the progressive businessmen of Fredericksburg, including Hugo Basse, William Habenicht, Otto Kolmeier, Louis Kott, H. H. Sagebiel, Edward Stein, and Joe Stein. They were not at all impressed with the whimsical addition, and in spite of some local opposition, they removed all the Victorian features. Edward Stein, an architect, builder, and investor in the project who had worked for several years for the architect Leo M. J. Dielmann in San Antonio, remodeled it into a more sober and businesslike Mission (or Spanish Colonial Revival) style.

Where once the ship-like upper deck had boldly protruded into Main Street, a straight-edged gable tentatively tried to emulate the curvilinear gables of the San Antonio missions. The principal material

Circa 1890. Courtesy of the National Museum of the Pacific War, Fredericksburg.

Circa 1935. Courtesy of the National Museum of the Pacific War, Fredericksburg.

was a buff-colored brick, not unlike the brick was would be used in the next decade on the Fredericksburg National Bank [15] and the Gillespie County Courthouse [3], both designed by Edward Stein. Two demure rows of red tile at the roofline and above the mezzanine windows gave the hacienda a touch of Mexico, and colored tiles were strategically deployed across the façade. The ground floor, however, was all business, with large plate-glass windows and mezzanine windows above the awning which ran across the front. No beer could be brewed or sold in the new hotel, thanks to Prohibition, but after the repeal of that law became effective in December 1933, the hotel was able to proudly advertise the availability of Grand Prize Lager Beer from the Gulf Brewing Company in Houston, a regional brewery owned by Howard Hughes.

The hotel finally closed in October 1963; a year later it was

acquired by a new nonprofit organization, the Fleet Admiral Chester W. Nimitz Naval Museum, Inc. They wished to honor a native son, a grandson of the hoteliers Charles and Sophie Nimitz who was born one block to the west in the Basse-Henke house [22] and had gone on to become commander of the Pacific Fleet in World War II. However, the group fell far short of its fundraising goal of $1 million. The museum opened February 24, 1967, in an unrestored building with exhibits that consisted of letters, pictures, uniforms, and weaponry.

In June of 1970 the museum was given to the State of Texas and placed under the auspices of a special commission, the Fleet Admiral Chester W. Nimitz Naval Museum Commission. In the early 1970s the upper floors of buff-brown brick were painted white, two red stripes were painted across the façade, and blue lettering announced that this was the Admiral Nimitz Center. The Nimitz Museum Commission was decommissioned in 1981, and the museum was placed under the jurisdiction of the Texas Parks and Wildlife Department. At this time it was decided to restore the building to something like its Victorian appearance, and all evidence of the 1926 remodeling was removed. Project architects Tom Price, Mike Penick, and Robert Coffee attempted to restore the exterior based on historic photographs and surviving walls, but the interior was designed to modern museum exhibit standards.

The restored building was dedicated November 11, 1983. The museum and historic site have since been transferred to the Texas Historical Commission, and with a series of major expansions the museum complex has been designated as the National Museum of the Pacific War.

33 Victor and Clara Keidel House
403 East Main Street
1928

This is a two-story house in the Spanish Colonial Revival style, which is quite unusual for the Hill Country. Houses in this style were more popular in urban areas of Texas that experienced more growth between the two world wars, especially in San Antonio and Austin. The architect was Edward Stein, who attended school in San Antonio and then the Armour Institute of Technology in Chicago before working as a draftsman for Leo M. J. Dielmann in San Antonio for three years. He returned to Fredericksburg in 1917. At that point the regional version of the Spanish Colonial style had not been fully developed; nearly a decade later the architectural firm of Ayres & Ayres of San Antonio designed homes in this style for Thomas Hogg and P. L. Mannen. Stein and his clients, Victor and Clara Keidel, were clearly aware of the latest San Antonio fashion.

 The building was made of concrete blocks, covered with a thick

coat of white stucco and with a red tiled roof, which was characteristic of the Spanish Colonial style. The one-story entry porch has scalloped decoration above, while the cantilevered balcony to the left brings a bit of Monterey, California, to the Hill Country. The light fixture beneath the balcony is also very characteristic of the Spanish Colonial style. The house is set back from the street—further back than the entire depth of the Kiehne house [34] next door—allowing for a spacious front lawn, which was also atypical for the Main Street of Fredericksburg.

Inside was a squarish entry hall. Both the railing of the staircase and the hanging light fixture were made of wrought iron; the light fixture was said to have been made in San Antonio. To the left was the living room, with a prominent fireplace on the front wall and a picture window on the east side. Through an arched doorway on the south was the dining room, which also had generous eastern-facing windows. Both the living room and dining room have wood-paneled ceilings. The master bedroom is downstairs; upstairs were two more bedrooms and a sitting room. The public rooms through the house had floors of golden oak, and there are numerous French doors throughout, both features found in well-to-do houses of the 1920s.

Dr. Victor Keidel, a son of Dr. Albert and Matilde Keidel, grew up in his parents' Victorian house on East Main Street [24]. He was one of the earliest students at the San Antonio Academy, graduating in 1900—a decade before Ed Stein—and then attended the University of Texas. Victor married Clara Stieler, daughter of Hermann Stieler, a pioneer in nearby Comfort, and sister of Adolf Stieler, the rancher who was known by the 1940s as the "Goat King of Texas." For a while Victor and Clara lived in a story-and-a-half frame house that was built on the front part of this lot; when the new house was built in 1928, the old house was moved behind it and became a guest house. Nearby is an excellent example of a limestone smokehouse, built into the hillside, and a rock barn, both remnants from the earlier house.

At various times, Dr. Keidel had his offices upstairs in the Keidel Drug Store [23], in the Lungkwitz Store [25], and in the Keidel Clinic [26], but he also used the northwest room of the 1928 house to meet patients with emergencies. His brothers Kurt and Felix had built matching houses on South Washington Street in 1914 that blended the Queen Anne and Arts and Crafts styles [113 and 114]. Clara was one of the founders of the local public library and the Gillespie County Historical Society, both originally housed in the replica of the Vereins-Kirche [1].

34 Friedrich and Maria Kiehne House
405 East Main Street
1850–51, circa 1858

This two-story rock house is one of the oldest remaining houses in town and quite possibly the first rock house. The names of Friedrich and Maria Kiehne and the date 1850 are found in the keystone above the main door; that date for the start of construction is confirmed by tax records. Friedrich was a blacksmith and a farmer and acquired a great deal of land in the country around town. Much of the hardware in the house, most notably the hinges on the front doors, has been attributed to him. Originally the house had two rooms down and two rooms up; the exterior walls were stone, but the partition dividing the interior was *fachwerk*. Most striking was its two-story front porch, not common in Germany but a necessity in Texas, a feature that Germans quickly learned from Anglo-Texans, though there were doors into both front rooms and no central passage. The front porch at one time contained a staircase, but it is uncertain as to whether this was original, as there may have been an external stair on the back; at any rate an internal stair was built when rooms were added to the rear around 1858. In 1850 the household also included the couple's three sons and two other people: a fourteen-year-old German girl (who may have been learning the art of keeping house from Maria) and Maria's seventy-year-old father Conrad Kreinsen—which may explain the highly unusual use of her maiden name on the keystone.

Friedrich and Maria worshiped with the Protestant congregation in the Vereins-Kirche, and the baptismal records of the church show association with a number of craftsmen who may have been involved in the construction of their house. Johann Joseph Walch and John Ruegner were likely to have been the stonemasons on the building, and Christian Altgelt and Christian Staats the carpenters. Walch's house still stands on East Austin Street [121], and Ruegner's house on West San Antonio Street [5].

Photo by Richard MacAllister, May 29, 1936, for the Historic American Buildings Survey, Library of Congress.

Remarkably, Friedrich was still alive in 1896, so Julius Splittgerber, another old pioneer, could interview him. Splittgerber wrote: "With increasing prosperity came the desire to enjoy the blessings thereof.

The primitive houses were replaced by better ones. Mr. Kiehne erected the first stone building, using the soft stone which he quarried at Cross Mountain." Friedrich died in 1898, and his heirs sold the house in 1904. The exterior was photographed by the Dallas architect David R. Williams and by the Historic American Buildings Survey in the 1930s, when its rugged simplicity once again began to be admired. Maria and Ronald Herrmann bought the house in 1973 and had it restored by William Kargan "W. K." (or "Keggy") Perrett with assistance from Tyrus Cox. The deteriorated floors were removed, random-length planks were laid over new electrical conduits and air conditioning ducts, and a modern kitchen was built in the west rear room.

35 Carl and Margarethe Weyrich House (Weyrich-Arhelger House)
420 East Main Street
1867–68, 1870–72

Though long thought to date to 1853, this large and impressive house was clearly built more than a decade later. Carl and Margarethe Weyrich were living on this lot by 1853, but this house is extremely large, well built, and, most importantly, has numerous Anglo features that were not adopted in Fredericksburg until after the Civil War. Carl pursued diversified activities such as gunsmithing, locksmithing,

trading in buffalo hides, and sheep raising, while Margarethe tended to their own large flock of children. Margarethe's sister, Elise Heuser, had married the tinsmith and silversmith Adolf Lungkwitz and lived further west on Main Street [25]. In 1866 he sold his other town lot— on Lincoln Street—to the stonemason Lorenz Schmidt, who soon built a story-and-a-half rock house [73], and Weyrich set to work building a new house, possibly with the assistance of Schmidt.

The Weyrich house was a full two stories—still very rare for Fredericksburg in 1867—with large six-over-six windows like those Weyrich had seen in Austin and San Antonio. He made the locks on the double doors, decorated with a five-pointed star and a lyre. Just as striking was the central passageway, which most German Texans considered to be a waste of space. In a nod to traditional ways, Weyrich placed French doors in each of the front rooms so that each room could be directly accessed from the street. A second set of rock rooms, with somewhat lower ceilings, were added around 1870–72.

The house was later purchased by F. W. Arhelger, whose wheelwright shop faced the Marktplatz on North Adams Street. The biggest change made by the Arhelger family was the removal of the two-story porch that fronted the central bay, which they replaced with a spacious concrete porch which stretched across the entire front. In the 1970s the house was purchased by Patty and Gerald Harvey Jones—he paints under the name "G. Harvey"—and the porch was restored to something like its original configuration. Other improvements included a two-car garage on the west side and a guest house to the rear.

---

36 African Methodist Episcopal Church
520 East Main Street
1887

Though Fredericksburg was overwhelmingly German, the population did include some Anglo-Texans and a few Afro-Texan families. This small frame church is virtually the only remaining evidence of that community. It was built in 1887 for a small African-American congregation. The pulpit was at the north end, and above it is painted on the wall, "Make a joyful noise to the Lord." (from Psalms). A flue cover in

the center of the ceiling (and the pipe chimney on the ridge outside) shows that a cast-iron stove was placed in the center of the space.

This not only distributed heat evenly throughout the space but also cut down on having to clean up creosote that dripped from the joints of horizontal stove pipes. The trustees included Cyrus Russel, who farmed in the area around Fort Martin Scott, and James Tinker, who farmed in the northwestern part of Gillespie County. At some point a one-room schoolhouse was built just to the east; a better structure was erected in 1922. The schoolhouse was moved in 1981 to a site next to 107 East Schubert Street [144] and adapted for use as a guest house. The church building was restored in 1976 and given a Texas historical marker the next year, but little has been done with it since. In spite of intense commercial development in the area, the little church remains on its original site on the eastern margins of town.

PART 3

Main Street, West of the Marktplatz and Courthouse Square

37 Heinrich and Elise Ochs House
215B West Main Street
1870–71

Though it takes some careful looking to see the original house, this is
an important smaller house. Its original owner, Heinrich Ochs, was
one of the first schoolteachers in town and was county clerk of Gillespie County from 1859 to 1869. He and his wife Elise bought this lot
in 1868 and built the house in 1870 and 1871. Originally it had a front
porch, but in the 1960s this was enclosed to create more space. The
original front door, with its fanlight, sidelights, and sloping pediment,
is visible just inside the present front door. The house had a central
passage; along with the Weyrich house on East Main [35] and the
Brockmann house on East San Antonio [122], it was one of the earliest
houses in town to have such a space. As a one-story house, there was
no need for a staircase in the hall or elsewhere. The house originally
had one room on each side of the passage (there is a window on the
rear wall of the right front room), but another large room was added
beyond on this side. The house was renovated in the 1960s by Milton M.
Moseley, a semiretired architect, and his wife Johnnie Moseley, an

interior decorator; they had both worked on the restoration and adaptation of the Victorian courthouse as the Pioneer Memorial Library [2] and in the 1970s owned the A. L. Patton Building [41] across the street from the Ochs house.

38 William and Elise Wahrmund House
214 West Main Street
1877–78

This charming little house is the last remnant of the Wahrmund family complex, which ran all the way to Crockett Street. William L. Wahrmund was a son of William Wahrmund, longtime chief justice of Gillespie County and later county judge. The elder Wahrmund had a rock house and store at the corner of North Crockett Street, facing the Marktplatz. In 1870 the younger William was clerking in his father's store. This corner house and store was demolished between 1915 and 1924 to make way for a filling station. William L. Wahrmund married Elise Hopf in 1874, and their new house was built in 1877 and 1878.

Originally it was a two-room house. Entry was into the *stube*, which occupied the eastern two-thirds of the house; a bedroom was to the left. A later rock addition, built before 1896, created a bedroom on the east and a kitchen on the west. This may have been added by William's brother Henry and his wife, the former Meta Nimitz, who married in

1886, moved into the house, and raised their family there. Henry and Meta's son Henry later built a house on West Austin Street [131]. In the 1970s the house was adapted as a savings and loan; as part of this project, local restorationist Tyrus Cox oversaw the adaptation of the house and the recreation of the Victorian front porch. Later still the house was adapted for others uses, but the drive-through window and the envelope depository on the west side were preserved as mementos of its 1970s usage.

39 Schwarz Building
216 West Main Street
1907–8

This early twentieth-century commercial building with a residence above replaced an earlier one-story rock structure that was associated with the Schmidt Hotel next door [40]. Maria, a daughter of Ludwig and Katharina Schmidt, married Charles Schwarz in 1888. They built this edifice to house his mercantile company, and the family lived above the store. The building is predominantly limestone, with red

granite cornerstones at both front corners. The stonework of the walls is very regular; the top of the main façade is the most ornate part of the building, with a broken-scroll pediment rising in the middle and smaller cartouches with a "C" in one and "S" in the other. At the base are blocks of red granite—inscribed with "Chas. Schwarz" and "1907"—presumably from Nagel Brothers Monumental Works [6]. Local contractor Franz Stein furnished the materials for the building and probably oversaw its construction. Originally the building did not have a front gallery, though there was a two-story gallery with staircase in the back; a wooden front porch was added between 1910 and 1915; later still this was replaced by the current cast-iron gallery. Another later addition was an external staircase on the east side, which was installed when the upstairs was turned into apartments. The stair has since been removed; the balcony is the only reminder of that era of the building's history.

---

40 Schmidt Hotel (Dietz Hotel)
218 West Main Street
1869–70

The Schmidt Hotel was one of the uptown rivals to the Nimitz Hotel [32]. Ludwig Schmidt, like his brother, Lorenz, trained as a stone-mason and acquired the property in 1857. He immediately built a one-story rock house, with two large rooms in front and two behind. This was next door to the present building, where the Schwarz Building [39] now stands. The rooms on the east were a *stube* and the kitchen; eventually, the two west rooms were used as the dining room for the hotel, but this may have been used by Ludwig, Maria Katharina, and their six children, born between 1856 and 1874.

The building at 218 West Main was built between 1869 and 1870, when Schmidt's property taxes went from $700 to $1,500 to $4,000. Its hipped roof was quite rare for Fredericksburg—one of the few other examples is on the house of another stonemason, Charles Jung [143], also from the 1870s. The six-over-six windows of the lower floor were symmetrically balanced to each side of the centrally placed double doors. These doors opened into the hotel lobby; behind this was an

Courtesy of Institute of Texan Cultures, University of Texas at San Antonio, 075–0229.

office. The western two-fifths of the building was rental property, usually occupied by a physician. The upper floor was more evenly divided, with a passage running down the middle; there were two large rooms on the west side and four smaller rooms on the east. The Victorian porch was not added until the 1890s.

Ludwig Schmidt passed away in 1879 or early 1880; in the summer of 1880 his widow, Katharina, was keeping the hotel, aided by their twenty-four-year-old son Otto. The yard behind the hotel and house had a barn and frame sheds. The hotel was a stagecoach stop in 1880, and the census recorded six stagecoach drivers in residence there.

Later, it was the Dietz Hotel, run by Louis Dietz, though by 1896 it was called the Central Hotel. By 1902 the hotel building was being used as a general store, and the one-story rock structure as a dwelling. In 1910 the hotel was a warehouse, but by 1915 it was a drug store. It was purchased in 1957 by Arthur Stehling, who converted it into his home and office.

41 A. L. Patton Building
222 West Main Street
1897

This building, a simple evocation of the Richardsonian Romanesque style, combined commercial space on the ground floor and residential space above. Albert Lee Patton was a native of Independence, Missouri, but grew up in San Antonio. He came to Fredericksburg in the early 1870s and opened a tin shop. He married a local girl, Emma Auguste Wahrmund, sister of William L. Wahrmund [38] in 1875, and they started to build a house on North Orange Street [43] around 1880. The downstairs of the Main Street building was rented to Citizen's Bank by 1905. (Patton's general mercantile was in a one-story room adjoining on the west.) This bank was run by members of the Bierschwale family—William and his sons Walter and Max [see 136, 134, and 161]. The bank fell victim to the Great Depression, going out of business on February 19, 1932—the same day that the Bank of Fredericksburg closed. The gallery featured cast-iron posts and railings, and large plate-glass windows provided ample light and considerable display space. Upstairs were the living quarters: the living room and dining room were on the west, separated by the stair hall and bathroom. The kitchen was east of the dining room; in front of this was the parents' bedroom; the girls' bedroom was at the front.

42 Hoerster-Blum Building
244 West Main Street
Circa 1897–1901

This is yet another good example of a Victorian commercial building with ground-floor retail space and a residence upstairs. J. Anton Hoerster bought the lot in 1878–79 and quickly built a log house, roughly eighteen by fourteen feet; around 1881 he added a rock kitchen, and later still more rooms to the east. The present structure was built after 1896 and before 1902. The building has rock side walls; in front are large plate-glass windows and a cast-iron front from Mesker Brothers of St. Louis, a pressed metal cornice, and a two-story frame front porch with slim cast-iron columns. Several buildings on East Main Street also have storefronts from Mesker Brothers [see 23], indicating that Fredericksburg merchants were happy to take advantage of manufactured parts and an improved transportation system. Hoerster sold the

building in 1910 to Max Blum, a lawyer who served as county judge from 1904 to 1914. Presumably he rented out the retail space while the Blum family—wife Elizabeth and four kids—lived upstairs. On the west side, facing Orange Street, were a parlor, dining room, kitchen, and bath; on the east side were bedrooms.

Around the Corner on North Orange Street

43 A. L. and Emma Patton House
107 North Orange Street
Circa 1880, circa 1890

This simple post–Civil War rock house was thoroughly Victorianized twenty years later. A. L. Patton was a native of Missouri, grew up in San Antonio, and was in Fredericksburg by 1872. Marrying Emma Wahrmund in 1875, he bought part of town lot 102 in 1877. At first they lived in a log house, then built the north part of the present house, consisting of four rooms. The south wing, which added two more rooms, has a bay window and sets of paired brackets in the gable, making it more fully Victorian. The large size of the windows in the

bay and on the south side wall is in stark contrast to those on the original part of the house. As continued to be typical with German Texas houses, the new rooms did not have fireplaces, but flue openings in the party wall, above which was a brick chimney. This new south wing was built by stonemason A. W. Petmecky, who worked on a number of other notable buildings in Fredericksburg, such as the White Elephant Saloon [21], the Albert and Mathilde Keidel house [24], and an addition to his own house [70]. The Patton family moved to the upper floor of their Main Street building [41] circa 1897. The Victorian trim on the front porch, while relatively recent, is a fairly plausible take on what might have been there originally. The Pattons' daughter Elizabeth married Anton Norwall Moursund in 1899; his parents lived at 302 North Kay [138].

44 Wisseman-Gentemann-Hanisch House
301 West Main Street
Circa 1855, 1858, 1871–72, early 1890s and later

The western half of this building was the home of the cabinetmaker Conrad Wisseman and his wife Luise. The first rock room was

completed in 1855; the kitchen behind it was built in 1858. The front
room had a centered door and with a window to each side. Conrad and
Louise were friends with Heinrich and Auguste Kammlah, who lived
two doors down [46]. Indeed, Conrad may have been involved in the
construction and furnishing of the Kammlahs' house. Wisseman sold
the property in 1862 to another cabinetmaker, Friedrich Gentemann.
Friedrich and his wife Margarethe were Catholics, and they certainly
appreciated that this lot backed up to St. Mary's Church [84], then
under construction and on which Friedrich worked. In 1870 Gentemann told the census taker that his property was worth $800, and
he made improvements to the property circa 1871–72. Gentemann sold
the house to Paul Hanisch in 1879; a few years later the Gentemanns
built a small rock Sunday house a little more than a block to the west
[87]. In the early 1890s Hanisch doubled the front part of the house.
The old house became a pharmacy, while the new block contained a
parlor and a bedroom. The stonework, notably the window sills and
lintels, is markedly different and decidedly Victorian, as are the new
porch posts added at that time.

45 Meckel House / Hanus Sanitarium / Sisters of Divine
Providence Convent
307 West Main Street
Late 1880s, circa 1909, circa 1949

This building started out as a one-story rock structure built for Henry B. and Mathilde Meckel, which looked nothing like it does now. Henry was a son of pioneer Conrad Meckel, who had been killed by Indians in 1866. Henry ran a saddlery in town. He and Mathilde were Catholics and, like the Gentemanns and Fassels, appreciated the proximity to St. Mary's Church [84]. They built a one-story, three-room rock house sometime between 1886 and 1896. It had a front porch just in front of the door.

Dramatic changes came sometime before 1910. A second story was added, which allowed for a two-story front porch with white columns and balustrades on both floors. This gave the house something of a Colonial Revival appearance. Henry Meckel died in 1909 and Mathilde Meckel in 1913, and the house was sold to Felix Walch. In 1924 it was serving as the Dr. J. J. Hanus Sanitarium, and in 1927 Dr. Hanus bought the structure. At that time an elevator was installed toward the back of the central passage. The hospital was closed during World War II and never reopened.

In 1949 the building was sold to the Catholic Diocese of San Antonio, which used it as a residence for the Sisters of Divine Providence, who taught at St. Mary's School [83]. At that time more dramatic changes occurred: the two-story, Colonial Revival porch was removed and replaced with the more nondescript one-story entrance in the center of the façade. By 1990 it had been turned into an office building; at this writing it houses the offices of St. Mary's Church.

---

46 Heinrich and Auguste Kammlah House
309 West Main Street, Pioneer Museum Complex
1853–54, circa 1858, circa 1867, 1869, circa 1902–10

The Kammlah house embodies a remarkable story: it is one of the oldest houses in town, but also a house to which a pioneer family made extensive additions over the course of five decades and which has survived in its present state for another century.

The phases of the house move chronologically from front to back. The front room is the earliest surviving room and has long been thought to date to 1849. The family was certainly living on the lot by then, but in a log house set back from the street. Tax records strongly suggest that three front rooms were built around 1853–54, and the physical evidence of the house, specifically the lack of a kitchen, suggests that the log house continued to be used for that purpose. These rooms are now open as one, as perhaps they have been since 1870,

Photo by Richard MacAllister, May 29, 1936, for the Historic American Buildings Survey, Library of Congress.

when this part of the complex became commercial space. This earliest part of the house was in *fachwerk*, the traditional German manner of building a frame that was then infilled with brick, stone, or even adobe. The builder may well have been Conrad Wisseman, a carpenter and cabinetmaker who lived on the same block at the corner of West Main and Orange [44].

The entire rest of the complex was built of native rock, starting with a lean-to on the eastern end. This is called the first kitchen, which it may have been; it was definitely the first room with a fireplace. As cooking hearths go, it is rather small. Another, larger room, known as the second kitchen, has a large hearth at its south end, raised two feet off the ground. This is a Germanic feature seen in only a few other Fredericksburg houses, such as the Tatsch house [132]. Traditionally the second kitchen has been thought to date just before the Civil War, and the evidence of the tax records is inconclusive. It may date to 1859–60, but could also be postwar, like the Tatsch kitchen.

What is certain is that Heinrich Kammlah built what he called a "new" house after the war, probably in 1869. The stonemason for the new house may well have been Carl Henke, who was a friend of the family and who had worked on the buildings at Fort Concho in San

Angelo with Heinrich Kammlah's younger son Willie. The construction of the new house allowed him to convert the original house into a general store. This store operated from 1870 until the death of Henry Kammlah II, the eldest son of Heinrich Kammlah, in 1924. The new house also took the form of a story-and-a-half rock house, many of which were being built in the late 1860s and 1870s. Like the original, the new house had three rooms. A new parlor was on the east, a bedroom was in the middle, and a sort of utility room was on the west. A large swinging door separated the parlor and bedroom and could be swung open for social occasions. The west room later became a bathroom. Unlike the old house, which had unlighted attic space, the new house had a half story lit by numerous windows. Beneath the east and center rooms was a large basement space, ideal for storing foodstuffs and other goods. A porch on the back side of the complex was enclosed sometime between 1902 and 1910.

After a century of ownership by the Kammlah family, the house was acquired by the Gillespie County Historical Society in 1955. Restoration work was done under the direction of local antiquarian and restorer Albert Keidel, the son of Dr. Victor Keidel and his wife Clara [see 33] and grandson of Dr. Albert Keidel [see 24]. In the front part of the house a window on the east wall was removed, apparently to accommodate shelves for the display of museum artifacts. Perhaps the most drastic change was replacing the roof on the second kitchen. The original roof, visible in the HABS photograph of the 1930s, had collapsed, and Keidel found another old roof to replace it. In 2007 the Gillespie County Historical Society contracted with Volz and Associates of Austin to prepare a historic structures report on the Kammlah house, and the preservation of the house is ongoing.

---

47 Matthias and Maria Fassel House (Fassel-Roeder House)
325 West Main Street, Pioneer Museum Complex
Circa 1876, 1890, 1900

Although this house is quite small, with only three rooms, it was originally even smaller. Heinrich Kammlah, who lived on the next lot over [46], acquired this lot in 1852 and later sold one quarter of it to Franz

Koehler and another quarter to Moritz Hartmann in 1871. Matthias
Fassel, a wheelwright who came from Germany in 1871, married Maria
Baumann in 1875 in the old St. Mary's Church [84]. By 1880 the family included Sophie, three, and Anna, four months old. Fassel bought
Koehler's share of the lot in 1876, and Hartmann's in 1884. Matthias
and Maria may have appreciated the fact that this lot was located on
Main Street—which was good for business—and was very near to their
church. In fact, a daughter of the Fassels, Lina Dupray, recalled that
after Midnight Mass on Christmas Eve, a large group would come to
the house for coffee.

The house was built one room at a time. The southwest room is
said to be the earliest and may predate the Fassel ownership; this
is now interpreted as a bedroom. Next came the kitchen, just to the
east of this. The two back rooms were present in 1896; the large front
room was added between that date and 1902; finally, the porch was
added before 1910. Maria's brother, John Baumann, is said to have
been one of the stonemasons of the nearby Sunday house of Friedrich
and Margarethe Gentemann [87]; he may have worked on his sister's
house as well. Members of the Fassel family sold the house in 1967 to
the Gillespie County Historical Society, which restored the building
and opened it to the public in May 1975.

A small frame building originally stood between the house and the
street, which is why the present house is set back from the street. At
first this was Fassel's wheelwright shop; by 1902 it was a blacksmith's

shop, which also shows up on Sanborn fire insurance maps through 1915. By 1924, however, the shop was gone.

48 August and Alwina Weber Sunday House
325 West Main Street, Pioneer Museum Complex
1904

This excellent example of a Sunday house was built in 1904 by August Weber, who grew up in the country south of town, and his wife, the former Alwina Wehmeyer, whose father, Conrad, owned a bakery in town. The couple received the lot as a gift from Alwina's mother,

Louise Klingelhoefer Wehmeyer. Like the Jenschke Sunday house [155], the Weber Sunday house was built in a new subdivision, the West End division on West San Antonio Street just beyond Cherry Street. The Webers belonged to Zion Lutheran Church—in fact, August was serving as one of the administrators of the church in 1896—so this lot was on the right side of town.

This little house sufficed for August, Alwina, and their children, Bertha and Adelbert. It had only one room, and there was only one door into it. There was a window on each side of the door, and one window on each side wall. There was no running water (the family had to bring jugs with them) and no electricity (oil lamps and candles provided some light). The chimney near the back left corner connected to a cast-iron stove inside. The advent of cars and trucks made Sunday houses obsolete by the 1920s. The widow of Adelbert Weber gave the house to the Gillespie County Historical Society in 1972, and it was moved to its current site. She also donated several pieces of furniture and plates used in the house, including the kitchen cupboard.

---

49 White Oak School
325 West Main Street, Pioneer Museum Complex
1920s

The White Oak School is a good example of a one-room schoolhouse. It was built in the 1920s in the White Oak community in the southwestern part of the county, near the Kerr County line, replacing a structure built in 1890. The new school building used board-and-batten construction (vertical boards butted together, with battens or strips covering the joints) and is topped with a hipped tin roof. The door is angled at one of the corners. The grouping of four windows in one wall and three in another, which was typical in early twentieth-century American houses, allowed for use of the other two walls for a blackboard and bookshelves. The school closed in 1950, when it merged with the Morris Ranch School. Mr. and Mrs. Charles Feller donated the school to the Pioneer Museum; Charles had attended the school, as had his brother, Stanley, and his father, Bruno.

50 Anna Besier House (Dambach-Besier House)
325 West Main Street, Pioneer Museum Complex
1893

This house stood for many years at 515 East Main Street before it was dismantled rock by rock and moved to the museum complex in 2005. Its history is not well documented; its most interesting years were when it was owned by a young widow with four children. The lot was

previously owned by Friedrich Dambach, from 1867 to 1869, and it has been suggested that he built the house; however, he sold the lot for only $450, which is very low for a rock house that is nearly two stories, and suggests that the lot contained only a small log or *fachwerk* house. Moreover, the L-shape plan of the house and the two-over-two windows are characteristic of the 1890s or even the first decade of the twentieth century in Fredericksburg, and, indeed, the largest increases in the property values came in 1893 and 1907.

Whenever this house was built, the property was bought in 1881 by Anna Besier, the widow of George Besier. Anna was the eldest daughter of John Schmidtzinsky, a farmer and carpenter who had worked on the Marienkirche [84] in the early 1860s. Her mother, Anna Maria, had contributed two dollars to the fund to pay for benches in the new church. Anna's husband George died in July 1880, one month after the census taker recorded that George, thirty, and Anna, twenty-nine, had three children, Thekla, Joseph, and Emily. A fourth child, Bertha, was born in September. For a while they lived on the farm of Anna's brother, also named John Schmidtzinsky, but Thekla was already attending school and Joseph was approaching school age, so Anna decided to move to town. She was a devout Catholic, and her children would all attend St. Mary's School.

In 1882 Anna Besier owned ten cows worth $70, so she could sell milk, butter, and cheese to people in town; the children were put to work delivering milk to the Nimitz Hotel [32] and to private homes before school. They also had a large vegetable garden and sold what the family did not eat. In 1882 Anna Besier also claimed $600 in goods and merchandise, suggesting that she had a little store attached to her house. This house may have been built in the hope that she could rent rooms to boarders. Moreover, Anna's father died in 1893, and her mother may have had thoughts of moving to town. She may also have seen building a large new house as an investment in her children, and, indeed, in 1924 she gave the house to her son Joe. She died two years later.

In 1967 the house was converted into part of the Sunday House Restaurant; in 2005 it was dismantled and rebuilt as the new entrance to the Pioneer Museum complex and as a welcome center for the Fredericksburg Convention and Visitors Bureau.

51 Oscar Krauskopf Building
312 West Main Street
Circa 1896

This building is the last remnant of the Krauskopf family on this block of West Main Street. The patriarch, Engelbert Krauskopf, was skilled at many of the mechanical arts, particularly gunsmithing, locksmithing, and cabinetmaking. He and his family first lived in a log house, then a story-and-a-half rock house at the eastern end of this block. Engelbert died in 1881, and his wife Rosa in 1884, but the business was carried on first by their son Oscar and then by their grandson Lawrence. The houses of Engelbert and Oscar are long gone, but the house of Lawrence and his wife Meta still stands on North Bowie Street [134]. The building on Main Street was extant by 1896 and was where Oscar sold buggies and carriages. The back room was a warehouse for agricultural implements. The rest of the Krauskopf building was demolished in 1961 and was adapted for use as a restaurant and beer garden in the late 1970s.

52 Itz Hotel, Saloon, and Residence
320 West Main Street
Circa 1870 and later

This building has had many uses: store, hotel, saloon, meeting hall, and residence. The lot on which this structure is built was purchased by Peter Itz in 1865. The Itz family had been farming in the Palo Alto community since before the Civil War; their farm was on Lower Crabapple Road just across Palo Alto Creek. (Their 1850s log house, done in the Anglo-Southern manner, and their circa 1875 story-and-a-half rock house are just visible from the road.) Peter was sixty-eight in 1870, and his son Carl thirty-eight. The two-story structure was probably built as a store and residence for Carl, his wife Henriette (née Evers), and their thirteen children, nine of whom survived into adulthood. The little log house that is connected to the building on the back side may be the oldest building on the property and may have

served as a retirement home for Carl's parents, Peter and Christine. Beneath the log room is a basement, which can be reached by doors on the front porch. The little rock addition on the west and north was built between 1902 and 1910 when Carl and Henriette let the next generation take over.

The Itz family married into other families with strong craft traditions, like the Jungs and Arhelgers; moreover, the Itzes themselves were involved in craft-related activities: before the war they made shingles on the Guadalupe River, and in 1889 they worked on the new Evangelical Church, of which they were members.

The front part of this two-story rock building was built around 1870. Peter Itz reported owning $4,000 in real estate when the census taker called in 1870, and this date is further supported by tax records and the six-over-six windows with sloping, pediment-like window frames. The back wall mirrors the front wall, having a centered door with a window to each side. The back section was added before 1896, when it was shown on the Sanborn fire insurance map. At that time the front part still had a shingle roof, while the rear unit had a tin roof. The original back windows were converted into cabinets. In 1896 the building was labeled as McDougal's Hotel, and the front room was a saloon. This was probably the establishment of William McDougal, who had been a farm laborer in 1880 at the Lorenz place [see 167]

---

and was working on his own farm in 1900. In 1899 it was "Herman's Saloon—A Popular Men's Resort." Rudolph Itz, grandson of Peter and son of Carl, married Emma Lehne in 1902, and it became Rudolph's Saloon.

The saloon was in the large front room; in the newer part of the building were a small room to store kegs, the dining room, the kitchen, and a bedroom. The stairway rose out of the bedroom. Upstairs in front there was a living room on the east and a bedroom on the west. Behind this were two more bedrooms on the west side, and on the east side a meeting room for groups, bands, and choirs. The saloon went out of business at the beginning of Prohibition in 1920. Much restoration has been done since the late 1970s, including the reconstruction of the front porch.

53 August Itz Store
330 West Main Street
1908

August Itz, the youngest son of Carl and Henriette [52], built a two-story commercial building next door to the west in 1908. Around 1904 August married Celestine Schlaudt, who was born and reared in a house one block to the west [58]. The storefront had large plate-glass windows and a pressed tin cornice, features as modern as you could get, but the side walls were limestone, a feature as traditionally Hill Country as you could get. In 1910 the entire first floor was a general store; in 1915 the east half of the building was a grocery store, and the west half a billiards hall. August proudly described himself as the proprietor of a general merchandise store in the 1910 census, but his business career was somewhat rocky. In 1920 he was a clerk in a grocery store in rural Bexar County, of which San Antonio is the county seat. Ten years later August, Celestine, and their three children were back in Fredericksburg, and he reported that he was a clerk in a dry goods store, presumably their own building, which was worth a very substantial $7,500. Around 1935 the family moved one block to the west to take care of Celestine's eighty-two-year old mother, Sophie Schlaudt. Sophie's husband John had died in 1901.

54 Ludwig and Paulina Evers Store and Residence
342 West Main Street
Circa 1870–71 and later

Ludwig Evers was a brother of Henriette Itz, the wife of Carl Itz, and Ludwig married Pauline Itz. Carl and Pauline's father, Peter Itz, owned this lot and the two to the west [52, 53]. The Itz family had farmed in the Palo Alto community just north of town, and the Evers family in Cherry Spring in the northwestern part of the county. After the Civil War both families moved to town. The Itzes and Everses owned the three lots jointly and paid taxes on them jointly until 1887, when the lots were partitioned. This two-story rock structure was built around 1870–72, and by 1896 there was a one-story rock lean-to on the back side. Sometime between 1915 and 1924 the front porch was enclosed with side rock walls and a front with show windows, with a new projecting porch roof, suspended on chains, above which was a band of windows to light the new front room.

55 William C. and Emma Henke House
402 West Main Street
1886

The date stone above the door proudly proclaims that this story-and-a-half house was built in 1886. In plan it was quite American: a central passage with two rooms on each side. The living room and a spare

bedroom were on the west; the parents' bedroom and kitchen were on the east. Upstairs were bedrooms for their ten children. William Henke went into the family business and opened an uptown meat market. In the early days he sold meat from the front porch. By 1924 the meat market was in a wood-frame structure attached to the rear wall of the kitchen. Beyond this, in another frame building, was a rendering kettle; presumably Emma Henke was relieved when the market moved next door to what is now 407 West Main in 1925.

---

56 George Wilhelm and Sophie Crenwelge House
415 West Main Street
1871–72

George Wilhelm Crenwelge and his wife Sophie were parents of three young children, two boys and a girl, when they built this house in 1871–72. They had built the smaller rock house [57] just to the west

---

the year before, and after the completion of this house they used the neighboring one as a rent house. Their family grew to include two boys and four girls; in addition, Wilhelm's parents, Peter and Henriette, who were in their seventies, lived with them. Peter Crenwelge was a farmer and a wheelwright, as was Wilhelm. Another son, Philipp, was a wagoner. These were men who worked with their hands, and these two sturdy rock houses show that their craftsmanship was appreciated by others in the community. Wilhelm and Sophie's daughter Dora was married in this house in 1898 to Otto Kolmeier; they started their own house in the center of town [28] in 1901.

This two-story rock house originally had a front porch. The double doors with attractive transoms opened onto the porch on both the first and second floors. They were clearly made by someone who was a cabinetmaker, as each door has handsome diamond-shaped panels; moreover, there is a false stile—a strip of wood attached to one door to cover the spot where the two doors abut—a construction feature also found on the Schmidt-Gold House [73]. There was one room in front on the ground floor, behind which were two corner rooms separated by a little passage with a staircase. Later, partition walls were added to the front section to create two rooms and a central passage through the entire house. The southwest room served as the Crenwelges' kitchen and dining room. Upstairs were four bedrooms. There was also a basement along the east side of the house.

In 1939 the heirs sold the house; the porch was removed sometime after that date, though the stone steps and floor of the porch remain. After 1945 the house was used for storage for the Fredericksburg Coca-Cola Bottling Company and Pearl Beer Distributing Company; the latter was at the west end of the block, facing Zion Lutheran Church [61].

The earliest structure on this lot was a two-room log house. The back room, perhaps earlier, was traditional log construction with chinking between the logs; the front room used the German technique of interlined logs and rock, firmly mortared together. There was a porch on the east side of the building, facing toward town. Although Zion Lutheran was just to the west, in 1870 this was a lightly settled part of town. The log and rock house was a carpenter's shop in 1896 and in 1910 but was again a dwelling by 1915.

57 Crenwelge Rent House
419 West Main Street
1870

George Wilhelm Crenwelge bought this lot in 1865 for fifty dollars and soon built a one-room log house with a porch facing the street. Its southwest corner almost touched the porch of the log house next door, soon to be owned by Johann and Sophie Schlaudt [58]. Around 1870 Crenwelge and his wife Sophie decided to build this two-story rock house behind the log house. It had two rooms down, and two upstairs; because the log house stood perhaps two feet in front of the west room, the rock house did not have a front porch. The east front room was the parlor, and the west front room the kitchen; upstairs there was a small bedroom on the east and a larger one on the west. This house, like the one next door, has a large basement. Its valuation in the 1870 census, $1,500, was consistent with most houses of this size.

After the Crenwelge family completed the larger two-story rock house next door [56], they lived in that house and used this one as a

rent house. Among the early tenants were Professor Charles F. Tansill, who came to Texas as part of the US Army Signal Corps in the late 1870s and served as principal of the Methodist College in Fredericksburg in the early 1880s [see 151].

The log room was still present in 1896 but had been demolished by 1910. As a result, the house is set back from the street, which allowed for a garden in front. (The one-story porch is a relatively recent addition.) In 1939 the other descendants sold this house to their brother Adolph Crenwelge, who mainly lived on his ranch. In the early 1940s Adolph, his wife Sarah, and their children often used this as their Sunday house when attending Zion Lutheran [61] across the street.

58 Johann and Sophie Schlaudt House
421 West Main Street
1871–72, circa 1915

As with so many Fredericksburg town lots, the first building on this site was a log house. The property was purchased from Wilhelm and Sophie Crenwelge in 1871 by a blacksmith, Johann Schlaudt, and his wife Sophie (née Honig). The Schlaudts soon built a story-and-a-half rock house, attached to the single-story log structure, which remained the front room of the house until perhaps as late as 1924. The back

room was the kitchen, and the two bedrooms upstairs were accessed from a narrow staircase in that room. Among their children was Celestine, born in the house in 1881, who married August Itz, who built a general store one block to the east in 1908 [53].

John Schlaudt died in 1901, and Sophie and her unmarried daughter Anna lived for a while with another of her daughters, Hulda (who had married W. R. Eckert), on a ranch in the Eckert community. When Sophie and Anna returned to town around or after 1915, they made big changes to the old house. They added a western wing made of concrete blocks, fronted by a porch, giving the old rock house a newer (but not too modish) Victorian form. (In the years between 1910 and 1925 building with concrete blocks was at its peak in Fredericksburg.) In 1920 Sophie and Anna were living in Fredericksburg, and twenty-six-year-old Anna was working as a milliner.

Around 1935 her daughter Celestine, her husband August Itz, and two of their children moved in to take care of Sophie. In 1940 August was a clerk in a general merchandise store, his son Raymond, twenty-five, was a machinist in a garage, and daughter Lucille, nineteen, was a salesclerk in a jewelry store. Celestine cared for her mother, turning the old rock trough from her father's blacksmith shop into a flower planter. The house was valued at $1,000, sharply less than the Kammlah house [46] at $6,000 or the Kraus Building two doors down [59] at $10,000. Sophie died in 1950 at age ninety-eight.

---

59 Kraus Building
423 West Main Street
1870–71, 1906

At the western end of the block, facing Zion Lutheran Church, is the Kraus building, a two-story rock structure. In 1867 this lot was one of four owned by John Fuhrmann, which together were valued at eighty dollars. Wilhelm Luckenbach acquired this lot and hastily built a house, set back from Main Street and facing South Edison, which had one room of rock, one of log, and another of *fachwerk*. This was removed between 1902 and 1910 and replaced by a frame barn. In 1870–71 Luckenbach built the part of the present building that is at

---

the front corner of the lot. The walls were rock, with two stories in front and a story and a half behind. The pair of double doors opening into the front room suggest that it was built as a store. Before 1906 the building did not have a front porch.

In the early 1890s the merchant Balthazar Blum was renting the building and may have been contemplating opening a soda water bottling plant. In 1892 Blum's son Max and Jacob Kraus bought the equipment for bottling soda water, and a few months later Blum sold out to Kraus. Max Blum later bought the Hoerster Store two blocks to the east [42], and Kraus bought the building from Luckenbach in 1898. Kraus had grown up on the farm of his parents, Christian and Mary Ann Kraus. At the time of the 1900 census he was thirty-seven, unmarried, and living with the family of his sister, Augusta Kraus Metzger. Kraus married Theresia Segner in 1901 in the old St. Mary's Church [84]. They used the front rooms of this building for a soda water bottling plant and raised their family in the back rooms. Among the soda waters bottled here was a new brand called Coca-Cola. A painted advertisement for Coke still graces the west side of the building.

By 1905 Jacob and Theresia had three kids, and another three would arrive later, so in 1906 they had the building enlarged. The contractor was the Weber Brothers, the local builders who also built the

Striegler house on East Main [29]. In the center of the façade, where the old and new parts meet, is a staircase that leads to the upper floor. The new section had rock walls and a tin roof and became their new residence; the old residence in back became part of the bottling plant. The 1906 remodel also included a gasoline engine to power the bottling plant, a one-story frame building with a water tower above, and a Victorian porch that unified the complex. Jacob died in 1922, but Theresia continued the bottling business with her sons Paul, Erwin, and Jacob Theodore.

60 Zion Lutheran Parsonage
424 West Main Street
1922

In 1878 a story-and-a-half rock house, with a kitchen projecting back from the rear, was built next to Zion Lutheran Church [61] to serve as a parsonage.. Although it did not originally have a front porch, one had been added by 1896. The parsonage was essentially rebuilt in 1922, with rock walls and a tin roof, from the designs of local builder Arthur Kuenemann, son of the carpenter and cabinetmaker Heinrich Kuenemann [see 106]. The result was a two-story foursquare with a generous front porch. Though the proportions and massing are typical

for a foursquare, the windows are smaller. Moreover, most American foursquares were built of wood rather than stone. A similar four-square, albeit more ornate and made of Basse blocks, was built as the parsonage for Holy Ghost Church [76] at exactly the same time.

61 Zion Lutheran Church
424 West Main Street
1854, 1884, 1907–8

Lutherans have worshiped at this site since 1854; the current appearance of the building dates largely to an enlargement in 1884 and a second enlargement and remodeling from 1907 to 1908. The cornerstone was laid March 7, 1854, and the building was completed by the end of the year. The work was overseen by the founding pastor, Philip F. Zizelmann. Members of the congregation were deeply involved in the work: Johann Phillip Klaerner, his son Phillip, and Heinrich Strackbein were the most active in preparing the building lumber, preparing the building stones, and hauling those stones to the construction site. In addition, one master mason and one carpenter were hired to supervise the work. The masonry has been attributed to Matthias Schmidt, and

Circa 1905. Courtesy of Institute of Texan Cultures, University of Texas at San Antonio, 099–0318.

the carpentry to Gottfried Ottmers. As originally built, the church was a simple rectangular structure with a pitched roof. Its windows with rounded tops were a simple frontier echo of the mid-nineteenth-century German mode of building known as the Rundbogenstil.

The first enlargement came in 1884, when the walls were raised two feet, a balcony was installed, and the interior was given a proper ceiling. Henry Kuenemann, builder and cabinetmaker, supervised the work. In 1907–8 a new seventy-five-foot tower and steeple provided a new vestibule for the church and the transepts and a semi-octagonal apse were added, giving the church a cross shape in plan. Supervising the work were, once again, Henry Kuenemann, Julius Klingelhoefer, and Henry Basse. Klingelhoefer was the son of J. J. and Elizabeth Klingelhoefer, whose *fachwerk* house [65] was just blocks away and who were members of the congregation. Basse was the grandson of pioneering Lutheran minister Henry S. W. Basse and his wife, Charlotte [see 22]. The steeple in particular but also the new sills added to all windows suggest an awareness of the relatively recent Holy Ghost Evangelical Lutheran Church [77] across town. The rounded arches of the windows are the only feature remaining from the 1854 church. The interior of the church was modernized in 1959. The altar and pulpit were the work of Werner Weber, who carved them in 1962 in the workshop behind his house [see 69] a few blocks away.

There are a number of other buildings on the campus of Zion. A small rock one-room schoolhouse was built in 1865, though it served that function only until 1871. This building is just behind the sanctuary and is visible from North Edison Street. In recent years the congregation has purchased three other houses adjoining the campus. The Feller house at 415 West Austin, a rock house of the 1890s, now serves as the church office. Across the parking lot to the east at 409 West Austin is the Arhelger house, an attractive bungalow built circa 1923, which is at this writing a rental property, as is the Rosenbach house at 422 West Main.

62 Loeffler-Weber House
508 West Main Street
Circa 1855–69, circa 1872, 1905

Although the historical marker in front of this house claims that it was built in 1846–47, this type of log and rock construction did not develop until the mid-1850s, and such houses were built into the 1870s and even the 1880s [see 125, 127, and 116]. Moreover, the original owner of the land, Gerhard Rohrig, sold the property to John William Schupp in 1851 for only $40, not sufficient for a solid if small log and rock house. This house could have been built anytime in the late 1850s or the 1860s; it was certainly present by 1870.

   The carpenter and cabinetmaker Johann Martin Loeffler came to Fredericksburg with his wife and three children in 1854; his wife was Johanna Christina Zizelmann, daughter of Philip Zizelmann, founding minister of Zion Lutheran Church [61]. When Zizelmann left to become minister at St. John's Lutheran Church in San Antonio, the Loefflers followed him, but Johanna Loeffler died on January 1, 1856,

and her husband returned to Fredericksburg. Four years later he married a widow, Juliane (Jung) Stalp, and they bought the lot at the corner of North Edison and built a log house, which they soon expanded with a second room and a dogtrot. The use of a dogtrot on a house in town was unusual; the only other known example is the *fachwerk* front part of the Klingelhoefer house [65], built in 1854–55.

The Loefflers did not acquire the lot on which this little house was built until 1868. In 1870 Johann's property was valued at $600, suggesting that that the little log house was there, though it is difficult to say with certainty whether it was built by Schupp or Loeffler. The front room, with its alternating layers of logs and rock, insured a room that was snug and also permanent. The more spacious rock room, most likely built in 1872, has a raised hearth built into the west wall. Both Johann and Julia died in 1891, and the property, which stretched all the way to Edison Street, was given to their youngest son, Adolph Loeffler, and Carl Weber, husband of their daughter Caroline. In 1905, when the property was partitioned, Adolph took the corner lot and the Webers the little house; the lean-to room on the right dates to that year. In 1909 the Webers moved the log house with the dogtrot out to their farm in the Pedernales community south of town. The Weber family kept the little house until 1964, when it was purchased by George and Gloria Hill and restored with assistance from local restoration expert Albert Keidel. They reopened the fireplace in the rock kitchen and placed a bathroom in the front lean-to. The Hills found a small coffin in the attic of the house, presumably made by Loeffler himself, which they donated to the Gillespie County Historical Society.

---

63 Henry and Amalia Kammlah Rent House
West Main Street
1871–72

Sometimes known as the Betz-Kammlah House, this property was purchased in 1854 by the blacksmith Peter Betz and his wife Elizabeth, though they almost certainly lived in a small log house on this lot. Unfortunately they did not prosper economically, and the marriage ended in divorce. They certainly could not afford a large and expensive

rock house like this one. Peter died in 1862, and Elizabeth in 1867; the property was inherited by their daughter Amalia, who had married Heinrich (Henry) Kammlah II in 1859. Henry and Amalia were most likely living in the original Kammlah log house, because the census taker in 1860 listed them in a separate household next to Heinrich Sr. The story-and-a-half rock house was not under way when Henry talked to the census taker and valued their real estate at $300; the valuation of the property more than tripled between 1870 and 1872.

Their stay was quite short, as they moved to the old Kammlah house down the street around 1874; however, they retained ownership of this house and used it as a rent house. In 1923, the year before his death, Henry Kammlah sold the house to his brother Louis. It remained in the Kammlah family until 1968, nearly one hundred years. The house has a single front room (a *stube*) and a kitchen with a raised hearth on the east wall. Access to the half story above was via a staircase in the kitchen built against the wall shared with the *stube*. This was similar to the arrangement in the Heinrich Bierschwale house [126] of 1872–73.

64 Georg and Clara Peter House
618 West Main Street
Circa 1869–75

Georg Peter followed his father into the stonemasonry business and worked for the US Army at Fort Concho as well as on prominent local houses such as the Heinrich and Margarete Bierschwale house [126]. A squarish *stube* with a kitchen behind, a very common post–Civil War floor plan, characterizes the earliest part of this house. The *stube* was fairly typical in size; less typical was the small size of the kitchen and the way in which the roof ridge ran perpendicular to the street, creating a shallow gable in front. Later a new kitchen and two more bedrooms were added. Peter may well have helped add the two rear rooms to the Klingelhoefer house across Main Street [65]. The Peter family worshipped at the Vereins-Kirche; when the congregation split and built new structures, they chose to join the Evangelical Church on Austin Street.

65 Johann Jost and Elisabeth Klingelhoefer House
701 West Main Street
1854–55, circa 1869

The Klingelhoefer house is one of the oldest in town; its significance, however, lies not in its age but because it is an excellent example of the traditional German building method known as *fachwerk*. As with many of the other pioneering families, a log house was quickly built in 1847 to house the family. The present front rooms, built in 1854–55, have exposed framing and served as a parlor and a bedroom, as the log house retained the cooking function. Both front rooms have a principal beam running from side to side, into which shorter joists are fitted; this is one of the more complicated ceilings in town and may reflect a shortage of long timber even at this early date. The framing was infilled not with stone, as was found in most other surviving examples, but with adobe, a material unknown in Germany but common in the Hispanic Southwest.

The non-Germanic features include the front porch, a necessary shady living space in Texas, a dogtrot (an open passageway in the middle of the house, which in German would be called a *durchgang*), and six-over-six sash windows. The two rock rooms added to the house after the Civil War effectively closed off the dogtrot, and so a front

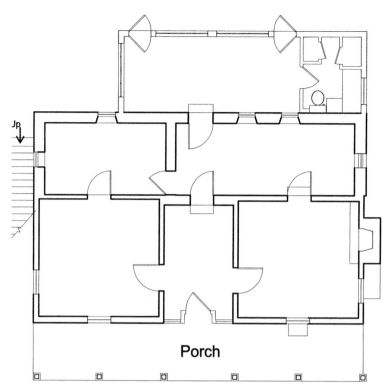

Measured floor plan by John Klein.

door was added as well. The staircase to the attic, however, remained outside, at the east end of the house. The house is thus a fascinating blend of German and Texan features. The rock addition at the rear was completed by 1870, when J. J. Klingelhoefer informed the census taker that his property was worth $2,360.

The likely builders of the house were Hermann Hitzfeld, a carpenter who married one of Klingelhoefer's daughters from his first marriage, Elizabeth, and Jacob Arhelger, a carpenter who was born in Germany in the next town over from Klingelhoefer. The rear rock rooms were most likely built by the Klingelhoefer's eldest son, Julius, who identified himself as a stonemason on the 1870 census. (Younger son William identified himself as a farm laborer, meaning that he was in charge of growing the family's food supply.)

Johann Jost Klingelhoefer was an early county judge and community leader. Julius inherited the house, while William built his own house [119] further west on the road to Mason. Julius married Sophie Tatsch, daughter of the cabinetmaker Johann Peter Tatsch [see 132].

Although Julius died in 1917, Sophie lived in the house until her death in 1949, at age ninety-two. Julius and Sophie's daughter, Lyne, was a painter and provided drawings of houses and historic artifacts for both volumes of the Gillespie County Historical Society's *Pioneers in God's Hills.* Lyne added two additional rooms, a studio and a bathroom, laid new floors throughout the house, and added the fireplace in the west front room around 1955. The house remains in the family and is cared for as the historic treasure that it is.

66 Frederick and Hulda Walter House
709 West Main Street
Circa 1896

This simple rock house exemplifies the latter phase of the German Texan rock house. It was built for Frederick Walter, who was a grandson of Peter and Margaret Walter, whose *fachwerk* house is on West Creek Street [108] and who grew up in the house of his parents, John and Maria Walter, on West Austin Street [127]. The house on West Austin Street began as one room of log and rock but was enlarged with rooms made entirely of rock. When Fred married Hulda Saenger around 1891, they decided to build a house entirely of rock. The stonework includes rusticated sills and lintels. It is a simple,

side-gabled structure with a single-bay Victorian porch leading into an entry hall. Though the entry hall is a concession to mainstream norms, the use of flues for cast-iron stoves had been a German Texan trait for decades. Fred and Hulda lived there with their daughter Elsa, who was born around 1892, and Hulda's mother, Harriet Klingelhoefer Saenger. Harriet was a daughter from the first marriage of Johann Jost Klingelhoefer [see 65] and lived just down the block until her marriage. Harriet died in 1910, Fred in 1914. Hulda lived in the house until her death in 1929. Elsa continued to live there, occasionally giving piano lessons to bring in extra money.

The Walter house is now surrounded on all sides by houses of a newer style, bungalows from the first quarter of the twentieth century, at 707 and 711 West Main to each side and 706 and 708 West Main across the street. Each has a prominent porch and windows in pairs and triplets; three have multiple gables, while 708 has a roof that curves upward over the front door, giving it a more picturesque and unusual appearance.

---

67 Ludwig and Catherine Schneider House (Schneider-Klingelhoefer House)
714 West Main Street
1873

Fachwerk houses were popular in the early 1850s but were rarely built for another fifteen years or so. This house is part of a small group that was built in the early 1870s, which seems to be a fairly self-conscious revival of a distinctively German building tradition. Ludwig Schneider, a watchmaker, bought this town lot and five adjoining ones in 1869 for $300 cash. They were valued at $400 in 1870 and rose to $1,050 in 1873. Schneider, his wife Catherine, and their seven children lived there for only a few years. Apparently they had a financial setback, as the house, a neighboring lot, and an out-lot were sold at a trustee's sale in 1879 for $575 cash. It was purchased by the brothers Charles and Louis Priess in 1883, and Louis bought out his brother in 1887. Both brothers had experience in stonemasonry but had become merchants. They seem to have bought this house as an investment, for Louis sold it in 1890. From 1924 to 1976 it was owned by Arthur W. and Lilly Klingelhoefer.

The construction is *fachwerk*, with rough-hewn rocks serving as the infill between the framing. The original finish of the front wall is not entirely certain; probably the frame was painted and the rocks plastered over. At a later date, probably during the Priess ownership, the front was plastered and scored to resemble finely carved blocks of stone. There was precedent for this both in San Antonio, on the John C. Beckmann house, and the August Arhelger house in Mason. At the time this decorative treatment was done, the porch was open to the ceiling; at a later date the porch was given a beaded ceiling. At that point or later still a second plaster coat was applied, perhaps because the earlier plaster had degraded. This also had scoring in imitation of stone but with much more shallow and irregular grooves.

In true German Texan fashion the house has two front rooms, each with its own door onto the porch, and no central door or passage behind it. Behind this was one long lean-to room; the larger western room served as a kitchen and the eastern room as a bedroom. The western room was later subdivided to create a dining room and a bathroom. There was certainly a front porch originally, but the decorative railing was added by later owners, given that such gingerbread ornament was at the height of its popularity in Fredericksburg in the late

1880s and 1890s. Another late example of *fachwerk* is the John and Anna Speier house [89] at 408 West San Antonio Street.

68 Emil and Alma Gold House (Gold-Morris House)
801 West Main Street
1904

This house is another example of a late Victorian house, but unlike many of this era it was made of wood rather than rock. The builder was Franz Stein, who founded one of the local lumber companies. Emil Gold bought the lot in September 1904 and contracted with Stein to build it for $986. Emil was twenty-nine that year and was the son of a farm couple, Peter and Henriette Gold. This was to be the house of Emil, his wife Alma, their little son Milton, and maybe his sister-in-law, Lina Haufler. However, Gold sold the house to Clayton and Carrie Morris in February 1906, still owing Franz Stein $901.54, which Morris agreed to pay off. Clayton and Carrie were both natives of Michigan; he worked as a bookkeeper and later in a feed store and as a farmer. The house has a T-shape plan, with a shallow porch on the

northeast corner. This small, frame Victorian house was somewhat forward-looking compared with the house that Stein was building at the same time for Emil and Bertha Riley on North Adams Street [162], with its two front doors opening onto the porch. However, it paled in comparison with the Victorian rock house that Stein had built for one of Emil's older brothers, Adolph, on the other side of town [149].

Around the Corner on Cherry Street

69 Emil and Mathilda Weber House
110 North Cherry Street
1902

This late Victorian house was built by its owner, the stonemason Emil Weber, in 1902. According to his account book, it cost $1,338 to build. The plan is a simple L-shape, with large, regularly carved blocks of limestone. Under the eaves in each gable are pairs of brackets, virtually the only concession to the Victorian demand for ornament. The walls are high enough for a half-story, at least in the south wing, as is indicated by the window in the upper part of the front gable and the staircase leading to a door in the south side gable. Also on the south side one can view a one-room limestone outbuilding over a cellar; this was for storage of various foodstuffs and wine. Emil and his wife Mathilda

had married late: he was thirty-three and she was thirty. They had three children, Lilly, Werner, and Edwin. Emil consistently gave his occupation as a stonemason who built houses; in 1930 and 1940 Emil and Mathilda's son Werner described himself as a laborer doing "odd jobs." At the time of the 1940 census the house was valued at a modest $1,500. Werner used the outbuilding as his workshop; he made altars, pulpits, and baptismal fonts for many local churches, including Zion Lutheran [61] in 1962.

PART 4.

South of Main Street

70 Mueller-Petmecky House
201 South Washington Street
1850s, 1895

This two-part house has a *fachwerk* section built for a pioneering German couple and a rock part built for a granddaughter and her husband. Heinrich Mueller was a member of the team of surveyors sent by John O. Meusebach from New Braunfels in December 1845 to lay out a road to the future site of Fredericksburg, and he also accompanied Meusebach when he negotiated a peace treaty with the Comanche tribe. Heinrich was granted this land on the south bank of Baron's Creek in payment for his service on the surveying committee. He and his wife Margarethe (née Mohr) settled into a little *fachwerk* house and raised a family of ten children. Members of the Arhelger family were often witnesses at the baptism of Mueller children, and it seems likely that the Arhelgers took a leading role in building the earliest part of this house. (Daniel Arhelger had also been part of the 1845 surveying party, and his brother Jacob Arhelger built the first Gillespie County Courthouse in 1855, demolished in 1939). Around 1882–83 their fourth son, Rudolph Mueller, later built one of the last *fachwerk* houses in town on South Creek Street [112]. The rock portion was added in 1895 by A. W. Petmecky, who married Heinrich and Margarethe's granddaughter Augusta in 1892. Petmecky was one of the stonemasons who built the White Elephant Saloon in 1888 [21]. The stones on the Mueller-Petmecky house are large and regular, consistent with an 1895 construction date.

71 William and Olga Rausch House
107 South Lincoln Street
Circa 1906

This lot was the site of the first house of Adolph and Elise Lungkwitz before they moved to their shop and residence on Main Street [25]. In 1894 William and Olga Rausch, who had married two years before, bought the old house. William grew up in the southeastern part of the county, near Grapetown; he was a stonemason and a carpenter. Olga was the daughter of August and Wilhelmina Schmidt and lived nearby on Llano Street [74]. Between 1896 and 1906 William and Olga had three boys, Erwin, Willie, and Arnold. William and Olga lived in the old rock house for about a decade and then built this late Victorian rock house between 1902 and 1910. The main roof ridge ran from side to side, but a prominent central gable with a single window gave the house something of a Victorian feel. William and Olga may well have admired the new house of Adolph and Auguste Gold [149], built around 1901. The main roof of the Rausch house was covered with shingles, a rather traditional material, while the porch roof was covered with the more modern tin. The door opened into a central passage, with a living room on the north and a dining room on the south. Behind the living room was a bedroom; behind this was the kitchen. The staircase rose from the central passage into the larger of the two bedrooms, which took two-thirds of the space, while the smaller bedroom took the remaining third of the space on the south. In 1920 William and Olga were living in San Antonio, where he continued to work as a carpenter, but they were back in Fredericksburg a decade later.

72 Schmidt-Gold House
106 South Lincoln Street
1869–71, 1906

Somewhat obscured by a later addition is a classic story-and-a-half rock house built by Lorenz Schmidt for his own family. Schmidt was one of those men from Fredericksburg who helped to build Fort Concho in San Angelo after the Civil War. Schmidt had long been married to Louise Sauer and had six children in addition to Louise's daughter

by her first marriage. Lorenz Schmidt almost certainly built his own house, aided by his son Louis, who was an apprentice stonemason. In 1870 their property was valued at $800, higher than a log or *fachwerk* house but not as high as most story-and-a-half rock houses. The handsome double doors with diamond-shaped panels led into one of two front rooms; there was another room to the rear and a half story above. Like the Basse-Henke house on East Main Street [22], entry was directly into the larger room on the right, the *stube*; on the left was a bedroom. In 1906 the next owner, Jacob Gold, raised the house to a full two stories, adding a much more elaborate Victorian two-story porch. At about the same time that Schmidt started this house, he also built a house for his stepdaughter Louise and son-in-law Heinrich Moellering [73].

73 Heinrich and Louise Moellering House
216 East San Antonio Street
1871–72

Although it has been suggested that this house is one of the oldest in town, in actuality it is an excellent example of a story-and-a-half rock

house of the early 1870s, a classic Hill Country house type. Moreover, the later date also allows this to be recognized as the work of the stonemason Lorenz Schmidt. The lot was originally owned by Wilhelm Sauer and his wife Louise; when Sauer died, Louise married the afore-mentioned Schmidt. Lorenz, Louise, and their children lived on this lot in a *fachwerk* or log house until they acquired a lot at 106 South Lincoln Street and built a story-and-a-half house between 1869 and 1872 [72]. Their daughter, Louise Sauer, married Heinrich Moellering in 1868, and Lorenz Schmidt built them this new rock house in 1871–72. It had a *stube* in front with kitchen behind. Originally a staircase rose from the kitchen into the half-story above. In the years after 1920 a new generation of Moellerings added a new kitchen and created more space in the old kitchen by removing the staircase and creating a new external staircase on the west side.

Around the Corner on South Llano Street

74 August and Wilhelmine Schmidt House
208 South Llano Street
Circa 1852 and later

Many Fredericksburg houses were added on to over time, and this house is an excellent example. August Schmidt, a tailor, and his wife, Wilhelmine, lived a simple existence in this little house. The lot was deeded to Schmidt in 1852, and a little log house was built soon thereafter. This earliest part, on the north side, was later covered with clapboard. It served as a *stube*—a combination bedroom and sitting room. Later a rock kitchen was added to the rear, and then a rock front room on the south side, before the Victorian porch was added in the 1890s. Behind the south front room was a frame porch, which was later enclosed for bathroom, closet, and pantry.

At the time of the 1880 census August and Wilhelmine were living with their five children, three boys and two girls, ages twenty to nine. August died in 1888, Wilhelmine in 1907. The older daughter, Olga, married William Rausch and lived nearby [71]. The other daughter, Pauline, never married and lived here for the rest of her life. In 1946

her heirs sold the house to Dorothea Kolmeier, who lived just on the other side of Main Street [28]; she used it as a rent house. It was purchased in 1983 by the architects Barry Wagner and Stanley Klein, who restored it and used it as their office. They created additional space to the rear, thus connecting a stone outbuilding to the main house. The stone outbuilding once had a water tower on its roof. In recent years the house has been adapted again to serve as an art gallery.

75 Stoffers-Lochte House
107 South Llano Street
1892 and later

In 1892 Henry and Amanda Stoffers built this three-room rock house with a T-shaped floor plan and porches with Victorian trim. The cornerstone is visible in the modern addition on the northwest side.

Henry, like his father, Fritz Stoffers, ran a saloon on Main Street. Apparently Henry and Amanda were in over their head financially, because they sold the house in 1896, and the new owners assumed payment of a note to the Lone Star Brewing Co. of $1,298.57. Friedrich W. Lochte bought the house in 1897. Lochte was a merchant who had partnered with Felix Reinbach in a store just up South Llano at Main Street; he married his partner's daughter, Marie, in 1895. Friedrich and Marie had six children, which necessitated adding rooms on the east side. Friedrich died in 1908, but Marie lived until 1941. Later owners plastered the rock walls and tore down the front porches.

---

76 Holy Ghost Lutheran Church Parsonage
117 East San Antonio Street
1922

This two-story parsonage for the Evangelical Protestant Holy Ghost Church next door [77] was erected in 1922 to mark the seventy-fifth

---

anniversary of the founding of the congregation. It is an example of the house type known as a foursquare, characteristic of the first quarter of the twentieth century. The foursquare is essentially a two-story version of a bungalow, which is confirmed by the trim on the front porch. Its mass is a simple cube, with a hipped roof. Windows are paired, and entry is into a stair hall, which is the right front room. The house is made of concrete blocks—made locally and known as Basse blocks—shaped to resemble stone. The Basses were members of the congregation. Foursquares made of concrete blocks could be seen in 1908 and 1911 in Sears and Roebuck and Company's *Modern Homes* catalogues. Zion Lutheran built a similarly proportioned parsonage [60] in the same year, but it was built of limestone rather than Basse blocks.

77 Holy Ghost Lutheran Church
115 East San Antonio Street
1888–93

The Evangelical Protestant Holy Ghost Church (originally the Evangelical Protestant Church, which was one wing of Fredericksburg's Protestant church and a longtime occupant of the Vereins-Kirche [1]) was the first Hill Country congregation to hire a big-city architect. James Wahrenberger was a native of Austin who studied at L'Ecole Polytechnique in Karlsruhe, Germany, for three years before settling in San Antonio. In association with Albert Beckmann, Wahrenberger had recently completed a new church building for St. John's Lutheran

Church in San Antonio (1886–88). The cornerstone for the Fredericksburg church, which was laid on June 6, 1888, features a dove and the initials "Ev. Prot. H.G.K.," which stands for Evangelische Protestantische Heiligen Geist Kirche. Financial difficulties forced the congregation to spread out the construction over five years. The church building was dedicated on March 21, 1893, which was Palm Sunday. In 1896 a local publication referred to the church as being "romanisch-gothischen-styl"—that is, a blend of the round-arched Romanesque and the pointed-arched Gothic styles, the two principal types of medieval architecture. However, the Gothic predominated in Wahrenberger's design. Not unlike St. John's Lutheran in San Antonio, Holy Ghost has a broad, open interior; but unlike St. John's, it has cut-off corners at the pulpit end so that the angled back walls cautiously create a sort of apse; Gothic windows in the angled walls frame the altarpiece. The 150-foot spire was not completed until 1903. It was the first spire in town to reach so high, which seems to have inspired (or provoked) both Zion Lutheran and St. Mary's Catholic to make dramatic improvements to their places of worship.

The roof was replaced in 1937, and the church was enlarged in 1949 to give the plan a cross shape. Once again the congregation turned to a San Antonio architect, this time Henry Steinbomer. The annex was also built of limestone and incorporated Gothic detailing. At that time the communion rail, baptismal altar, and lectern were added. New pews were made by L. L. Sams and Sons of Waco, Texas, and new gothic light fixtures were installed. The art windows in the annex were made by the Jacoby Company of St. Louis. Since 1949, the church has been known as Holy Ghost Lutheran Church.

---

78 August Wilhelm and Caroline Jordan House
109 East San Antonio Street
Circa 1869–75, 1924

Tailors were among the more specialized tradesmen in Fredericksburg, but they tended not to be well remunerated for their work. As a result, their houses were simpler and smaller and were improved upon at a slower pace. This house, and the house of August and Wilhelmine

---

Schmidt around the corner at 208 South Llano Street [74], are good examples of this. Wilhelm and Caroline Jordan, recent arrivals from Germany, acquired this property in 1860, when it had a small log house on it. In the 1860 census they valued their property at $120; the neighboring Schmidts valued their one-room log house at $150, a comparable figure. The valuation on the Jordan's property did not begin to rise until 1869, increasing to $900 in 1875. Their one-room story-and-a-half rock house must have been built around this time. Their son August was to build a larger rock house further down San Antonio Street only one decade later [80]. Wilhelm and Caroline lived in this little rock house for the rest of their lives. After Wilhelm's death in 1898, his sons sold this house to Henry Duecker; the frame additions on the west side and behind the rock room were added before 1924. The house was purchased by neighboring Holy Ghost Lutheran Church in 1941.

For the 100 block of West San Antonio Street, see entries 5–8.

79 Christian and Francisca Stehling House
204 South Crockett Street
1899

This Victorian house, built of native stone, was the first in town to have
Christmas lights festooned across the exterior. German Texans brought
with them their ancient tradition of a Christmas tree, which was
quickly imitated by Anglo-Americans, but for Christmas lights outside
one needed electric power. And Christian Stehling was the man who
brought electricity to Fredericksburg. Also a rancher and a merchant,
he built the first power plant in town in 1898. This was such a success
that he was able to buy town lot 355 on January 31, 1899. This was a
convenient one block from the Marienkirche [84], which was where
Christian had married Francisca Reinbach in 1891. They had eight
children. Christian was a founding member of the St. Joseph's Society
[82], the Catholic alternative to the Masons, and served on the building committee for new St. Mary's Church [85].

The Stehlings did not waste time once they bought the lot: the
circular attic vent has the date of 1899 in it, showing that the house

was begun in that year. It was a larger version of the simple Victorian house at 107 South Llano [75], which Francisca's sister, Marie Lochte, and her husband Friedrich had purchased in 1897. The Stehlings' rock house was T-shaped in plan; the central front room was the parlor. This room was flanked by north and south porches. Behind the parlor was the hall, then the dining room, which was windowless but which presumably was equipped with an electric light. To the north of the dining room was the kitchen, and to the south, a bedroom. Two rock rooms were added to the rear in 1914, a new kitchen and another bedroom, and the old kitchen was converted into a third bedroom. Christian Stehling died of typhoid fever in 1907, but the family continued to live there for many decades. The house sits on what was originally a corner lot until Francisca sold the northern part sometime between 1924 and 1938.

80 August and Caroline Jordan House
209 West San Antonio Street
1886–87

This lovely story-and-a-half rock house was built in 1886–87 and has been added to several times. August, a carpenter and cabinetmaker, was a son of Wilhelm and Caroline Jordan. He was born in Germany

but grew up first in their log house and then the one-room rock house further to the east at 109 East San Antonio Street [78]. He married Caroline Pfiester in 1881 (she had grown up in a house with one log room that was built for her grandparents and enlarged by her parents with several rooms of stone). Though the centered door looks as if it would enter a central passage, it now enters one large room. Originally a partition to the right separated a small bedchamber from the larger sitting room (known as a *stube*). Each front room had a window on the front, another on the side, but none on the rear wall. The high walls of the upper floor make it virtually a second full story. The first addition was another rock room on the south side. As a carpenter and cabinet-maker, August certainly worked on his own house and also made two large wardrobes (*schrank* in German) that once stood in the west front room; these heirlooms remain in the family.

81 William and Carolina Jordan House
211 West San Antonio Street
1871–73

This story-and-a-half rock house is smaller and earlier than its newer cousin to the east. William Jordan was a son of Heinrich and Anna

Jordan, and thus a cousin of August Jordan, who later built the house next door. William was a tailor, but he clearly did better economically than many of his fellow tailors [see 74 and 78]. He married Carolina Hasper in 1868, and they built this house a couple of years later. Although this house is very near to the old St. Mary's Church, the Jordans were not Catholic, having been married by the Reverend Burchard Dangers, whose Evangelical Lutheran congregation worshipped in the Vereins-Kirche. It is a more compact version of a rock house, with one large room (a *stube*) in front, and a kitchen behind, both built at the same time. The front room has a window on each side of the centered door and another window on the east. The kitchen had windows flanking the door on the south wall and another on the east. The staircase rises from the west side of the kitchen into the bedroom above.

82 St. Joseph's Hall
212 West San Antonio Street
1899–1900

The St. Joseph's Society is a Catholic men's fraternal organization. The Fredericksburg chapter was founded by Father Joseph Roch in 1899

as an alternative to societies of which the church did not approve—in particular, the Masons. A Masonic lodge had been chartered in 1896, and one year later the Masons agreed to help John Schandua build his new store on Main Street [19] in return for the use of a meeting hall on the second floor. In 1900 the St. Joseph's Society completed this simple rock building to serve as its meeting place at a cost of $7,000. It was also used for parish meetings and the activities of other Catholic societies. The Sanborn fire insurance maps of 1910 and 1915 show a small frame room on the back elevation marked "BEER STORAGE." This room disappeared from the 1924 map, apparently a victim of Prohibition. However, a new frame shed appears on the 1924 map at the very back of the lot; its use was not indicated.

Around the Corner on South Orange Street

83 St. Mary's School
202 South Orange Street
1923–24

This handsome building in the Colonial Revival style was built 1923–24, when St. Mary's School had outgrown its adapted home in the old Marienkirche across the street. The construction of this building required the demolition of a two-story rock house that had been built in the late 1860s by the Reverend Burchard Dangers; starting in 1873 it had served as St. Mary's School and as a residence for the nuns who taught at the

school. The new school was designed by Leo M. J. Dielmann of San Antonio, the architect responsible for the new St. Mary's Catholic Church [85] in 1905–6. St. Mary's School was built at a cost of $60,000. The main floor of the new building provided classrooms and other facilities, the upper floor, living quarters for the sisters, and the basement, a kitchen. The Colonial Revival style was at the height of its popularity nationwide in the 1920s, and the building had a reinforced concrete frame and walls made of brick from the little Alsatian town of D'Hanis, Texas, where a brick kiln opened for business in 1905. The building was wired for electricity but was still heated by individual wood stoves. After World War II enrollment expanded, and the residence for the sisters was moved to the Meckel Building around the corner on West Main Street [45].

84 Old St. Mary's Catholic Church (Marienkirche)
300 block West San Antonio Street
1861–64

The Roman Catholics of Fredericksburg were among the first to withdraw from the Vereins-Kirche, as would be expected given Catholic

doctrine that emphasized that the church building is sacred space. The earliest parish structure was built in 1848, most likely a *fachwerk* building, which was erected by the carpenter Peter Schandua. The only trace of this building is a red granite marker behind the Marienkirche marking the spot where it stood.

The Marienkirche was the most ambitious of the early churches of Fredericksburg. The church is cross-shaped in plan, with entry through a central tower that is topped by an ovoid dome. Most of the doors and windows have flat

Courtesy of the Gillespie County Historical Society.

tops, but Gothic arches are created by panels that feature a Maltese
cross. No architect is known, but the trained craftsmen were recorded:
Peter Schmidtz and Anton Krause were the principal stonemasons,
and Heinrich Cordes took charge of building the roof. Moritz Hartmann fashioned the stone cross atop the steeple and the baptismal
font at the rear of the church, and also installed the soapstone slabs of
the original floor. Friedrich Gentemann and Anton Kunz fashioned the
windows; Johann Staudt and John Schmidtzinsky acquired the wood
for the pews and may have made them as well. All of these men, with
the exception of Cordes, were also members of the congregation. The

women of the congregation were instrumental in raising funds to pay for the pews.

After the completion of the new St. Mary's in 1906, the old church was converted into St. Mary's School, replacing the old two-story rock house that stood across Orange Street, a purpose it served from 1913 to 1924, when a new school was built [83]. The choir loft was removed, and a floor was installed to create a second story. The building was documented by the Historic American Buildings Survey in 1934. The exterior was restored under the direction of architect Reuben E. Bohnert between 1970 and 1991.

A rock rectory was built across the street from the Marienkirche in 1868. This was a simple two-story rock building that later received a front porch with turned columns. When a new rectory was built in 1953–54, it made the old rectory expendable, and it was demolished for a new St. Mary's School, completed in 1959.

---

85 St. Mary's Catholic Church
300 block West San Antonio Street
1905–6

The longtime pastor of St. Mary's, Father Peter Tarrillion, retired at the end of 1899 and was replaced by his assistant, Father Joseph Roch. In 1901 the congregation decided to build a new and larger church. Father Roch turned to James Wahrenberger of San Antonio, whose design for the Evangelical Protestant Holy Ghost Church of a decade before seems to have impressed the locals. Plans were drawn, but then Father Roch fell ill with typhus and died in June 1904. His successor, Father F. Neissens, agreed that a new church should be built, but did not approve of Wahrenberger's plans. Instead he turned to Leo M. J. Dielmann of San Antonio, an architect who was a Catholic himself and who was just beginning a career specializing in the design of Catholic churches and institutional buildings. Jacob Wagner of San Antonio was chosen as the contractor for the project. The cornerstone was laid on July 14, 1905, and the church was dedicated on September 4, 1906, though it was not consecrated until 1908. The cost was $40,000. Like the old St. Mary's [84] and Holy Ghost [77], the new St. Mary's

---

was Gothic in style, but it was the first asymmetrical Fredericksburg church, as Dielmann placed its tower at the right front corner.

The exterior is largely limestone, except for the grey slate covering of the steeple and the polished columns of red granite that grace the main entrance. The stonework emphasized its rustic character, though the entrances had a much more smooth finish. On both the west and east sides are projecting rooms that hold confessionals, spaces dedicated to the sacrament of Confession (now called Reconciliation) in which a priest hears the confessions of the faithful and offers forgiveness of sins. Also on the west was a side door, typical of many German Gothic churches.

Dielmann designed a truly impressive interior, with Gothic arches supported by columns separating the nave from the aisles on each side.

Its interior paint treatment has led to St. Mary's being listed on the National Register of Historic Places as one of the "painted churches of Texas." Though it is sometimes suggested that these church interiors are works of folk art, most of the later examples were executed by professional artists, usually from San Antonio. In the case of St. Mary's, the designer was Fred Donecker, a German-born painter who had settled in San Antonio. Originally the columns were painted with blue veins to resemble marble, and all doors, windows, and arches were outlined and elaborated with stenciling.

In the same year that Dielmann designed St. Mary's, he also designed another great "painted church," the Nativity of Mary Catholic Church in High Hill, between LaGrange and Schulenberg. The pastor there was Father Heinrich Gerlach, who was then reassigned to Fredericksburg in August 1913. Father Gerlach continued the embellishment of the new church, procuring stained glass windows from Emil Frei Art Glass in St. Louis between 1914 and 1917 and adding several statues "to give the interior a more alive appearance." He also saw to the repair of the roof and the addition of an iron fence in front of the church. In 1936–37 a subsequent pastor, Monsignor Alfons Heckmann, hired Dr. Oidtmann Studios, Inc., of Linnich, Germany, to redecorate the interior of the church. The painted decoration was toned down somewhat; this included new stenciling on the walls and painting of scenes from the Old and New Testaments. New lighting fixtures were also added, and, perhaps most telling, the captions beneath the Stations of the Cross were changed from German to English.

86 Methodist Episcopal Church
312 West San Antonio Street
1855, 1923

The Methodist Episcopal Church was the second rock church to be constructed in Fredericksburg, after Zion Lutheran Church (1854) [61] but before the Marienkirche just to the east (1861–64) [84]. Among the founding families of the church were Johann and Margaritha Durst, whose son Johann C. Durst was a stonemason; he may be responsible for the building. The stone came from John Peter

Dechert's quarry on Grape Creek, southeast of town. The two openings
for doors and the four openings for windows on each side were all
originally tall rectangles. The two doors on the front suggest separate
entrances for men and women, but such gender distinctions may not
have lasted too long. The Neoclassical portico was added when the
building was remodeled in 1923, when such stylistic features were
again popular. The pointed-arch windows on the side walls and over
the doors were added at the same time, giving the building a rather
eclectic appearance. The church later became Methodist Episcopal
Church, South, and then Fredericksburg United Methodist Church.
The building is now owned by the Gillespie County Historical Society.
Across the street is a house that began as a one-room log building
in the 1850s and was given numerous rock additions over time; it
was owned by one of the founders of the church, Heinrich Friedrich
Kneese. The north and south congregations of the Methodist Epis-
copal churches reunited in 1970 and completed a new sanctuary on
North Llano Street in 1981.

87 Friedrich and Margarethe Gentemann House
108 South Milam Street
1885–86

This was one of the earliest of the Sunday houses, and a very rare example of a rock Sunday house. Friedrich Gentemann was a cabinet-maker and a devout Catholic. He made the windows for old St. Mary's Catholic Church [84], built 1861–64. From 1862 to 1879 Friedrich and his wife, Margarethe (née Petsch), owned the two-room rock house previously owned by Conrad Wisseman, which backed up to the church [44]. In 1879 they sold that house, and in 1880 the census taker found them on their farm. Apparently, however, the Gentemanns missed the convenience of a house so close to their church. In 1882 they purchased a sliver of land from John Claude Neraz, the Catholic bishop of San Antonio, one block from their old house and, conveniently, one block from their church. Work was begun on a tiny new house in 1885 and finished in 1886. There was one room on the ground

floor and a loft above. In 1886 the Gentemanns had seven children ranging in age from twenty-four to seven, so finding a place to sleep may have been a challenge.

West San Antonio Street

88 John and Mathilda Metzger Sunday House
406 West San Antonio Street
Circa 1901–7

This is a classic example of a Sunday House, diminutive, simple, and close to the owners' church. John Metzger Jr. had been born in a log cabin north of town, one of the earliest German children to be born in Fredericksburg. John built a story-and-a-half rock house just behind St. Mary's Church (no longer extant), but when his first wife died he moved to a 475-acre spread on Bullard Creek. He married Mathilda Sophia Emilia Schmidtzinsky in 1878 in St. Mary's Church [84]. Both of their fathers had worked on the rock church. In 1898 John and Mathilda bought a quarter of a lot on San Antonio Street, one block east of St. Mary's; sometime thereafter they built a Sunday house for

their weekend trips for shopping and church. The lot was valued at $50 the year they bought it, rose in value to $100 in 1901, to $150 in 1906, and to $300 in 1907. Originally it consisted of a single large room, with a loft above reached by stairs. The house was of the utmost simplicity: the exterior was of board-and-batten construction (that is, vertical boards with strips of wood covering the joints), and the roof was covered with wooden shingles. Inside a cast-iron stove was in the left rear corner, as evidenced by a patch in the ceiling and another patch on the west side of the tin roof. By 1907 they had added a back room, doubling the size of the house. New clapboarding was added all around, unifying the appearance, though original board-and-batten construction can be seen in the front wall of the kitchen, beneath later wallpaper. The new room had a tin roof, but since the shingled roof of the front room was less than ten years old, it was left that way for many years. A possible builder of this house was John Metzger Jr.'s cousin John Baumann, whose mother was Catherine Metzger, a sister of John Metzger Sr. The rock house of John Metzger Jr.'s sister, Margaretha Weidenfeller, was nearby [90].

---

89 John and Anna Speier House
408 West San Antonio Street
Circa 1872–75

This is not a Sunday house. That is to say, this house was built as the main residence of the Speier family. The difference is made clear by contrasting it with the size and materials of the Metzger Sunday house next door. However, the house did fulfill one important function of a Sunday house—it was very near the Speiers' church, St. Mary's. Moreover, the Speier house does have the distinction of being in the last group of *fachwerk* houses in Fredericksburg, along with the Ludwig and Catherine Schneider house on Main Street [67]. The Speiers were the original grantees of the lot, and they certainly were living there permanently. In 1865 John Speier married Anna Petsch, who was the sister of Margarethe Gentemann [see 87] and Catharine Kollett [see 95]. In 1869 John and Anna signed an agreement to take care of his father, Henry, in return for the gift of the lot. The valuation of the property doubled between 1872 and 1875, showing that a significant

upgrade had occurred. The new house was still small—two rooms with a half story above. The framing of the *fachwerk* is much thinner than in earlier *fachwerk* houses. Except for the corner posts, the framing is just under two inches wide and very regular, suggesting that it was cut in a sawmill, unlike wider, hand-hewn frames of the first generation of *fachwerk* houses. As a result, the stone seems to predominate; in fact, the Sanborn fire insurance map of 1910 noted that the front was solid stone. The house was expanded in two campaigns, both of which dispensed with the *fachwerk*.

90 Johann and Margarethe Weidenfeller House
419 West San Antonio Street
Circa 1880

This house was the home of Johann and Margarethe Weidenfeller. Johann had been married in Germany and had two sons, Johann and Adam, before coming to Texas in the late 1860s. He was living in 1870 with John and Maria Klein, along with his mother, Maria, his brother, Adam, and the two boys. In 1873 he married Margarethe Metzger, the

daughter of John and Gertrude Metzger, at old St. Mary's Church [84]. They purchased this land for $125 in 1874 and built this rock house around 1880. Both Johann and his brother Adam were stonemasons, and it is highly likely that they built this house, which was a story and a half, with the rooms heated by iron stoves with a flue leading to a chimney at each end. The front contained two rooms, with direct entry into the living room; to the left was a bedroom. A lean-to contained the kitchen and auxiliary spaces. The main floor has six-over-six windows on the front and side; the upstairs are lit by smaller six-over-six windows in the gable ends. By 1900 the household included Johann and Margarethe and their four children, along with Johann's grown sons from his first marriage. The youngest girl, Rosa, was born in the house in 1891 and lived there until her death in 1970. Margarethe's brother, John Metzger Jr., had a Sunday house nearby [88].

Around the Corner on South Edison Street

91 Heinrich and Eliza Ochs House
105 South Edison Street
1872, circa 1897, circa 1924

This one-room house with walls of log and rock demonstrates the classic German Texan technique for log construction. Heinrich Ochs Jr. was the son of the man who was an early schoolteacher and county clerk. The younger Heinrich was a stonemason, and in 1870, at age twenty-five, he bought this lot; by 1872 he had built the first room. At almost exactly the same time his father was building a small house on West Main Street, one of the first houses in town to have a central passage separating the two front rooms. Heinrich Jr.'s log house reminds us that such houses were often starter houses and also that log and rock houses were not a degenerate type of log house but one created by trained craftsmen. The rock section was added considerably later, possibly after Heinrich's death in 1897. The frame section was present by 1924, when it appeared on the Sanborn fire insurance map.

---

92 Methodist Episcopal Church, North (later Edison Street Methodist Church, now Greater Life Christian Center)
106 South Edison Street
1923–24

This church building exists because of a congregational split that happened more than fifty years before it was constructed. In 1871 the division of the Methodist Church into northern and southern branches, which

---

had happened elsewhere before the Civil War, finally hit Fredericksburg. The northern Methodists withdrew from the church, leaving the southern Methodists with the old building on West San Antonio Street [86]. Most of the southern Methodists lived in town, while many of the northern Methodists lived on ranches outside of town.

A rock church was built on this site for northern Methodists in 1872, supervised by the local stonemason Charles Jung, and was later known as the Edison Street Methodist Church. The building was later expanded, but a new building was begun in 1923 at the same location and was dedicated the next year. Among the founding members were Ludwig and Wilhemina Kneese, who were among the earliest German Texans born in Fredericksburg.

This red brick building utilizes the Tudor Gothic style, which was very popular in the twenties, and was also used for the new Fredericksburg High School in 1922 [152]. A shortcut was using segmental arches instead of the more stylistically correct Tudor Gothic arch. The two Methodist congregations merged in 1970 to become the Fredericksburg United Methodist Church, using this newer building. In 1979 the congregation decided to move to a new campus on North Llano Street across from Greenwood Cemetery. The new sanctuary was completed in 1981.

93 Johann and Louise Hoffmann House (Hoffmann-Keller House)

511 West San Antonio Street
Circa 1869–70

This little story-and-a-half rock house was home to Johann and Louise Hoffmann and their children, August and Anna. In 1870 Johann's brother, Carl, was also living with them. Johann Hoffmann was married to Louise Donhoefer in 1868 by the Reverend Burchard Dangers, who led the Evangelical Lutheran congregation in the Vereins-Kirche. Their son August came along the next year, and the Hoffmanns bought this town lot. On the 1870 census both Johann and his brother Carl listed their occupation as laborer. Perhaps Carl was living with them as payment for helping to build this house.

This type of house was very characteristic of the post–Civil War era. In front was the *stube*, and behind this was the kitchen; above was a bedroom and storage room. A narrow staircase rose from the east side of the kitchen, lit from the window above. Originally the beams were exposed. Later owners changed the staircase and replaced the original

floors, which had termite damage. Around 1970 plaster was removed from the rock walls, and a frame addition was put on above the kitchen. Later still the original casement window in the upstairs room was replaced with sash. The Hoffmanns did not settle permanently in Fredericksburg; in 1880 they were living in San Antonio, and both Johann and Carl gave their occupation as gardener on the census of that year. Such a specialized occupation was more viable in a large city such as San Antonio than a small town such as Fredericksburg.

94 Catharina Loth House
515 West San Antonio Street
Circa 1871–74, 1887

Although it has been claimed that this house was built by Peter Staudt and his wife Catharina before his death in 1852, or by her new husband Anton Loth before he died in 1869, Catharina lived on a farm during this time, first with Peter and then with Anton. After her second husband's death, she decided to move into town. This lot was valued at a mere $20 in 1869, but increased to $250 in 1874. Catharina continued to keep house, but she also owned six cows and, with the help of her teenage son Anton, was able to supply many of her neighbors with milk and other dairy products. A rock room was added to the

rear around 1887; she sold three of her cows in that year, presumably to help pay for this new room. Her son John Lott (who changed the spelling of their name to accord with the pronunciation) sold the house to Barbara and John Weidenfeller (son of Johann Weidenfeller by his first marriage [see 90]) in 1908, and the family retained ownership until 1974. The Weidenfellers built the little board-and-batten house between this one and the Hoffmann house [93] in the 1920s.

95 Joseph and Catherine Kollett House
516 West San Antonio Street
1885

This block of West San Antonio was thinly settled at the end of the Civil War, and the houses on the block were all built in the 1870s and 1880s. Joseph Kollett married Catherine Petsch in 1876; her sister Margarethe married Friedrich Gentemann [see 87], her sister Anna married John Speier [see 89], and her sister Maria married Anton Weinheimer [see 110]. Joseph and Catherine had six children, one of

which died in infancy. The lot was acquired from Catherine's family. The house was built by Joseph Moritz, a stepson of the stonemason Peter Schmitz [see 120], with whom he apprenticed.

Joseph Moritz completed the stonework on the Kollett house in three months, May, June, and July of 1885. This consisted of erecting the walls and creating two chimney tops. He was paid not by the hour or the day but by the rod of stonework, which came to $115.80. The chimney tops were fashioned for $3, and he also whitewashed the stairs and ceiling for an additional $1.50. The total came to $121.30, which did not include roof, floors, windows, or doors. Perhaps the woodwork was done by Catherine's brother-in-law, the carpenter and cabinetmaker Friedrich Gentemann, who crafted the windows for old St. Mary's Catholic Church [84], or one of his sons. For his part, Kollett paid off $7 of the cost by digging (or repairing) a well for Moritz. The door and six-over-six windows were set within opening with segmental arches at the top, the only hint of its late nineteenth-century date of construction.

96 Martin and Maria Heinemann House (Heinemann-Moritz House)
714 West San Antonio Street
Circa 1871–74

This is another classic example of a post–Civil War rock house, with two rooms downstairs and one room upstairs, though its appearance was seriously compromised by an addition on the east side in the mid-twentieth century. It is also another example of a house that was conveniently located near the family's church, in this case St. Mary's Catholic Church [84]. Martin and Maria Heinemann paid $100 for the lot in 1871. Though this was on the edge of town, it was only a couple of blocks to St. Mary's. Martin's father, Valentin Heinemann, had helped to build the original St. Mary's Church in 1848. Maria was the daughter of John and Margarethe Raulz, who bought the Dangers house [102] in 1873 and who probably added the front rooms to that house. The Heinemann house has two dates carved into one of the rocks—1871 and 1874—which presumably mark the beginning and end of construction.

Perhaps Peter Schmitz, one of the principal stonemasons on St. Mary's, was involved in this project as well. The house was sold to Joseph Moritz (a grandson of Peter Schmitz) and his wife Amalia, from whom it passed to their daughter and her husband, Walter and Auguste "Gugu" McKay. They expanded the house with help from a Fredericksburg authority in restoration, Albert Keidel, in 1945 and again in 1968.

South Adams Street

97 Peter and Caroline Bonn House
206 South Adams Street
1868–69

This is a classic story-and-a-half rock house, one of the most popular house types in Fredericksburg in the decade just after the Civil War. In 1859 Peter Bonn, a farmer, married Caroline Lochte, a daughter of Friedrich and Dorothea Lochte, one of the wealthiest couples in the county. The Lochtes owned a store in town but also a ranch on Meusebach Creek south of town. Peter and Caroline lived near her parents in the country [165]. By 1869, however, both of her parents had passed

away, and Peter and Caroline bought a rock house in town from Ernst Schaper. This house was built by Schaper, perhaps with help from his father, the cabinetmaker Christoph Schaper, sometime between 1865 and 1868. The house had one large square front room and a rectangular room to the rear. An external stair on the north side led to another bedroom; this was a typical treatment in the Hill Country, though soon other houses would have staircases leading upstairs from the back room. The Bonn house also had a large rock outbuilding with a roofline perpendicular to the street, not unlike the "second kitchen" at the Kammlah house [46].

98 Adolf and Auguste Bonn House
210 South Adams Street
Circa 1905

For the children of the pioneers, the story-and-a-half rock house no longer had its allure. They preferred something more modern in the arrangement of rooms and in its ornamentation. Adolf Bonn, the fourth son of Peter and Caroline Bonn, grew up in the story-and-a-half

rock house next door [97]. In census records Adolf gave his occupation as bartender in 1900, as salesman of general merchandise in 1910, and as clerk in a general merchandise store in 1910. He and his wife Auguste (née Heimann) built this rock house around 1905, but with a late Victorian T-shaped plan. The south wing contained two rooms, the north wing an entry hall and another room. The large limestone blocks provide most of the character. There are no decorative window sills or lintels of the type found in other late Victorian houses; the trim of the porch provides the only decoration.

West Creek Street

99 Johann Nikolaus and Caroline Tatsch House
101 West Creek Street
1874

Johann Nikolaus Tatsch was a cabinetmaker, as was his considerably more famous contemporary, John Peter Tatsch [see 132]. The fame of the latter rests on the numerous examples of his craftsmanship that have descended in the family; few examples of furniture by J. N. Tatsch are known to have survived, but this house occupies a prominent corner at West Creek and South Adams streets. At first Johann, his first wife Margarethe (née Lorenz), and their two sons lived in a log house

that once stood to the east of the present house. Margarethe died in 1859, and Johann married Caroline Dannenberg in 1860. By 1870 the household included four children; they told the census taker that their real estate was worth only $150, evidence that they were still in the original log cabin. Caroline's parents, Heinrich and Frederika, were living in a neighboring house to the west. Johann and Caroline built this story-and-a-half rock house beside their log house in 1874.

100 Emil Nagel House
106 West Creek Street
1907

Emil Nagel, along with his three brothers, founded Nagel Brothers Monumental Works [6] in 1904. They owned a quarry near Bear Mountain that provided a ready source of red granite for grave markers and for cornerstones on buildings in town. Emil bought this lot on Creek Street, which backs up to the lot of their business at 113 West San Antonio Street. Emil married Lina Karger around 1904, and they had four children. In 1907 he built a wood-frame Victorian house with

a simple T-plan. In style it is indistinguishable from late Victorian houses anywhere in Texas. Quite unique, though, is the retaining wall at the front of the lot, which incorporates a variety of stones and serves as a form of advertisement for the brothers' business.

On the 1910 census Emil gave his occupation as proprietor of a monument yard, and the household included Lina, the three children, and his younger brother Arthur, who listed his occupation as stone cutter at a monument yard. Older brother Willie was a boarder at the hotel of Louis Dietz and, like Emil, gave his occupation as proprietor of a monument yard. Emil died in 1914 and is buried under a red granite marker in Der Stadt Friedhof. Lina married Walter Meckel, who gave his occupation as printer at the time of the 1910 census, but in 1920 he was a granite cutter at a marble works. He not only worked at the Nagel brothers' company but moved into Emil and Lena's house.

The second son of Emil and Lina, Chester Nagel, studied architecture at the University of Texas in Austin, then attended graduate school at the Harvard Graduate School of Design, studying with modern masters Walter Gropius and Marcel Breuer. He later taught at Harvard, worked with Gropius in the Architect's Collaborative, and had his own private practice. He and his wife Lorine are buried with Emil in Der Stadt Friedhof.

101 Peter and Elisabeth Wunderlich House (Wunderlich-Fritz House)
198 West Creek Street
Circa 1868, circa 1900

At first glance this might seem to be a two-story late Victorian house to which someone later added a one-story addition, but the reverse is true. The German Emigration Company, or Adelsverein, deeded this lot to Johan Peter and Elisabeth Wunderlich in 1852. Peter was a blacksmith and carpenter. They quickly built a small house, probably of log; but then between 1866 and 1872 they added a rock house with one large room, presumably north of the log house. The rock room had its own entrance on South Crockett Street; a fireplace was centered on the north wall. Their son Adolph built a house for himself and his bride Martha in the late 1880s, first a log house [116], then a rock house [117], perhaps with help from his father. Both Peter and Elisabeth died in 1899, and their sons sold the house to Caspar and Elise Fritz, who added the two-story frame part.

102 John and Margarethe Raulz House (Pape-Dangers-Raulz House)
213 West Creek Street
1855–56, circa 1875

This is a beautiful, simple, but poorly documented small house. Unfortunately, the historical marker placed on the house in 1974 is a compendium of inaccuracies. It seems that the front room dates to the 1870s and that the back room was earlier, perhaps from the 1850s. The town lot was originally granted to Friedrich Pape, who almost certainly built a log house on it soon after his arrival in 1846. This house was most likely very close to the street, unlike the little windowless log house that sits in the side yard. Nor is it likely to have been built with alternating logs and rocks, a method for which there is no well-dated example before 1855. In the sketches that Captain Seth Eastman made of Fredericksburg in 1849, none of the log houses depicted show alternating rows of stone. Moreover, the Sanborn fire insurance maps of 1924 and 1938 do not record a log structure on this lot, and it was not mentioned by Ella Gold when she wrote about the Dangers house.

Friedrich Pape sold the lot to the Reverend Gottlieb Burchard Dangers in 1850, when Dangers arrived to lead the Evangelical Lutheran congregation in the Vereins-Kirche. The price was $250, which was

consistent with the value of a one-room log house. The rear two rooms of the rock house were most likely an addition to the log house. They were built around 1855 and 1856, when Dangers sold three of the six lots he owned, yet increased the value of his property. This ell faced west, rather than north toward Creek Street. Ella Gold characterized it as "rectangular," which is a good way to describe its simplicity. It had two rooms, one of which was a kitchen. The partition wall contained the kitchen fireplace as well as built-in shelves. The west wall, facing the porch, has a door into the kitchen but no windows; the rooms were lit by windows in other walls. Underneath the other room was a cellar with rock-lined walls. This part of the house still had a shingled roof in 1938; the front part of the house had a tin roof (not the current one) by 1924. The beams in the front room of the ell have notches in them in the wrong places, which suggest that they were reused from an earlier building.

Reverend Dangers also bought a property across Orange Street from St. Mary's Church, now the site of St. Mary's School [83], on which stood a two-story rock house. Dangers died in 1869. His widow, Mathilde, was living in Fredericksburg with two daughters, and the combined value of the two properties was $1,500.

Mathilde Dangers sold the house on West Creek Street to John Raulz, a carpenter, in 1873, and Raulz demolished the original log house and built two new rooms. In 1873 John was fifty-one, his wife Margaretha (née Zenner) was forty-five, and they had two adult children, Maria and John. Their daughter Maria married Martin Heinemann, and they built their own rock house on West San Antonio Street [96]. The new part of John and Margaretha's house had a front room and a second room under the lean-to roof. The front wall was very typical of the 1870s, with a central door flanked by one window on each side. There is a distinct echo of the Ruegner house [5] on West San Antonio Street, also built in the early 1870s. Perhaps John Ruegner was the stonemason of the Raulz house as well.

103 Goebel-Meckel-Roos-Wissmer-Staudt-Jenschke House (George and Lena Jenschke House)

223 West Creek Street
Circa 1850–55, circa 1904, circa 1914

This little house, originally even smaller, was home to working-class Catholic families for more than a hundred years. The oldest part is a single log room, with a centered door and two windows. It was built for a blacksmith, Heinrich Goebel, and his wife Catherine, who had six children by 1850. They sold it in 1856 for $170 to Bernard Meckel, a cooper, who in 1855 had married Sophie Weinheimer, daughter of Catholic pioneers Jakob and Theresia Weinheimer. Her brother was Anton, whose rock house was on Baron's Creek [70]. They valued their property at a mere $150 on the 1860 census.

Heinrich Roos Jr. bought the house in 1865, L. Wissmer in 1879, and Peter A. Staudt in 1903. Staudt and his second wife, the former Mary (or Maria) Leindecker, added a new rock kitchen behind the original log room and the group of rock rooms on the west side. In 1910 Peter told the census taker that he was a laborer doing odd jobs, and Mary had no occupation, meaning that she did all the work in the house; they sold it in 1914. The new owners, George and Lena (née Kunz) Jenschke, were a farming couple and used this as their Sunday house. They added two more rooms, of frame construction, on the east

side, both rooms being bedrooms; in 1920 they had thirteen children, so this was something of a necessity. The house was never much to look at, but it was extremely close to St. Mary's Catholic Church [84 and 85], a convenience that most of its owners greatly valued.

104 Charles and Ida Hotopp House
301 West Creek Street
1914

This red brick house, which now seems quaint, was the height of modernity when it was built in 1914. A brickyard opened in D'Danis, Texas, in 1905, and this house may be an early use of this material, which was most prominently used on St. Mary's School of 1923–24 [83]. Two red granite date stones both give the date of construction; one also gives the name of the owner. Carl Hotopp was born in Texas during the Civil War to a farming couple, Heinrich and Henriette, who were both natives of Braunschweig. As Fredericksburg became more anglicized, Carl became Charles. Charles married Ida Schmidt, daughter of Ludwig and Maria Schmidt, who ran a hotel on Main Street [40]. By 1900 he was working as a horse and cattle dealer and the household included five daughters. The front part of the L-shaped house is only three rooms, but the rock rooms to the rear are older, perhaps the house of Charles's parents. At the time of the 1930 census

Charles Hotopp gave the value of the house as $5,000, which was comparable to the Max and Lydia Bierschwale house [133].

---

105 Sophie Spaeth House (Ahrens-Spaeth-Langehennig House)
314 West Creek Street
Circa 1883–84, circa 1905

The oldest remaining part of this complex is the two-room rock house on the west side.

The lot was owned by Conrad Ahrens Jr. from 1874 to January 1883, but its valuation for tax purposes was quite low. A large jump in valuation occurred the year after the lot was purchased in 1883 by the widow Sophie Spaeth. The daughter of Peter and Sophie Behrens, she married Ludwig Spaeth in 1853, but he had been killed by Indians in 1870. By 1883 she was forty-five, and her oldest children were grown; in September 1883 her second-oldest, Louis, married Lena Schmidt. She may have been thinking of enticing Louis and Lena to live with her, like Charlotte Basse on Main Street [see 22].

The house has the arrangement typical of the 1870s and 1880s— front porch, large front room, smaller back room. The attic was

accessed by a hatch in the west wall—there is no evidence of external stairs. Later, probably after 1904, a frame addition with porch was added to the east, set back from the rock house. The east window in the front room of the old house was converted into a door that opened onto the porch of the frame addition. The new part contained two bedrooms, both of which opened onto the porch. After Sophie's death, her five surviving sons and one daughter sold the house to Christian Segner, whose family owned it from 1904 to 1943. The Erhardt Lange-hennig family owned it from 1943 to 1977, when Richard and Maxie Hoerst bought the house and had it restored. The front door dates to the restoration but is said to be a replica of the original.

106 Henry and Elizabeth Kuenemann House
413 West Creek Street
1896–97

This is a splendid late Victorian house that incorporates a late *fach-werk* house. It has sometimes been characterized as one of the oldest houses in town, but this is wildly inaccurate. Apparently the 1847 date is based on when the town lot was assigned to Heinrich Schupp,

which proves only that it could not have been before 1847, and on the fact that it is *fachwerk*, although *fachwerk* houses were built in Fredericksburg in the 1870s [see 67 and 89]. Moreover, even if the *fachwerk* part is from 1847, this is now less than 25 percent of the house, which is predominantly from the Victorian era.

Friedrich Kuenemann and his family came from Germany with the original group of pioneers; they lived and worked on their farm for two decades. As their children came of age, they decided to move into town and bought the lot formerly owned by Heinrich Schupp and then Ludwig Kuhlmann. In 1869 their son Heinrich (later known as Henry) married Elizabeth Tatsch, daughter of the cabinetmaker John Peter Tatsch [see 132], for whom Heinrich worked. Soon thereafter, he built a *fachwerk* house, the remains of which are visible on the east side of the house. The ground floor six-over-six windows were not used in Fredericksburg until after the Civil War; the upper floor four-over-four windows are even later.

Henry Kuenemann was master of a number of crafts. He described himself as painter, carpenter, and cabinet maker in 1880, cabinetmaker in 1900, and retail lumber and furniture dealer in 1910. Ultimately the furniture shop was on Main Street, but the lumberyard surrounded this house, and the house in turn served as an example of the materials the factory could produce. The 1915 Sanborn map shows that across the street to the north was the planing mill, while catercorner from the big house was a long lumber shed with an attached to store shingles and another room to store window sash and doors, and beyond this was a pile of cedar posts. The office and two additional lumber sheds were built on the Kerrville Road (now South Adams Street). After 1887, when the railroad reached Kerrville, goods were hauled along this route; in 1913 it became the terminus of Fredericksburg's own railroad depot.

At the time of the 1910 census, three sons and one daughter, all in their twenties, were living at home, and another son, Charles, was living next door with his wife. Charles was the manager of the lumberyard, Max was a house carpenter, and Arthur was a clerk in the furniture store. Their father's grand Victorian house demonstrated both his financial success and his hearty embrace of mainstream American taste. Between 1915 and 1924 the entire operation was moved to the

Kerrville Road location, taking advantage of Fredericksburg's recently completed railroad connections.

The complicated floor plan and Victorian ornamentation of the porch of the Kuenemann house were at their height in Fredericksburg in the 1890s and remained popular into the first decade of the twentieth century. Especially striking are the steps on the west side of the porch—beyond the door is an enclosed staircase to the second floor. This is a highly unusual variant of the external stairs on the side of some Fredericksburg houses. When the house was restored, the earlier *fachwerk* framing was left uncovered, which is instructive for those curious about the early days of the house but also misleading about how the house would have looked after its enlargement: Kuenemann did not intend the *fachwerk* to be visible, as it detracted from his grand Victorian advertisement for his business. Indeed, it was built at the very time when the town fathers were demolishing the most prominent remaining example of *fachwerk*—the Vereins-Kirche. The house stands in contrast to other two-story houses in Fredericksburg, which are built of rock, Basse blocks, or a combination of the two. Again, this was because Kuenemann was showing potential customers the beautiful work his lumber mill could do.

Kuenemann also built the small frame house at the other end of the block for Joseph and Meta Klein in 1908–9, and he may have been responsible for the houses in between as well.

---

107 Adam and Eva Krieger House (Krieger-Henke-Staudt House)
512 West Creek Street
1851, 1855, 1864

Like many of the earliest houses in Fredericksburg, this one started small and was added on to over time. The original owners were Adam and Eva Krieger. They built a one-room *fachwerk* house in 1851—this is the left front part of the house. It amounted to little more than 200 square feet of living space. Like the Walter family one block to the west, they probably started out in a one-room log house on the rear of the lot. The front left room is the only part of the house that

---

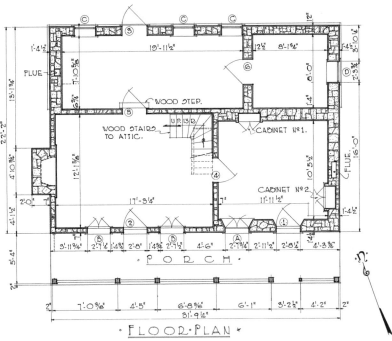

Floor paln based on measured drawing by Bartlett Cocke and Anton Heisler Jr. for the Historic American Building Survey.

is *fachwerk*—the other three rooms have rock walls. The original *fachwerk* room had centered doors in the front and back walls and windows flanking the door in the front wall. The fireplace on the west side wall is fairly unusual for Fredericksburg, given the long-standing popularity of cast-iron stoves for cooking and heating. In the right rear corner was a staircase, though it had disappeared by the time the house was documented by the Historic American Buildings Survey in 1934. The first rock room was added in 1855, the two rear rooms around 1862. Adam Krieger sold the house to Karl Henke in 1869. The earliest room almost certainly had a porch, but the ornamental trim between the posts clearly date to the Victorian era.

The Historic American Buildings Survey documented this house with measured drawings and photographs, all of which are very useful, but erroneously referred to the house as the "Staudt Sunday House," even though it was built as a full-time residence and not by the Staudt family. Photographs taken at that time show that the house had been plastered, but the *fachwerk* is proudly displayed today.

New owners Rodolph and Roberta Smith made several changes after they purchased the house in 1968. They added the external staircase and door into the attic on the east side to provide access to the air-conditioning unit in the attic. The Smiths also removed layers of linoleum from the floor, only to discover that the original floor was in bad condition. They removed the floor boards and then set slabs of stone in between the floor joists. This was by no means a return to the original state, but it was a highly original solution. They also converted a back bedroom into a bathroom. The original log house was long gone, but Roberta, the daughter of Fritz and Lillian Stieler of Comfort, was able to find a log building from Comfort to place in the backyard. It is said to have been built by Edward Steves and was later owned by Herman Ingenhuett of Comfort before being moved to Fredericksburg. A significant log house from Comfort has less significance once it has lost its original context.

108 Peter and Anna Margaret Walter House
601 West Creek Street
1853, 1859

This little house, though heavily restored, is one of the oldest surviving houses in town and demonstrates how a *fachwerk* house would be enlarged with a rock addition. Peter Walter purchased a group of town lots at the west end of Creek Street—eight by 1850 and eleven by 1852—and promptly began to farm on them. The earliest structure was a one-room log house, which was followed in 1853 by a two-room *fachwerk* house with a rock infill. As usual, the *fachwerk* was Americanized with an Anglo-Southern front porch. At an early date the *fachwerk* was plastered over, perhaps so that the *fachwerk* and rock sections would blend together. Peter and his wife Margarethe (née Rubbin) had six children by 1859, and they expanded to the rear with a room made entirely of rock. Peter died in 1865, and the eldest son, Heinrich, took over the farm. After Heinrich's death the farm went to his younger brother, William. Their brother John had already built his own log and rock house on West Austin Street [127], and his son Frederick later built a rock house on West Main Street [66].

The little house remained in the family until 1954, when they sold it to St. Barnabas Episcopal Church. At that time it was remodeled to

Circa 1920s. Courtesy of Institute of Texan Cultures, University of Texas at San Antonio, 075–0246.

serve as a chapel. The plaster on the front wall was removed to expose the *fachwerk*, while the side walls were covered with shingles. Later still, the shingles were removed from the side walls, exposing all of the *fachwerk*. Early photographs show a small window on the east wall just to the front of a center post; at some point another window was added just to the rear of this post, and new, larger windows were installed. (Presumably this happened on the west wall as well.) Interestingly, the new windows were casement windows rather than double-hung sash, which made the house look older and more German. Inside, the partition in the *fachwerk* section was removed, creating a single front room. Lady Bird and Lyndon Johnson worshipped here from time to time when they were at home in nearby Stonewall.

109 Friedrich and Sophie Behr House (Behr-Fiedler House)
212 South Acorn Street
1891–93

This is a late example of a house with two doors opening onto the front
porch rather than a single door opening into a central passage. Friedrich and Sophie Behr bought this lot on the outskirts of town, town lot
296, in 1882 for $300, but the lot appreciated significantly between
1891 and 1893. Like the nearby Peter Walter family [see 108], the
Behrs farmed on what was supposed to be a town lot. The house was
rock with four rooms—two in front and two in back. The only thing to
suggest such a late date was the large size and even shape of the stones
on the front wall. In 1916 the house was sold to Adolph Herbort for
$1,100. It was sold again to Bernhard Fiedler in 1931, then to Willie
Fiedler in 1934.

110 Anton and Anna Maria Weinheimer House
514 Franklin Street
Circa 1869

Anton Weinheimer, son of pioneering Catholics Jakob and Theresia Weinheimer, married Anna Maria Petsch in 1854. Anton and Anna Maria purchased three out-lots from Friedrich Kiehne in 1868, where they farmed and ranched. The farm was bounded by Baron's Creek, South Creek Street, and Franklin Street. Anna Maria's brother-in-law was the carpenter and cabinetmaker Friedrich Gentemann [see 87], who may have crafted the house's floors, doors, and windows (all of which disappeared long ago, the victims of time and neglect). The stone walls may have been erected by one of Gentemann's coworkers at St. Mary's Catholic Church [84], Peter Schmitz, who built his own rock house between 1872 and 1874 [120]. Anna Maria's younger sister Catherine married Joseph Kollett in 1876, and in 1885 they built a rock house on West San Antonio Street [95]; the stonemason for that house was Joseph Moritz, the stepson of Peter Schmitz.

   The house has all the attributes of a post–Civil War rock house: one and a half stories, sash windows, and direct entry into the parlor. The parlor was the east front room; the west front room was a bedroom. The lean-to also had two rooms—a kitchen on the west, with a chimney on its west wall, and a smaller bedroom on the east. The walls

between the front and rear rooms were rock, but the wall between the two back rooms consisted of adobe block. (All evidence of adobe has been removed in the course of various restorations.) The kitchen has a raised hearth, another postwar trait seen at the additions to the Kammlah house [46] and the Tatsch house [132]. Both rear rooms have a south-facing window. The stair to the loft is in the west front room, on the inner wall, again similar to its placement at the Tatsch house. The loft is a single space, with two windows at the west end and one on the east. Anna Weinheimer died in 1923, after which the old rock house was used mainly to store hay. By the time the property was sold to George and Marjorie Garretson in 1968, the roof had collapsed, windows, doors, and the floor were decayed or gone, and the adobe block partition wall had virtually melted away. The Garretsons built a new, sprawling ranch house on the property in 1969, but also restored the rock house to something like its original appearance. The house faces Baron's Creek to the north and is just visible from the street. Remember not to trespass!

---

111 Arthur and Anna Danz House
514 Franklin Street
Circa 1913–14

The eldest daughter of Anton and Anna Maria Weinheimer, named Anna Maria like her mother, married Arthur Danz, a son of Caspar

and Dorothea Danz, who farmed in Stonewall [204]. After Anton Weinheimer died in 1910, Arthur and Anna came to live with her mother. Around 1913 they began work on a new house closer to the road. There they raised three children, Clara, Willie, and Edwin. In the 1920 census Arthur identified himself as a farmer; in 1930 he was a stockman. The new house was built of concrete blocks, the locally made Basse blocks, but the bulk was lightened by an abundance of Victorian gingerbread trim. The arrangement is quite symmetrical: three rooms in east and west wings, connected by a hallway that may have originally been an open breezeway. This would be extremely late for a dogtrot, but it should be noted that when Emil and Emma Beckmann built their dream house in Stonewall in 1915 [207], they created a breezeway between the earlier rock kitchen and their new Victorian rooms. From the recessed front porch of the Danz house one can enter the hall or either of the front rooms. The kitchen seems to have been the middle room on the east side, which has a side entry. To the rear are bedrooms; the room on the northeast corner has a built-in wardrobe in a back corner. Pretty clearly, it was no easier to insert closets in a house made of Basse blocks than in one made of limestone.

112 Rudolph and Helene Mueller House (Mueller-Reinbach House)
South Creek Street at southeast corner of East Highway Street
Circa 1882–83 and after, 1925

This sprawling complex started as a two-room farmhouse in 1882–83 for Rudolph and Helene Mueller. Rudolph was the son of Fredericksburg pioneers Heinrich and Margarethe Mueller, and he grew up in their *fachwerk* house on South Washington Street [70]. In 1879 he bought fifty acres on this site as his farm. He married Helene Hopf in 1882. The earliest two rooms are perhaps the last example of *fachwerk* construction in the county. The frame is infilled with rock. These two rooms were a *stube* and a kitchen; there was a loft in the half story above. As the family grew (two sons and a daughter), a frame addition of two rooms was built on the north side. The house was sold in 1910 to Felix and Elise (née Henke) Reinbach. Felix died 1916, and Elise

married Charles F. Kiehne in 1925. Around this time the back rooms were added: a hall, a bathroom, and two bedrooms. The swept yard was later replaced by white gravel.

113 Kurt and Margareta Keidel House
114 Felix and Hattie Keidel House
614 and 616 South Washington Street
1914

This pair of houses was built for two sons of Albert and Mathilde Keidel, who built the impressive Victorian house on East Main Street [24]. Kurt was trained as a pharmacist, and Felix as a dentist. In 1909 Kurt opened a drug store in partnership with Hugo J. W. Kallenberg in a building that his father, Dr. Albert Keidel, had built just west of his home [23]. Kurt bought the land on which these two houses were to be built in 1910. The two houses were designed by a San Antonio architect, Leo M. J. Dielmann, who had earlier designed St. Mary's Catholic Church [85] and a number of houses for young people with old Fredericksburg names, such as Wahrmund [131] and Bierschwale [161]. Kurt and Felix married sisters from Selma, Alabama, Margareta and Hattie Pfeiffer. In 1920 Felix and Hattie had two daughters, while

Kurt and Margarate had three daughters and a son. Apparently pharmacy was more profitable than dentistry, because Kurt and Margareta could afford a live-in servant girl.

The houses, which are mirror images of each other, invoke the late version of the Queen Anne style, combining a studied asymmetry and a prominent equilateral triangular gable with columns characteristic of the Colonial Revival style. (The columns at 614 have been replaced with slim cast-iron posts; those at 616 are original.) Perhaps the feature most associated with the earlier Queen Anne style is the front window in which the upper sash has twenty smaller panes of glass, consciously invoking an old-time feel. Perhaps the most up-to-date feature, still intact at 616, is the porte cochere, which was very popular in the teens and twenties as more Americans purchased cars. The internal arrangement of rooms reflects an awareness of the recent popularity of bungalows: there is direct entry into the front room, with no entry hall; behind this are the dining room and kitchen. In 1941 a family room was added and the kitchen enlarged at 614. At this time a number of windows were replaced with modern windows with a stationary central pane and casements to each side that are opened by a crank.

Next door to the Keidel houses, to the north, is the Henry and Alice Grote house, a brick house that is a more canonical version of a bungalow: prominent gables on each side, another gable covering the porch, generous overhangs of the roof supported by brackets, a fireplace bracketed with small windows on the north wall of the living room, and, behind this, the dining room with a bay projecting to the north.

---

115 Heinrich and Marie Lehne House (Lehne-Itz House)
402 Whitney Street
1885–86

This is a fine story-and-a-half rock house, the 1880s edition. Earlier such houses tended to be one room in front and another behind; this one was two rooms wide, each with access from the front porch. This is not unlike the William and Maria Klingelhoefer house [119] of the same decade, and indeed Klingelhoefer may have done the stonework on this house. Heinrich (Henry) Lehne was the son of pioneers Christian Lehne and his wife, the former Sophie Kuenemann. Sophie's brother (and thus Henry's uncle) was Henry Kuenemann [see 106], the carpenter and cabinetmaker, who may have done the woodwork on this house. Henry married Anna Barth in 1885, and the house was begun soon thereafter. Sadly, Anna passed away soon thereafter, and

Henry married Maria Spaeth, daughter of Ludwig and Sophie Spaeth. Henry and Maria's youngest daughter, Sophie, married Ernest Itz in 1931, and they improved the house by adding the frame addition to the back, which had a more modern kitchen and another bedroom. In recent years the house has been used as a restaurant and shop; in its latest permutation the partition between the two front rooms has been removed to create one large dining room.

116 Adolph and Martha Wunderlich Log House
117 Adolph and Martha Wunderlich Rock House
55 and 59 Post Oak Road
1886, 1889, 1892

This little house is a late manifestation of a log-and-rock one-room house with a fairly tall half story above, to which was added a rock kitchen to the rear. Adolph was a son of Johann Peter and Elizabeth Wunderlich [see 101], and Adolph's blacksmith-carpenter father may have helped get his son situated in his new house.

Adolph and Martha's growing family encouraged them to build a larger house just a few years after erecting the log and rock house next

door. The new house, built entirely of rock, has a date stone proudly marking 1892 as its date of construction. Like an earlier generation of houses, the *stube* was in front and the kitchen behind, but now there was a second room in front. Both rooms had its own front door, a late example of a feature found in many German American houses. Earlier

houses to take this approach were the Lehne house on Whitney [115] and the William and Maria Klingelhoeffer house [119]. These were all built by children of the pioneer generation, and this new generation was less invested in the older ways of arranging space. Nevertheless, the additional half story echoes the classic story-and-a-half rock house of twenty to thirty years previous.

118 Rudolph and Louise Eckert House (Eckert-Seipp House)
805 South Bowie Street
Early 1870s, 1890s

Rudolph was the oldest son of Ludwig and Christine Eckert, immigrants from Baden. When Ludwig and Christine divorced in 1860, Ludwig got the four oldest boys; Christine got Christiana, Mary, and the youngest son, Ernst. Christine deeded the land to Rudolph in 1871; he married Louise Dietz in that year. Rudolph and Louise farmed the land for many decades—in the 1910 census the sixty-seven-year-old Rudolph still listed his occupation as farmer. In 1920 their youngest son, Edmund, had taken over management of the farm. Rudolph died in 1925, and Louise in 1926.

This house is extremely hard to date, but it seems to have been begun

in the 1870s, not too long after their marriage. The earliest part consisted of the three rooms on the north side. Originally there was a staircase on the south side. The front room was the *stube*, and the back room the kitchen; the use of the middle room is not clear. The south wing and a porch at the angle were added later, possibly in the 1890s. The front porch was enclosed to make a sitting room. The house was struck by lightning in 1972, and fire caused much damage. It has since been restored to its appearance when the south wing was added. The property was purchased in 1928 by Meta Seipp, the wife of Otto H. Seipp, and he built a dance hall adjacent to the house known as Seipp's Dance Hall, which burned to the ground on Christmas Day 1947, just before a big dance. The hall was rebuilt, and later owners renamed it Pat's Hall in 1953. At some point the original front porch was enclosed to make another bedroom, but the house retains its turn-of-the-century appearance.

119 William and Maria Klingelhoefer House
US 87 north, just west of intersection with US 290
1883–84, 1887–88

This house was formerly thought to have been built in 1879, but tax records show that it was built in two phases; the first was most likely the rock outbuilding, one large room with another room beneath it partially below ground. The big house is larger and has much finer stonework. William Klingelhoefer was the younger son of J. J. and

Elisabeth Klingelhoefer and grew up in their *fachwerk* house on Main Street [65]. Like his older brother, Julius, he was trained as a stonemason and presumably assisted his brother in building the lean-to of their parents' house in 1869. In 1870 he gave his occupation in the census as "farm laborer," which meant that he was working the out-lot where he would eventually build his own house. In 1879 he married Maria Eckert, the next-to-youngest child of Ludwig and Christine Eckert, who farmed and ranched nearby.

William and Maria's own story-and-a-half house has two front rooms, both with their own door onto the porch, a late example of this feature. Behind this is a lean-to with a kitchen. The west front room, the *stube*, has a built-in cabinet on the side wall. This echoes the built-in at the home in which Julius's wife, Sophie, had grown up, the house of the cabinetmaker John Peter Tatsch [132], though the Klingelhoefer cabinet is simpler in construction. The side wall of the kitchen has a raised hearth, another feature found in the Tatsch house as well as the Kammlah house [46]. William Klingelhoefer continued to work as a stonemason and was most proud of his work on the Bank of Fredericksburg [16], built in 1898. He was one of four stonemasons from Fredericksburg who built St. Peter's Lutheran Church [175] in the Doss community.

PART 5

North of Main Street

120 Peter and Therese Schmitz House
502 East Austin Street
1872–74

This is the house of Peter Schmitz, a stonemason and one of the principal stonemasons who built the Marienkirche [84]. He married Therese Hatcher Moritz, the widow of Edmund Moritz, sometime between 1864 and 1870. Presumably he built his own house, perhaps with the assistance of his two oldest stepsons, Joseph and Franz Moritz. On the 1870 census Franz was listed as "apprentice to

stonemason;" ten years later Joseph's occupation was "stonemason." According to the cornerstone, Schmitz started work on the house on January 15, 1872. Tax records suggest that he finished it in 1874. In the year Peter started the house, Franz turned eighteen and Joseph turned eleven. The house apparently had one large front room and a large kitchen to the rear. Schmitz also built the rock outbuilding and the rock fence around the property. Peter died in 1888, and Therese in 1902. At a later time—probably early in the twentieth century—two gables were placed on the front side of the roof, giving it an appearance similar to that of the Ellebracht house on West Austin Street [130], but these were later removed to take the house back to its original appearance. The Schmitz family was Catholic, and in 1926 the heirs sold the house to another Catholic family, Mr. and Mrs. James Ruff (Mrs. Ruff being a daughter of Anna Catharine Moritz Petri and thus a granddaughter of Therese Moritz Schmitz), who kept it until 1971.

---

121 John J. and Wilhelmine Walch House
400 block of East Austin Street
1850s, 1870–71, 1905

The buildings on this lot reflect the evolution of more than half a century, from 1847 to 1905. John Walch was one of the earliest settlers of Fredericksburg and did work for John O. Meusebach on his ranch at Comanche Spring. He was a stonemason but also owned a sizable

---

farm and ranch in the country. The earlier, one-story building has sometimes been dated to 1851, based solely on Walch's marriage to Wilhelmine Gaertner in that year. However, on the census of 1870 Walch reported that his property was worth only $400, consistent with the presence of a log house, and tax records show that the largest jump in value came in 1870 and 1871. A historic photograph of the property shows a three-room log and rock house, with the middle room possibly an enclosed dogtrot, which stood in front of the rock building that survives today. The rock house had only two rooms, thought to be a *stube* on the east and kitchen on the west. The most unusual feature was the placement of the fireplace against the north wall of the kitchen. The eastward-facing two-story building to the west of this house is said to have started out as a barn but was remodeled into a house by John and Wilhelmine's son Felix around 1905. For the one-room log-and-rock house of John's younger sister, Anna Regina Walch Hahn, see 141.

---

122 Julius and Mina Brockmann House (Brockmann-Kiehne-Keidel House)
209 East Austin Street
1871

Julius Brockmann was the postmaster of Fredericksburg, and as someone who dealt with postal officials from other parts of Texas and

---

the United States, he seems to have been open to outside ideas. He purchased this lot in February 1870 and apparently got right to work, as the house was completed by 1871. Along with the Heinrich Ochs house on West Main Street [37], this is one of the first houses in town to have a central passage, which earlier German Texans had considered a waste of space. The Brockmann house has two rooms to each side of the passage. Another Anglo-Texan feature was a kitchen separate from the main house. The rock kitchen had a cellar beneath it; later it was connected to the main house. At that time the original paneled front doors were moved to the side so that doors with glass panes could admit some additional light into the passage.

123 John and Bertha Schandua House
111 East Austin Street
1885

This little house is a remarkable survivor: a basic starter house of the 1880s that has never been enlarged or modified. John Schandua was the son of Peter Schandua, one of the carpenters who built the *fach-werk* St. Mary's Church in 1848. Bertha was the daughter of farming couple Christian and Gertrude Klein. The house has just two rooms: a *stube* (a combined parlor and bedroom) and a kitchen. The front room

is nearly square, the back one smaller and rectangular. It has never been electrified, nor does it have running water or a bathroom.

In 1897 John built a store with a residence above at 203 Main Street [the western half of 19], but he died of a heart attack in 1900. Bertha married his brother, Henry, and they enlarged the new store and created living space for the family above the new part of the store. They moved out of the house on East Austin in 1903 but continued to own it until 1921. San Antonio businessman Burt L. Joiner purchased the house in 1963 and gave the house to the Gillespie County Historical Society that same year. It was restored over the next decade.

124 Friedrich Wilhelm and Anna Marie Elizabeth Schumacher House
104 East Austin Street
1873

Unlike some other Fredericksburg houses of the early 1870s—for example, the Brockmann house one block to the east [122]—the Schumacher house adheres to the local vernacular. For many years the Schumachers lived in a house just to the east of this one, which

started out with one *fachwerk* room, then another, and finally a rock room to the rear of the western one. It was valued at only $360 at the time of the 1870 census. This *fachwerk* house may now be seen at the San Antonio Botanical Gardens. The two-story rock house that the Schumachers built in 1873 follows a typical Hill Country pattern: a squarish front room with a smaller rectangular room behind, and a lower-ceilinged room above the front room. It differs somewhat in two respects: the second floor also has a back room, and there is a two-story front porch, which had previously been seen only on the Kiehne house on East Main [34]. Helen "Shatzie" Stieler Crouch and her husband, John R. "Hondo" Crouch (see 193 and 194), purchased the Schumacher house in 1969, and Shatzie opened a shop called the Rumpelkammer. The site where the *fachwerk* house stood is now occupied by a two-story log house moved to Fredericksburg from Pennsylvania; it has little in common with German Texan log houses and serves only to confuse the architectural history of the town.

For the 100 block of West Austin Street, see entries 10–11.

Around the Corner on North Crockett Street—North of Austin Street

125 Heinrich and Wilhelmine Cordes House
210 Mistletoe Street, rear (visible from North Crockett Street)
Circa 1857–59, circa 1874

This house exemplifies the German version of a log house and the way in which Germans added rooms to their houses. It was built by Heinrich Cordes, a native of Hanover who came to Texas in 1845. His parents settled in New Braunfels, but Heinrich settled in Fredericksburg. He married Henriette Sophie Kothmann, but she died while giving birth to their daughter Sophie in 1856. He married Wilhelmine "Minna" Henke in 1859, and they had four children. Heinrich was a carpenter who was responsible for roofing St. Mary's Catholic Church [84] in the early 1860s and later the Heinrich and Margarete

Bierschwale house [126] nearby on West Austin Street. For his own house, built around 1858, he started with a room in which hewn logs alternated with rows of rocks; this was at once more airtight against winter cold and rain and more permanent. An opening for a flue indicates that a stove was installed in the northeast corner. Cordes added to his house over time: first came the rear rock room, with a small cooking hearth on the east side wall, and later came a second front room and expansion of the porch; last came a space behind this, open at the rear, for performing laundry and other household chores. The rock rooms may have been built with the assistance of Minna's brother, Carl Henke, who was a stonemason.

After Heinrich died in 1875, Minna continued to live in the house with the children. Their son Heinrich Jr. married Emma Crenwelge around 1888 and continued to live in this old log house until they built their own rock house at 204 West Schubert Street in 1893. At that point Minna went to live with her daughter Mina and her husband Fred Koennecke, but she continued to own the house. In 1922 Fred subdivided their land as the Koennecke Addition and built the frame bungalow at 201 Mistletoe, which backs up to the old house. The property was purchased in 1971 by Helen "Shatzie" Stieler Crouch, who also served as president of the Gillespie County Historical Society, and her care for the house has been ongoing.

West Austin Street

126 Heinrich and Margarete Bierschwale House
209 West Austin Street
1872–73

This house is not only an excellent and well-preserved example of a story-and-a-half German Texan rock house; it is also one of the best documented houses in town. It was begun in 1872 and completed in 1873 for Heinrich and Margarethe (née Treibs) Bierschwale. Originally they lived in the German settlement known as Hilda in southeastern Mason County, but they moved to Fredericksburg so that Heinrich could serve as the county clerk. Heinrich, Margarethe, and their children lived in a one-room *fachwerk* house while their new house was being built. It turns out that Heinrich's meticulous record keeping did not stop when he left his office in the old rock courthouse on the Marktplatz; his private account book gives a detailed record of workmen and materials for the construction of the house.

The walls of the house were built by Georg Peter, a second-generation Fredericksburg stonemason who also worked on the building of Fort Concho in San Angelo. He would soon build his own house [64] on Main Street. Heinrich Cordes, who lived in a little log and rock house just around the corner on North Crockett Street [125], built the roof, just as he had on St. Mary's Catholic Church [84] in the

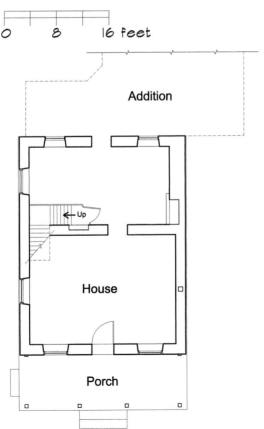

Measured floor plan by John Klein.

early 1860s. Jacob Schneider, a carpenter and cabinetmaker, made the doors, windows, floors, stairs, and porch. Locks for the doors were supplied by Engelbert Krauskopf, the gunsmith and mechanic whose shop was a few blocks away on West Main Street.

Like the Weihmiller house [9] around the corner on North Crockett Street, the Bierschwale house has a squarish front room that served as the *stube* (parlor-bedroom) and a rectangular room behind this that was probably a bedroom for some of their children. (As was usually the case with early log houses, the *fachwerk* room probably remained as the kitchen.) Both the front and rear rooms were heated by cast-iron stoves on the west side wall, as the flue openings inside and chimneys outside attest. And as with the Weihmiller house, the staircase is in the rear room, starting on the wall between the front and back rooms and turning to rise against the side wall. The tall half story above the *stube* had more space for beds, as did the attic space behind. At a later date the rear bedroom was converted into a kitchen. In the early twentieth century cabinets were built on the west wall, to the right of which was a fireplace with a raised hearth.

---

127 John and Maria Walter House
408 West Austin Street
Circa 1869–70 and later

This house was built by John and Maria Walter, both children of the pioneer generation. John was the third son of Peter and Margarethe

Walter and grew up in their little *fachwerk* house on West Creek Street [108]. Maria was the daughter of Heinrich and Dorothea Brandes, a farming couple. John served as county sheriff and tax collector from 1874 to 1888. John and Maria bought this lot in 1867, and by 1870 it was worth $350. It has been added onto several times, the first addition being the rock rooms on the east side.

The log room is a classic Hill Country log house: the logs were held together by V-notches, as Texans from Tennessee had taught the German immigrants, but between the logs are courses of mortared rock, which answered the German desire for a snug, air-tight, and permanent building. The two rock rooms, a squarish *stube* with a lean-to room behind, may have been built by Georg Peter, whose sister Wilhelmine was married to John's brother Henry. The very different log and rock front rooms are somewhat unified by the front porch. John and Maria's son Frederick married Hulda Saenger and built a house entirely of rock—a late version of the local vernacular—on West Main Street [66].

---

128 Christian and Katherina Strackbein House
(Strackbein-Roeder House)
414 West Austin Street
1872–74

This is one of the simplest and most charming houses in Fredericksburg. Christian Strackbein was a stonemason who met Katharina Eckert while working on a construction project at her father's ranch in the Beaver Creek community in southeast Mason County. They married at the Hilda Bethel Methodist Church in Beaver Creek in 1870 and, in the same year, bought this lot in Fredericksburg from John Walter, who was just building his log and rock house next door. The two-room house with a loft above was completed by 1874. The front porch was inset beneath the main roof, a feature that German builders had learned from Creole carpenters on the Gulf Coast. The house is built of rock; the front wall is plastered, while the sides are not. It has an external stair to the attic, a space-saving feature that was very helpful in a house this small. The little house in town allowed him to participate in

---

the post–Civil War building boom that happened in Fredericksburg, but he also did projects in the surrounding country. They later lived in the communities of Cherry Spring and then in Doss before returning to Fredericksburg in 1913. Presumably Christian built his own house and the large two-story rock house at Cherry Spring of Martin Dittmar and his wife, Elizabeth, who was Katherina's sister.

129 Elise Vogel Sunday House
418 West Austin Street
Circa 1903, 1907

A historical marker and brochures claim that this house was begun in the 1880s by Christian Vogel and enlarged around the turn of the century by his son Amandus Vogel and his wife, the former Elizabeth Weber. An examination of property tax records tells a different story. Christian and Magdalena Vogel lived on their farm, as did their son Amandus, who married another farm girl, Elise Weber, in 1880 in St. Mary's Catholic Church. By 1889, the year in which he apparently died, Christian had amassed 825 acres worth over $1,900. Moreover, he and Magdalena had

given Amandus and Elise 325 nearby acres worth $1,610. Christian and
Magdalena also owned several lots in town, including Lot 50 on Austin
Street, but it was only worth $80–100. It stayed at that level after the
death of Christian around 1889 and the death of Amandus in 1898.

Not until 1903 did the value rise from $80 to $200, and then to
$400 in 1907, a value comparable to the Metzger Sunday house [88]
and Jenschke Sunday house [155]. Elise continued to farm with the help
of her five children, but clearly she began to think about spending more
time in town. First she built a one-room house with a tall half story so
that they could come to town on Sundays. A staircase on the west wall led
to the room in the half story. The eastern section of the house was added
circa 1907, when Elise was forty-nine, making it a full-week house rather
than a Sunday house. It was a mirror image of the first room, so that both
front rooms have a window and a door opening onto the porch, a fairly
typical German Texan façade. The Victorian porch was also added at this
time, and the entire house was covered in metal siding soon thereafter.
This particular metal siding is pressed to look like stone, using a pattern
similar to that used on the Junction School near Stonewall [208]. Later
still a small back porch was enclosed to create a bathroom.

When Elise died in 1944 at age eighty-six, the house was sold and
became a rental property. In the late 1960s or early 1970s the entire
house was painted purple, a testament to the taste of the psychedelic

era. In 1976 Randy and Marilynne Cox bought the house and fixed it up as their retirement home. The metal siding was removed from the west room and given board-and-batten siding, which was another typical wall treatment at the beginning of the twentieth century. The original room became a modern kitchen, and the east room their living room. The Coxes added a sitting room behind this and also another bedroom that was to be a mother-in-law suite with separate bathroom. They installed closets between the two bedrooms upstairs. In subsequent years the house has been used as a bed-and-breakfast, which in Fredericksburg has been a popular way of giving a new use to an old house while retaining its historic character.

---

130 Henry and Sophie Ellebracht House (Ellebracht-Sagebiel House)
420 West Austin Street
Circa 1901–7

This house is an excellent example of a late Victorian story-and-a-half rock house. Peter Maurer built a small house on this lot in 1875; newlyweds Henry and Sophie (née Dittmar) Ellebracht bought it in 1897 and lived in it for several years before building this house sometime between 1901 and 1907. The main roof line runs from east to west,

that is, from one side gable to another, but two prominent front gables with windows provide additional light and headroom in the half story. Victorian trim ornaments the front porch and the peaks of the front gables. The most traditional feature is the presence of two front doors, announcing quite plainly that this family would not waste money on a central passage. Behind the left door was the parlor, later a dining room; behind the right door was a bedroom. Herman Henry Sagebiel, an attorney, and his wife Eugenie (née Kuemmel) bought the house in 1920 and lived there with their four children. The home was valued at $4,000 in the 1930 census. In 1926 Henry was one of the investors in the Hotel Nimitz Company, which purchased and remodeled the old hostelry [32]. He died in 1938; she lived until 1970. Even after her death the house stayed in the family.

---

131 H. E. and Augusta Wahrmund House
509 West Austin Street
1916

Henry Emil Wahrmund, who had this house built in 1916, when he was a single man of just twenty-one, wanted to be modern but not too modern. He was the son of Henry and Meta Wahrmund, who lived in the rock house with Victorian ornamentation on West Main Street

[38]. Henry E. was born in 1895. He was a stock farmer but chose to live in town. His wife, Augusta Reeh, had grown up on the farm of her parents, Adolph and Louise.

Henry and Augusta's house was designed by the San Antonio architect Leo M. J. Diehlmann, who had previously designed the new St. Mary's Catholic Church [85] and who would later design the new St. Mary's School [83]. It was one of the earliest to use red brick made available in Fredericksburg by the coming of the railroad in 1913. It stands in dramatic contrast to the creamy limestone of the house in which he grew up. Also notable was the use of concrete for the front porch, which allowed for the initials "HEW" and the date "1916" to be prominently displayed. Many of the other red brick houses in town are bungalows, reflecting the Arts and Crafts movement of the early years of the twentieth century; this house is a bit more conservative, in the later version of the Queen Anne style, which often incorporated classical columns on the porch. It closely relates to the William and Cora Habenicht house on North Llano Street [156]. Next door to the west at 511, 513, and 515 are a trio of well-kept bungalows, built of wood rather than brick. The house at 515 was designed and built by Edward Stein for Lawrence Knopp.

Around the Corner on North Bowie Street

132 John Peter and Maria Elizabeth Tatsch House
210 North Bowie Street
1858–59, 1869–70

John Peter Tatsch was one of Fredericksburg's best-known cabinet-makers, and his house is one of the best known in town. Tatsch and his family arrived in Texas in 1852 and bought this town lot in 1854. A log house served as a temporary home, then as a freestanding kitchen, then as Tatsch's workshop. The front two rooms of the present house were built in 1858 and 1859, and the addition to the rear, with its humongous chimney stack, was added 1869–70. Typically German Texan were the casement windows, a built-in cabinet in the south front room, and the rejection of the idea of a central passage. The front two

Courtesy of Institute of Texan Cultures, University of Texas at San Antonio, 075-0247.

rooms were a *stube* and a bedroom (which contained an internal stair to the attic); the main room in the rear was a kitchen with a raised hearth. The external expression of that fireplace has become one of the symbols of the town, even though it was the only house in Fredericksburg that ever sported such an outsized chimney.

Peter and Maria's daughter Sophie married Julius Klingelhoefer and moved to the *fachwerk* house that Julius inherited [65]. Daughter Elise married Henry Kuenemann, the carpenter and cabinetmaker who worked with her father; they lived in a little *fachwerk* house that was later enlarged into a grand Victorian house [106]. Middle

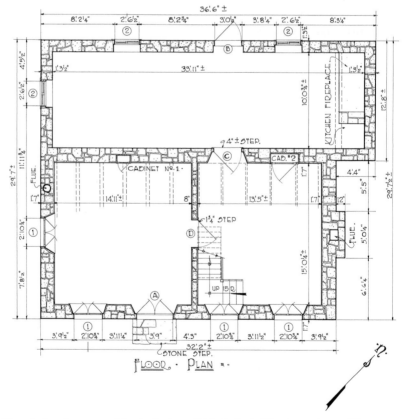

Floor plan based on measured drawing by Anton Heisler Jr. for the Historic American Building Survey.

daughter Caroline never married and cared for her father until his death in 1907. After Caroline died in 1928, the house was sold to a cousin, Walter Tatsch, who was committed to preserving the house in its original state.

The Tatsch house is one of the most widely published houses in the Hill Country. It was written up in Don Biggers's brief history of Fredericksburg, *German Pioneers in Texas*, in 1925. In anticipation of a meeting in San Antonio of the American Institute of Architects, Samuel Gideon wrote an article about Sunday houses in Fredericksburg for the national architecture magazine *Pencil Points* in April 1931 that included a photo of the Tatsch house. It was documented by the Historic American Buildings Survey in 1934, and the Keystone View Company produced a stereoptic view of the house in the 1930s, simply entitled "Texas—Old German Home, Fredericksburg." A cousin of Walter Tatsch, Esther L. Mueller, lived in the house for several years with her sister Emmie while teaching English and journalism at Fredericksburg High School, and she gave tours through the house. Still in private hands, it is well cared and for and is occasionally open for tours.

---

133 Max and Lydia Bierschwale House
206 North Bowie Street
Circa 1918

Max was the younger son of William and Lina Bierschwale, who lived one block to the south [136]. When his older brother, Walter, built a house, he ventured all the way to West College Street [161], but Max kept closer to home. Like his older brother, Max worked at the Citizens Bank of Fredericksburg with his dad [see 41]. But he was adventurous in the style of his house, which blends the Colonial Revival and the Queen Anne styles. The hipped roof was interrupted by gables on the front and both sides, an echo of the Queen Anne style. The use of shingles in the gables is also a Queen Anne touch. The porch, which stretched across the front, has the most elaborate form of Roman columns of the Composite order, which blends elements of Ionic and Corinthian capitals. Their use here was a Fredericksburg first. Max

---

and Lydia had two sons, William and Calvin. At the time of the 1920 census their next-door neighbor was Carolina Tatsch, the unmarried daughter of John Peter and Maria Elizabeth Tatsch. In 1930 they told the census taker that their house was worth $5,000, the same as Walter's but notably less than the red brick house of Lawrence and Meta Krauskopf next door to the south [134], which was valued at $6,000.

---

134 Lawrence H. and Meta Krauskopf House
204 North Bowie Street
1921

Somewhat incongruously sited between two nineteenth-century rock houses, this is a well-done example of a brick bungalow, showing a Fredericksburg resident adopting the popular style of the American bungalow. Lawrence H. Krauskopf was the son of Oscar and Rosa Krauskopf and the grandson of Engelbert Krauskopf, a gunsmith and cabinetmaker in Fredericksburg. Oscar had a farm implement store on West Main Street [51], which Lawrence and his brother Edward eventually took over. Engelbert lived in a German Texan rock house, Oscar in a house decorated with Victorian trim, and Lawrence in a house reflecting the Arts and Crafts style. The architect and builder was Edward Stein, who a few years later would build a brick bungalow for his own family [164]. The porch has squat Craftsman-style columns

---

resting on brick piers. The porch and steps are concrete, and to the side of the steps are the initials L.H.K. and the date 1921. This was a feature that Stein picked up from his former employer, Leo M. J. Dielmann, who had used it on the nearby Wahrmund house [131] in 1916. The windows of the Krauskopf house are paired, and the roof has several gables. The walls are red brick, probably from the kiln in D'Hanis, Texas, which had opened in 1905; they were definitely shipped into town on the railroad, which had arrived only in 1913.

The original blueprints, which have been passed down to the present owner, not only document the names of the rooms but also verify that the house has been little changed over the years. The front door leads into a reception hall, which has a built-in bench with a hinged top on the south wall. Straight ahead is the den, which has a fireplace and two windows to the south wall, a closet on the east, and a built-in bookshelf on the east. To the right of the reception hall is the living room, which has double sliding doors that open into the dining room. This latter room has a bay window on the north, with a built-in bench, and a built-in buffet on the west. Beyond the dining room are two pantries and the kitchen. From the den a hall leads to two bedrooms and a bathroom. The Krauskopf house has a close cousin at 502 North Llano, the Walter H. and Helen Kolmeier house [158], which was built in 1925.

135 Anton and Catharina Kunz House
602 West Austin Street
Circa 1871

This is yet another fine example of a story-and-a-half rock house built
by children of the early pioneers. Anton Kunz was the son of Peter and
Catherina Kunz and came to Texas as a young boy. Peter Kunz sold this
lot and the adjoining one to his son Anton in December 1870 for $75.
The *stube* and kitchen were on the ground floor, with an upper room
above the front room. The stair rises out of the kitchen on the east
wall. In 1885 Anton and Catharina Kunz sold the lot for $800 to her
half brother, Anton Loth, who married Anna Meurer in that same year.
They owned it only briefly, as they it sold to Mary U. Miller the next
year. She lived there until her death in 1904. Anton's brother William
built a similar rock house at 108 North Acorn Street around 1878
[137].

136 William and Lina Bierschwale House
110 North Bowie Street
1888–89

This Victorian house, designed by Alfred Giles of San Antonio, is a
remarkable contrast to the story-and-a-half rock house of William's
parents, Henry and Margarete, just a few blocks down West Austin
Street [126] and built just sixteen years earlier. Indeed, this house,
the Keidel house on Main Street [24], and the Moursund house on
Kay Street [138] must have announced quite boldly that the era of the
story-and-a-half rock house was over.

William married Lina Jung, the daughter of farmer Jacob Jung
and his wife Anna (née Keller), in 1884, and they bought two town lots
on North Bowie Street in 1886. They hired the English-born architect
Giles to design their house. This in itself was a radical departure
for Fredericksburg, where the design of a house was almost always
worked out between the owner and the builders. But Giles had already
designed elegant Victorian mansions on King William Street and

officer's quarters at Fort Sam Houston in San Antonio as well as the new Gillespie County Courthouse [2]. Indeed, for the Bierschwale house Giles's specifications called for "first class rustic rubble work . . . of rock from the best local quarries well laid in mortar."

That is exactly what the Bierschwales got: stonework that is not extravagant but dignified, solid, and sturdy. All doors and windows have sills and lintels that are vermiculated—that is, carved with a worm-like pattern—which was repeated on the quoins at each corner. The date stone at the lower right of the projecting southern bay states "1889." The Bierschwales built the house almost exactly as Giles designed it, though they economized a bit by not having the gallery wrap around on the north side.

The entrance leads into a stair hall, something that was still quite rare in Fredericksburg. To the left were an office and sitting room, both heated by fireplaces in the common wall. The office had windows on the front and the south side, with a separate entry off the porch (a small concession to local practice). Later the family used this room as a formal parlor. The sitting room was unusually shaped, as it received light from the angled window on the front porch, a matching angled window on the south wall, and another window on the back wall. To the right was the dining room, which had a fireplace in the north wall. The kitchen and a storeroom (essentially a pantry) were in a one-story rock room behind the dining room. Upstairs were three bedrooms. The two on the south were heated by wood stoves, while the room on the north had a fireplace connected to the same chimney as the dining room below. The lack of a bedroom on the first floor would have struck Fredericksburg old-timers as unusual, as would the presence of a dining room. In many ways the Bierschwale house set a new standard that locals would be emulating for years.

137 William and Anna Kunz House
108 North Acorn Street
1878–79

This story-and-a-half rock house was built by William Kunz, a son of
early immigrants Peter and Catherine Kunz, a farming couple, and
the brother of Anton Kunz, who built a similar (albeit more compact)
house on West Austin Street [135]. William was a carpenter and cabinetmaker—he identified himself as a joiner on the 1880 census, and
it is said that he worked with the carpenter and cabinetmaker August
Jordan, who also built his house [80] in the 1880s. William Kunz married Anna Meckel on August 21, 1878, at St. Mary's Catholic Church
[84]. The land on which he built the house had been owned by his
parents; they made the legal gift to William and Anna in 1879, though
he may have been working on the house beforehand. As was typical in
a house with two front rooms—including the August Jordan house—
one was the *stube* and one the bedroom. The kitchen is behind the
bedroom on the north and has a built-in kitchen cabinet that Kunz is
said to have made himself. An external staircase runs to the half story

on the north side. Behind the south front room was a porch, which was later enclosed. William and Anna had six children; she died 1892. He remarried and lived until 1932.

Around the Corner on Kay Street

138 A. W. and Henrietta Moursund House
302 North Kay Street
1888–90

Along with the William and Lina Bierschwale house [136] and the Albert and Mathilde Keidel house [24], this is an important and early example of a two-story Victorian rock house, built for one of Fredericksburg's leading attorneys. Albert Waddell Moursund was a native of Norway who came to Texas around 1870. He practiced law in Blanco from 1873 to 1883. In 1874 he married Henrietta Mowinckel, another Norwegian who was living in Oak Hill, near Austin. After becoming a naturalized citizen in 1876, he served as a Blanco County judge and served two terms in the state legislature during the early 1880s. A. W.

and Henrietta moved to Fredericksburg in 1883. He was elected district attorney in 1884 and then became a district judge in 1885.

Judge Moursund bought two ten-acre out-lots, 586 and 587, in 1886 for $725. A new house was well under way by 1888 but not completed until 1890, when the property was appraised for tax purposes at $2,500. The house is T-shaped, but with a projecting bay on the right side, a feature that had not been previously seen in Fredericksburg. Inside was an entrance hall; the parlor was the large room on the left. At the right front was Judge Moursund's study; behind this was a combined dining room and sitting room; and behind this was the kitchen. Later owners have added a new side porch on the north. Judge Moursund died in 1927, and his widow Henrietta in 1942. In 1955 their heirs sold the house and twenty acres so that it could be developed into a residential subdivision known as Oakcrest Manor. The house itself was sold two years later, and, surrounded by newer houses, has continued to serve as a private residence.

The Moursunds' third son, Albert Waddell Moursund Jr., opened his own title abstract business in Johnson City. In the 1960s he was principal trustee for the business interests of President Lyndon B. Johnson and was a member of the Texas Parks and Wildlife Commission when it acquired land for Lyndon B. Johnson State Park [see 203–7].

---

139 St. Mary's Catholic Cemetery
Catholic Cemetery Road
1875 to the present

It is a requirement of the Roman Catholic Church that Catholics be buried in sanctified ground and that such a burying ground must be reserved only for Catholics. On the frontier it was not always possible to meet this expectation, and so for the first fifteen years of Fredericksburg's existence Catholics were buried in Der Stadt Friedhof [140]. The first site for a Catholic cemetery, now known as St. Mary's Pioneer Cemetery, was less than a mile north of the current cemetery (north on Metzger Road, then left on Memory Lane) but was considered to be too far from town. There are over one hundred grave markers at

Pioneer Cemetery, but the majority are small red granite markers that
were placed there much later.

The oldest part of St. Mary's Cemetery is in the northwest corner.
The grave markers follow a similar pattern to those in Der Stadt Friedhof: the earliest are of local limestone, followed by a few of white marble imported in the 1880s or later, and then a very large number of red
granite, either from nearby Bear Mountain or from other points in the
Hill Country, such as Llano or Burnet. Presumably the great majority
of the red granite stones came from the shop of the Nagel Brothers
[6], as was the case at Der Stadt Friedhof.

The symbolism, however, differs from that in Der Stadt Friedhof.
Fredericksburg Catholics did not embrace neoclassicism to the same
degree as their Protestant friends, though one grave more nearly
approaches an ancient Roman sarcophagus than anything across town.
Most striking is an interwoven cross and anchor within a circle, a symbol of Our Lady of Sorrows. There is a greater proportion of crosses
among the early gravestones, some marked with the letters "IHS." This
stands for *In Hoc Signis*, meaning that the Gospel would be spread by
this sign of the cross. This symbol is found on early limestone markers
but also on the later red granites ones. Roses are also carved into some
markers, which is a symbol of the Blessed Virgin Mary.

The earliest part of the cemetery was enclosed with a rock wall laid without mortar. Later additions were enclosed with cast-iron fencing made by the Rogers Fence Company of Springfield, Ohio; this was reused from the 1882 Gillespie County Courthouse [2], probably after the new courthouse [3] was completed in 1939. A gate from the Rogers Fence Company is also at the St. Mary's Pioneer Cemetery, also probably reused from the courthouse grounds. On the south side, the most recent expansion of the cemetery, barbed-wired fencing was used, perhaps a legacy of the town's western heritage. As at Der Stadt Friedhof, many family groups and some individual graves are bounded with cast-iron fences. Fewer of these are marked with the name of the company that made it than across town. Though these seem to have been made industrially, some were augmented with ornament made locally of wrought iron. Several have hearts, out of which rise crosses or five-pointed stars. Terry Jordan, in *Texas Graveyards*, identified the latter as a *drudenfuss*, or witches foot.

Schubert Street

140 Der Stadt Friedhof (Town Cemetery)
East end of Schubert Street
1846 to the present

The land for the town cemetery was set aside by the founders in 1846. It is on the earliest plan of the city, dated 1846, where is it marked "Kirchhof." It is shown as being just east of the point where Town Creek flows into Baron's Creek; interestingly, the plan shows the road to New Braunfels as being on the north side of the cemetery rather than as a continuation of the Main Street. Until the establishment of a Roman Catholic cemetery in 1860, Catholics as well as people of other faiths were buried here. It is cared for by a cemetery board with members from Bethany, Holy Ghost, and Zion Lutheran churches.

The earliest rock fence is on the south side, along Baron's Creek; the segment nearest the entrance is said to have been built by the stonemason John Ruegner [see 5]. The oldest graves and grave markers are between the lane that leads from the main entrance and Town/Baron's Creek. In the southeast corner—section B—can be seen many

of the earliest gravestones, made of local limestone. These are some of
the most traditional forms, with a strong sense of neoclassicism, seen
in pedimented tops, often framed by acroteria at both corners. Also in
this section are some of the earliest imported stones, made of a white
marble that is clearly not local. One of these was made in San Antonio
by Frank Teich, who later moved to Llano and became a leading maker
of red granite monuments. These stones seem to have introduced
traditional Anglo-American funerary symbolism, such as weeping
willows, angels, doves, lambs, and the like.

In the 1890s and the early twentieth century German Texans
began to mark their graves with red granite, which is also native to the
Hill Country but was not usable until the development of industri-
al-grade stone cutters. Some of these may have been imported from
other towns in the Hill Country, such as Burnet or Llano, but by 1904
local red granite was being excavated at Bear Mountain by the Nagel
Brothers [see 6] for gravestones and cornerstones in buildings. Other
twentieth-century stones were made of gray granite, which had to be
imported from the east and represent the end of the local tradition.

Individual graves and sometimes the graves of couples were
bounded with curbing; early examples may have been in wood (though
none have survived in Fredericksburg), but all surviving examples
are either stone or concrete. Around 1900 local residents began to
purchase cast-iron fencing made in the Midwest. Though most are

not signed, at least thirty of these were marked by their markers. The greatest number came from the Stewart Iron Works in Cincinnati, but others came from Valley Forge Patent Fences of Knoxville, Tennessee, and Hinderer's Iron Works of New Orleans; still others came from Detroit, Michigan, Kenton, Ohio, and Springfield, Ohio.

Inscriptions are in German for the all of the nineteenth century; the shift to English seems to have happened around World War I, when German Americans found themselves in the awkward position of having roots in a country with which the United States was now at war.

Der Stadt Friedhof was designated a State Historical Cemetery in 2000.

---

141 Hahn-Burgdorf House
202 East Schubert Street
Circa 1870, circa 1881, circa 1905

This picturesque house was started by one pioneer farming couple and greatly enlarged by another. Ludwig and Christine Eckert acquired this lot in 1851; they sold it at the time of their divorce in 1860 to Conrad Hahn (also spelled Hahne) and his wife, Anna Regina (née Walch), who had married that same year and eventually had six children. While the log and rock portion may have been built by the Eckerts,

it is more likely to have been built by the Hahns. Such houses with alternating logs and rocks were built in Fredericksburg at least by 1857, when Heinrich Cordes built his house on North Crockett Street [125]. Anna Regina, younger sister of the stonemason John Joseph Walch [see 121], may have recruited her brother to provide assistance in constructing their log and rock house. At the time of the 1870 census their property was valued at $600, an indication that they were still living in a one-room log and rock house and had not yet built a rock addition. The household in 1870 included not only four children but also a farm laborer, John Billo.

In 1879 Conrad and Anna Hahn sold the property to August Burgdorf, who had immigrated from Hannover, Germany, to Texas in 1873. (In 1886 the Hahns bought the property at what is now 304 East Morse Street and built a rock house.) In 1881 August married Minna Weber, the daughter of John Weber and Wilhelmine (née Henke) Weber. They lived on their farm with their five children but used this house when they took trips to town. The second room to the rear, built of rock, probably dates to the early 1880s. By 1900 they were living in town, as Meta, Otto, and Dora were attending school. August ceased to farm around 1905, and the frame addition on the east side dates to around this time. Five years later August was retired and living off his savings, and Otto was a teacher in the public school. In 1920 neither August nor Minna were working, but their youngest daughter Margarette was a teacher.

142 Johann Friedrich and Dorothea Kneese House (Kneese-Gibson-Schoenewolf House)
112 East Schubert Street
1870s

This house of the 1870s has one foot in the future and one foot in the past. It is a full two stories and a central passage, but also external doors from both front rooms. Johan Friedrich Kneese and his wife, the former Dorothea Bierschwale, had a farm and ranch in the Live Oak community; they were also leaders of the northern Methodists [see 92]. Charles Jung built the original rock structure for that

congregation in 1872 and also built this house, along with his own house on the lot next door [143]. Much like the Weyrich house [35] on East Main Street, the Kneese house had double doors into the central passage and also doors into each of the front rooms. The central passage had a staircase to the second floor, but this was removed in the 1950s when an external stair was built to turn the house into a duplex. At this time the doors into the front rooms were converted into windows, giving it a more conventionally Anglo-Texan appearance. The present two-story front porch is a modern replacement.

143 Charles and Anna Jung House
108 East Schubert Street
1878

This house looks like no other in Fredericksburg. It is squarish, a full two stories, and has a hipped roof—perhaps the first such roof to be built in town. Charles Jung came to Texas from Germany with his aunt when he was five; he lived in San Antonio before coming to Fredericksburg and worked as a stonemason at Fort Concho. In both San Antonio and at Fort Concho he would have seen hipped roofs and other building elements favored by Anglo-Americans, such as large six-over-six windows. In 1872 he oversaw the construction of the Methodist

Episcopal Church (for the northern congregation) on Edison Street.
His wife, Anna, was a daughter of Wilhelm Tietze, a carpenter and
cabinetmaker in New Braunfels. Charles and Anna bought this lot in
1871, but Charles did not get around to completing it until 1878. The
rock for the walls was quarried around Cross Mountain on the north
side of town. Though the exterior was quite novel, the interior was
traditional: a single front room with a kitchen behind it and bedrooms
above, accessed from a staircase in the kitchen. The house was restored
in the 1970s with the assistance of local restoration authority Albert
Keidel; the cantilevered balcony over the front door and much of the
ornamental trim date to that time.

144 Theodore and Mathilde Langerhans House
(Langerhans-Kowert House)
107 East Schubert Street
1925

This pleasant Craftsman-style house, or bungalow, was built by carpenter Theodore Langerhans as his own home. Langerhans did the

carpentry on St. Anthony's Catholic Church in Harper in 1909. On
the west side are a living room, dining room, and kitchen, and on the
east are two bedrooms separated by a bathroom. Beginning in 1949
this was the home of Art and Elise Kowert. Art was the editor of the
Fredericksburg Standard, and Elise was the author of two important
books on the homes and other historic buildings of Fredericksburg.
To the right is a frame building with a roof that is hipped in the front
and gabled in the rear; it originally stood on the eastern edge of town,

where it served as a school for the children of the African Methodist Episcopal Church [36].

145 Gottlob and Christiane Fischer House
106 East Schubert Street
1873

This simple story-and-a-half rock house was built for Gottlob and Christiane Fischer by their neighbor, the stonemason Charles Jung, in 1873. Though the façade has a centered door with a window on each side, the front is divided into two rooms, as was the case at the August and Caroline Jordan house [80] and the William and Anna Kunz house [137]. As at those houses, the larger, west room of the Fisher house was the *stube*, and the smaller room was a bedroom. The staircase rose from the rear room, the kitchen. In 1973 the house was purchased by Oliver C. W. Kowert and his wife, Josie Mae Kothmann Kowert, who remodeled the house, adding frame one-story wings to

each side and extending the house to the rear. Milton Moseley was the architect for the remodeling. Later owners have removed the wings, restoring the house to something closer to its original appearance.

146 Julius and Sophie Splittgerber House
302 West Schubert Street
Circa 1870

Julius Splittgerber was one of the earliest settlers of Fredericksburg. He was a wagoner, a farmer, and a limeburner, according to the censuses of 1850, 1860, and 1870. At the time of the 1870 census he may well have been fresh from burning lime for use in constructing his own house; he told the census taker that his property was valued at $1,500, further suggesting that this house was newly finished. The house is two stories, but originally it had only one large room on each floor. The staircase was on the west wall. Not surprisingly, additions have been made over time: on the west, a kitchen, behind which was a bath and another room, and on the north, a conservatory and a carport.

147 Christian and Elizabeth Crenwelge House
307 West Schubert Street
1855–56, 1870, 1939

This great old house was built in three phases, though a later restoration obscured the sequence of the sections. Johan Christian Crenwelge, a carpenter and cabinetmaker, bought two lots on Schubert
Street just west of Town Creek early in 1855. He built a log house in
that year or the next, using the simplest form of log construction: the
logs were not hewn but left in the round. Christian married Elisabeth
Margaretha Mohr in 1860. After the Civil War the Crenwelges dramatically expanded their house to the east with a two-story rock addition.
The projecting roof provided some cover for the cantilevered balcony
below, which gave it some of the character of a Swiss chalet. The books
of the New Yorker A. J. Downing illustrated examples of Swiss, Italian,
Gothic, and other early Victorian styles; these books, though published
in the 1840s and 1850s, had their greatest influence in Texas in the
1870s. The ground floor originally had two rooms, heated by corner
fireplaces that shared a single chimney; this was quite unusual for the
Hill Country.

By 1930 additional rooms had been added to the north and south

of the log structure, sheathed in board-and-batten construction. Fredericksburg restorationist Albert Keidel purchased the house in 1937, and he remodeled the house over the next several years. He removed the board-and-batten walls, presumably because they were in a late Victorian style, and he built new *fachwerk* walls, giving this section a Germanic appearance that it never had. Keidel also removed the partition wall between the two rock rooms downstairs, creating one large room with a central fireplace; he also rebuilt the balcony and the roof that projects over it and added a bathroom upstairs. Sometime between 1937 and 1965 a garage was added at the west end of the property. In the latter year the house was purchased by Philip and Ruth Ann O'B. Montgomery Jr.; they and their children have cared for the house for several decades. Early in their ownership the garage was converted into a master bedroom with an attached bath.

148 Johann Joseph and Katharina Knopp House
309 West Schubert Street
1873–74

This is a great example of a small rock house that expanded with its original family and that has subsequently gone through several generations of remodeling and restoration. Johann Joseph Knopp, his wife Katharina (née Stein), and their three sons emigrated from Germany to Texas in 1869. In December 1871 Knopp bought the western half of town lot 22a from his soon-to-be neighbor, Christian Crenwelge [see 147], for $70, and that is the value of the property on which he paid taxes in 1872. Knopp contracted with Johan Kallenberg to build a house for $500. The tax value increased to $300 in 1873 and $350 in 1875, suggesting either that it came in well under budget or that it was conservatively appraised. Knopp identified himself as a stonemason on the 1870 census and may have decided to do some of the work himself. In 1871 Katharina's brother, Franz Stein, emigrated from Germany at age twenty. He lived with his sister and brother-in-law while working with Christian Crenwelge next door. Franz would later build a planing mill and house for himself [153] on Travis Street as well as many other houses, and two of his sons would be prominent in Fredericksburg

[see 154 and 164]. Johan Joseph and Katharina Knopp had fifteen children, and nine were still alive in 1900.

This small rock house originally consisted of one room, with additional sleeping space above, reached by an external stair on the east side wall. When a second room was added to the rear, the original room became a *stube* (parlor-bedroom), and the new room a kitchen. It did not have a porch, perhaps because the house faces north. A circa 1900 photograph showed another two rooms added to the rear and a standing-seam tin roof. A rock barn was built just to the east of the house, very near Schubert Street. Both Joseph and Katharina lived in the house until they died in 1917.

In 1939 local restorationist Albert Keidel restored the little house for his sister, Victoria, and brother-in-law, Dr. J. Hardin Perry. Some things were changed to emphasize (if not overemphasize) the antiquity of the house: the original sash windows were replaced with casement windows with fixed panes above, and new frames were placed around the windows and the front door. A cantilevered pediment—the only one of its kind in Fredericksburg—was added above the front door to shelter entering guests. On the east side Keidel added a bay window to provide more light to the front room, rebuilt the stair to the loft, and placed a shed dormer on the south roof to provide additional light upstairs.

Other changes to the interior provided modern comforts. In the front room Keidel converted the east window in the back wall into bookshelves and created a similarly styled fireplace where a west window had been. He covered all the floors with Mexican tile and created a bathroom on the east side of the kitchen wing. Beyond this he created a new sun-room. This had a wall of glass on the east that nicely framed a view of the Crenwelge log house, which he was also restoring. At the southwest corner of this room was a corner fireplace, doubtless inspired by similar fireplaces in New Mexico.

The family sold the house in 1956. Mrs. Marschall D. Altgelt (known as Honey) remodeled the house in the late 1960s, removing the bathroom to the east of the kitchen, creating a new one in the rear wing, and adding wall-to-wall-carpet throughout the house. In the 1970s Martin and Maurine Bogisch purchased the house and restored and remodeled it with the help of Albert Keidel. A new master bedroom and bathroom were created at the rear, and all carpet was removed. They also built a "garden house" on the property, using the old rock barn and adding rooms to the west and south.

Travis Street

---

149 Adolph and Auguste Gold House
212 East Travis Street
Circa 1901

The Gold house, like other late Victorian houses from the first decade of the twentieth century, has a central roof running from side to side and a smaller central gable; however, this house had the most fully developed Victorian ornament in town. The house was built by Franz Stein, and it is far more ornate than the other houses he was responsible for, even his own house [153]. The limestone blocks are quite large and play off the minute detail of the gingerbread on the porch. The central unit—underneath the gable—breaks forward from the plane of

---

the rest of the house, and the central part of the porch follows suit. The entrance led into a central passage, with a living room on the east and bedroom to the west. This house may have served as a model for the William and Olga Rausch house [71], which was built soon after this one.

Adolph Gold was in the mercantile business in the 1890s. He then purchased a one-quarter interest in the Bank of Fredericksburg [16], where he worked for thirty-one years, ultimately becoming president of the bank. He and Auguste Herbort were married in 1891 by Reverend Michael Haag, the pastor of Evangelical Lutheran St. Paul's Church [189] in the community of Cave Creek. By 1900 they had three daughters, Edna, Hedwig, and Cora. Their house is on the southeast corner of a ten-acre subdivision that Gold and Alfred van der Stucken [see 11] bought in 1900. It is bounded by a cast-iron fence from Stewart Iron Works of Cincinnati, Ohio, which also provided many fences for graves in Der Stadt Friedhof [140]. This impressive house may have inspired Adolph's younger brother, Emil, to hire Franz Stein to build his house on West Main Street [68].

150 Schmitt-Henke House (Carl and Minna Henke House)
116 East Travis Street
1874, 1911

This is a classic story-and-a-half rock house of the 1870s, given a more late Victorian appearance by the addition of the wing on the west in 1911. John Schmitt bought the lot in 1861, and stonemason Carl Henke built the earliest part of this house for him in 1874. In 1883 Schmitt sold the house to Minna Crenwelge Henke, wife of Carl Henke, for $400. Minna's dad, Christian Crenwelge, came to live with the family after he sold the place on West Schubert Street [147] in 1906. The Henke's son Max married Cora Schaper in 1911, and that led to the addition of the wing. The wing gave the house an L-shape that looks somewhat Victorian, but not a lick of Victorian ornament can be found. Two-over-two windows gave a more up-to-date appearance than the six-over-six windows in the old part of the house. Concrete blocks, manufactured locally by the Basse Brothers Cement Yard, were used in the new section.

151 Methodist College / Public School / Old Grammar School
152 Old High School (Fredericksburg Middle School)
110 West Travis Street
1876, 1922, and later

The campus of the Fredericksburg Middle School includes two earlier educational structures. In the center of the campus is the building erected for a college sponsored by the Southern Methodist Church; the college opened in 1876 and lasted until 1884. The building was sold and became the Fredericksburg public school. Though duration of the college was short, it gave its name to College Street, which survives to this day.

The college building was constructed of load-bearing stone walls. One of the stonemasons was John Ruegner [see 5, 8]; John Durst was perhaps another. It originally had a hipped roof that was later removed in favor of a flat one. The first principal was W.J.R. Thoenssen, the second Charles F. Tansill. In 1880 Thoenssen and two assistant teachers were in charge of four students between the ages of eighteen and twelve, all born in Texas but two with German parents and two with a father from Switzerland and mother from Prussia. In spite of the ambition that this institution should serve as a college, most of the students were of school age, and in 1885 all schools in Fredericksburg, except for the Catholic school, were merged into this location. Up until

this point, the principal school building in the town was the Vereins-Kirche, then situated in the middle of Main Street. When this building became the Fredericksburg public school, it held all grade levels. It did not take long until the building was crowded with students; a limestone annex to the building was added in 1905.

It was not long before another building was needed, and in 1921 it was decided to build a separate high school. This was completed in 1922. The earlier building thus became the grammar school. Whereas the grammar school was built with traditional materials and techniques, the high school was quite modern, with a concrete frame and curtain walls of brick. The style was Tudor Gothic, which became a popular style for the nation's school buildings in the 1920s. In Fredericksburg it was also used on the Methodist Episcopal Church on South Bowie Street [97]. However, the horizontal bands of windows gave the high school an unmistakably twentieth-century feel. When a new high school was opened for the 1964–65 school year, the old high school became the junior high school, now Fredericksburg Middle School.

153 Franz and Agnes Stein House
207 West Travis Street
Circa 1910

Franz Stein came to Fredericksburg after his older sister, Catharina, married Johann Joseph Knopp. He lived with them in their new rock house [148] at 309 West Schubert and worked with the cabinetmaker Christian Crenwelge, who lived next door [147]. Stein had moved to Boerne by the mid-1880s, where he worked as a cabinetmaker. After his first wife, Therese, and an infant son both died, Franz married Agnes Pfeiffer in 1887. They moved to Fredericksburg in 1892, and he opened a lumber yard and planing mill. He was also a partner in the electric light plant with Christian Stehling [see 79] and between 1902 and 1910 opened an ice factory. Franz's planing mill was between Schubert and Travis Streets and between Orange and Milam—thus one block north of his sister Katharina's house. The Steins' house fronted on Travis Street; originally it was frame, one-story and T-shaped; by 1910 the front part had been raised to two full stories with

a two-story porch. Agnes Stein not only raised their family and ran the household but was also bookkeeper for the lumber yard. Eldest son Joe built a Victorian house nearby [154]. Second son Ed, architect, builder, and banker, lived with his wife Minnie in a brick bungalow a few blocks to the north [164]. Youngest son Oscar, who worked at the ice factory, lived just a block west at 301 West Travis in a two-story house that blended Victorian asymmetry and Arts and Crafts detailing. Around 1921 Franz and Agnes's daughter Ruby married Eric Juenke, and Ed Stein built them an attractive bungalow at 111 West Travis Street, facing the campus of the Fredericksburg schools. In addition to the planing mill, ice factory, and electric plant, Stein also built a number of early twentieth-century houses in Fredericksburg, ranging from simple wood-frame structures, such as the Emil and Alma Gold house [68] and the Emil and Bertha Riley house [162], to limestone houses with Victorian trim, such as the Adolph and Auguste Gold house [149].

---

154 Joseph and Ella Stein House
302 West Travis Street
1910

Joe Stein, the eldest son of Franz and Agnes Stein, married Ella Baag in 1910, and this house was built at that time. The house is proof that in Fredericksburg the Victorian style came late and stayed late. The floor plan is L-shaped, with gables at the front and right side. These

gables were filled in with shingles. The door is at the corner where the two wings join; the porch, with ornate decoration typical of Victorian Fredericksburg, runs along the east side of the house. The front room on the left, the parlor, has an angled front wall, allowing for three windows. The rooms behind this have windows that are doubles or triples—an indication that the Steins were aware of bungalows that were popularizing this feature across the United States. Joe worked in the lumber business with his father, Franz, whose house was nearby [153]. He was a civic leader and the first mayor of Fredericksburg when it was incorporated in 1927. He was one of the investors in the Hotel Nimitz Company, which purchased the hotel in 1926 and remodeled it under the supervision of his brother, Ed Stein [see 32]. He was also president of the Fredericksburg National Bank [15], which was established in 1932 and also designed by his brother. Joe Stein died in 1957, and his widow Ella lived in the house until her death in 1981.

---

155 Robert and Maria Jenschke Sunday House
406 West Travis Street
1907

This is another good example of a true Sunday house. It sits on land that was owned by John and Maria Walter, who lived in a log and rock house on West San Antonio Street. Some who feel that age is the main significance of a building have suggested that the Walters built this house, but when the widow Maria Walter created the Walter Addition and sold this lot to Robert Jenschke, it sold for a grand total of $25. Over the next several years it rose in value to $150 and then $250. Originally the house had a board-and-batten treatment on the front and pressed metal on the sides, in much the same manner as the Emil and Bertha Riley house [162], built in 1904. The external staircase, which was important because the house was so small and interior space was at a premium, originally started at the rear. This is a true Sunday house because the Jenschkes lived on their 800-acre ranch and used this little house only when they came into town to shop, socialize, and attend St. Mary's Catholic Church [84 and 85].

Sometime after 1980 a number of changes were made. The external

---

staircase was rebuilt to start at the front to accommodate an air conditioning unit. At that point the board-and-batten treatment was continued to the side, covering the pressed metal, and the lean-to was given an additional room.

156 William and Cora Habenicht House
408 North Llano Street
Circa 1916

This red brick house, which has an exterior in the late Queen Anne style, with a wraparound porch, Neoclassical columns, a projecting front room on the right side, and a complicated roof. It is among the earliest houses in Fredericksburg to use imported brick, along with the Henry E. Wahrmund house on West Austin [131]. However, the interior is straight from the Arts and Crafts/bungalow playbook, with the exception that the front door leads into a narrow entrance hall instead of directly into the living room. William was the son of Rudolph and Lina Habenicht and grew up on the family farmstead near what later became Bankersmith, a community in southern Gillespie County. In 1926 he was one of the investors in the Hotel Nimitz Company, which purchased and remodeled the old hostelry [32]. He married Cora

Ransleben, the daughter of Guido and Minna Ransleben. Minna was the daughter of Peter and Caroline Bonn and grew up in their house in town [97]. When Guido died young, Minna married the jeweler Alphonse Walter. William and Cora had two sons and a daughter. William died in 1931, and Cora was left to manage the household during the Great Depression. By 1940 she was housing six boarders, most in their twenties, none of whom were Fredericksburg natives. In that year she told the census taker that the house was valued at $5,000, considerably less than the $8,000 value for the Kolmeier house across the street but comparable to the houses for Walter Bierschwale [161] and Max Bierschwale [133].

157 Gold-Grobe House
413 North Llano Street
1902, 1916

Peter Gold Sr. built a one-story house here with a central passage in 1902. Its walls were made of very large blocks of limestone, and each window had large and heavily rusticated sills and lintels. He sold the house to Friedrich William Grobe, a farmer, and his wife Clara (née Jacoby) in 1914. In 1914 both F. W. and Clara were approaching sixty and had been married for nearly forty years, so they must have looked at this house as their retirement home. Two years later the Grobes

added the second story and a wing to the rear, made of concrete blocks manufactured locally by the Basse Brothers cement company. The use of concrete blocks, along with other brick and frame houses on this side of town, indicate that the tradition of the rock house was being challenged early in the twentieth century.

158 Walter H. and Helen Kolmeier House
502 North Llano Street
1925

Walter Kolmeier grew up in his parents' rock house [28] and then built his own house of imported red bricks, showing a willingness to use materials different from those used in the local vernacular. Walter was the son of Otto and Dora Kolmeier; Otto had a hardware store on Main Street, and Walter continued the family business [see 27]. He married Helen circa 1925, which was also the year they built this red brick bungalow. Three gables face the street, and the porch roof is supported by squat columns resting on brick piers, which are also part of a low wall around the porch. The entry is directly into the front room, which is lit by a trio of windows on the front wall. Direct entry into the front room was a typical feature of bungalows, which were wrapped up in an ideology of simple living in which entry halls were useless

and thus pretentious; ironically, the Germans of Fredericksburg had arranged their houses with direct entry into the *stube* for decades—for exactly the same reason. This house relates closely to the Krauskopf house on North Bowie [134], designed by Edward Stein. However, the Krauskopf house was valued at $6,000 in 1940, whereas the Kolmeier house was valued at $8,000.

College Street

159 Our Lady of Guadalupe Catholic Church
302 East College Street
1917

The Mexican Revolution brought a new generation of Mexicans into Texas, especially into major cities like San Antonio, Dallas, and Houston but also into the Hill Country. While Father Heinrich Gerlach was pastor of St. Mary's Catholic Church, this small frame church was built in 1917 to serve these new Texans. Henry Kuenemann [see 106] provided $1,250 worth of lumber for the church; Gregorio Martinez, a member of the parish, is remembered as having done much of the carpentry. The first priest was Father Sebastian Galarza, who had been

expelled from Mexico, along with many other priests, by the regime
of the political boss Venustiano Carranza. Many changes have been
made to the church over the years, including the addition of stained-
glass windows and the remodeling of the porch and the steeple. Other
start-up congregations followed the Hispanic Catholics to East College
Street: an African American congregation at Gospel Tabernacle to the
east, and the original home of the First Baptist Church to the west
at the intersection with North Llano. Declining membership led the
Catholic Diocese to close Our Lady of Guadalupe in the 1940s, but
another surge of Mexican immigration led to its reopening in 1983.

160 Joseph Wilson and Ruth Huffman Baines House
102 West College Street
1906

This late Victorian house was inspired by dreams of an old age surrounded by children and grandchildren, but, alas, these dreams were
partially dashed. This house was built for Joseph and Ruth Baines.
Joseph W. Baines was born in Louisiana, but his family moved to
Anderson, Texas, when he was four. His father, Reverend George W.
Baines, was a Baptist minister and served for two years as president of
Baylor University in Independence, Texas, but the stresses caused by
the beginning of the Civil War led him to resign his position. Joseph
attended Baylor until he joined the Confederate Army in 1863. After
the war he taught school while studying law in McKinney, Texas. In
1869 he married one of his students, Ruth Huffman, and they had two
daughters, Josefa and Rebekah. Rebekah married Sam Ealy Johnson,
and their first son, Lyndon Baines Johnson, was to become president
of the United States. Joseph practiced law in the 1870s and then was

appointed secretary of state by newly elected Governor John Ireland in 1883. After this he practiced law in Blanco County, but financial reverses led Joseph and Ruth to move to Fredericksburg in 1904. Neither Joseph nor Ruth had any German ancestry; it seems that they moved to Fredericksburg in anticipation of the marriage of their daughter Rebekah, who would be living in Stonewall in a house that would become LBJ's birthplace [209]. On March 26, 1906, Baines purchased six lots in the new College Addition from Alfred van der Stucken for $450. Three lots fronted on College Street, and three on Centre Street. Apparently work on this house started right away, but on November 20, 1906, Joseph died after a three-month illness. There was no Baptist church in Fredericksburg at that time, and his funeral was held in the German Methodist Church [86], though the service was conducted by a Baptist minister from Kerrville. Ruth sold the house on July 6, 1907, for $3,250, a considerable appreciation. By 1910 she was living in San Marcos, where she ran a boarding house for students at the teacher's college. She died in 1936 and was buried next to Joseph in Der Stadt Friedhof [140]. Rebekah Johnson also long outlived her husband and at the end of her life stayed with her son Lyndon and his wife Lady Bird at the LBJ Ranch [210].

Whatever local flavor the house has comes from its use of Basse blocks—that is, blocks of concrete shaped in molds to resemble stone. Its general appearance—being raised on a very high basement and with some Victorian elements—echoes the houses of late nineteenth-century Galveston.

---

161 Walter and Lillie Bierschwale House
306 West College Street
Circa 1915

This is one of two third-generation Bierschwale houses to survive in Fredericksburg. Walter's grandfather, Heinrich Bierschwale, built a story-and-a-half rock house on West Austin Street in 1872–73 [134]; Walter's father, William, built a two-story limestone house to the designs of Alfred Giles in 1888–89 [136]. Walter and his younger brother Max worked under the direction of their father at the Citizens

Bank of Fredericksburg, which was in the A. L. Patton Building on West Main Street [41]. Walter married Lillie Keyser in December 1915, and they had two children, son Keyser and daughter Lucille. Their house was designed by Leo M. J. Dielmann of San Antonio and built by Dielmann's former employee, Ed Stein. Given that Ed Stein was the best man at Walter and Lillie's wedding, he is highly likely to have secured the commission for Dielmann. In 1923 Lillie's parents built a house at 315 West College, designed and built by Ed Stein.

Built of imported red brick, the house blends elements of bungalow style and the Colonial (or Neoclassical) revival. The curvaceous front porch features slim Doric columns. In addition to the front door there are two additional entrances on the right side. Substantial windows in the front and right-side gables indicate that rooms were tucked under the roof in the attic. In contrast to this bungalow with a classical porch, Max and Lydia Bierschwale's frame house was built with a porch supported by Composite columns [133], more fully in the Neoclassical style. In 1930 the homes of both Walter and Max were valued at $5,000. The Citizens Bank, where they both worked, closed in 1932, a victim of the Great Depression, and Walter described himself as a rancher on the 1940 census.

162 Emil and Bertha Riley House (Riley-Enderlin House)
606 North Adams Street
1904

This house was built for a young couple, Emil and Bertha Riley, but
became the home of an older couple, Charles and Louise Enderlin,
ready to live their golden years in town rather than on the farm. Emil
and Bertha were both native Texans; Emil's parents were born in Texas
and with a Deep South ancestry, while Bertha's were both born in
Germany. Bertha was the daughter of the merchant Charles Nauwald
and his wife Bertha; she grew up on East Main Street in the shadow of
the Nimitz Hotel. Emil, who worked for a while as an RFD mail car-
rier, married Bertha in 1902, when he was twenty-three and she was
eighteen. Two years later they hired local builder Frank Stein to con-
struct this house. It is a story-and-a-half house with two front rooms
and additional rooms to the rear. Quite remarkably for this date, it
had two front doors, a late example of this German Texan feature.
The front façade is sheathed with board-and-batten construction; the
north and south sides, however, are pressed metal shaped to resemble
stone. Both are typical of late Victorian Fredericksburg; the use of

board-and-batten on the front suggests that the Rileys preferred that to pressed tin. A similar treatment is found in the Robert and Maria Jenschke Sunday house [155] of 1907. The Rileys lived in this house for eight years, and then in 1912 sold it to Charles and Louise Enderlin, who had formerly lived southeast of town on South Grape Creek [192]. The purchase allowed their son, Charles Jr., to take over their farm. The house in town remained in the family for more than seventy years.

163 Moritz-Hitzfeld-Jacoby House
608 North Milam Street
1907

This late Victorian rock house was built for a young Catholic couple, Edmund and Anna Moritz. Edmund's father, Joseph Moritz, was a stepson of Peter Schmitz [see 120] and presumably learned the trade of stonemasonry from him. Anna's father, John Metzger Sr., was a carpenter. The rock work is solid and typical of German Texan work, the carpentry work on the porch frilly and Victorian. The house was originally L-shaped in plan, with direct access into two of the three rooms from the front porch. The placement of the chimney immediately above the window in the right front room indicates that there was

no fireplace but a flue for a cast-iron stove. By 1910 Edmund, Anna, and their three young children had moved to Austin, where Edmund worked as a stonecutter. In 1920 he was proprietor of a marble yard, a position he still held ten years later. In 1914 the house was sold to Levi and Caroline Hitzfeld. Levi was a carpenter and a grandson of Herman Hitzfeld, who was probably one of the carpenters who built the Klingelhoefer house [65] and the Walter house [108]. They probably added the room behind the south front room, which is visible on the 1938 Sanborn fire insurance map. The Hitzfelds had moved to San Antonio by 1930, probably searching for work in the construction industry in the midst of the Great Depression, and they were still there in 1940. Both Levi and Carolina had Jacoby ancestors, and in 1941 the house was sold to Felix and Emma Jacoby. Felix had been a salesman in a general merchandise store in 1910 but was later a farmer. In 1941 he was fifty-eight and Emma was fifty-two, and they were probably planning this as their retirement home.

164 Edward and Minnie Stein House
101 East Hackberry Street
1923

While his older brother Joe opted to build one of the last Victorian houses in Fredericksburg [154], Edward Stein chose to build a bungalow, which had become popular nationwide in the first quarter of the twentieth century. The Stein house used brick for the walls rather than wood, a concession, perhaps, to the German appreciation for permanence. The brick was not the red D'Hanis brick that Ed had used on a number of houses around town, including the Krauskopf house on North Bowie Street [134], but a lower-key brown brick.

Edward Stein was born in 1892 and came to Fredericksburg in 1894, when his father, Franz, opened a lumberyard on Travis Street [see 153]. Ed attended the San Antonio Academy, then spent three years in Chicago at the Armour Institute of Technology. Returning to San Antonio, he worked as an architectural draftsman for Leo M. J. Dielmann, who had designed the new St. Mary's Church in Fredericksburg in 1905–6 [85] and who would return in 1923 to design the

new St. Mary's School [83]. In San Antonio Ed also met Wilhelmine "Minnie" Grobe, a Hill Country girl who worked as a seamstress for Joske's department store in San Antonio. They were married in 1914 at St. John's Lutheran Church in the Alamo City, the church of many German Texan pioneers. In 1917 the couple returned to Fredericksburg. Ed gave his occupation as architect in the censuses of 1920 and 1930, but he was a very practical architect, involving himself not only in design but also in construction, which, of course, was his father's business.

He designed this house for his own family in 1923. Though it was typical for American bungalows to have direct entry into the living room, in the Stein house one entered into a small hall. To the right of this was a den, which may have doubled as Ed's office. Ahead and to the left was the living room, lit by a trio of windows on the side wall. The fireplace on the back wall had an oak mantel that incorporated shelves on each side. To the right of the living room was the dining room, which had a bay window in the side wall and a built-in oak buffet on the back wall. Originally there were sliding doors between the living room and dining room, but these were later removed when the opening was widened. Behind the dining room was the kitchen, and behind the living room was the breakfast room. The kitchen had cabinets and a sink on the outer wall and more cabinets between the kitchen and the breakfast room. To the left of the breakfast room was a small room with a concrete floor, known as the flower room. Behind the breakfast room was the master bedroom, the rear wall of which consisted solely of closets, a testament to the proliferating wardrobes of Americans in the early twentieth century. Behind the kitchen were the pantry, the master bathroom, and a smoking room for Ed. There was an additional bedroom to the rear and two more upstairs. The house also had a two-car garage, which was quite unusual for 1923. Stein converted the garage into an apartment for his son and his new wife in 1948.

Soon after designing this house, he redesigned the Nimitz Hotel [32] in a more up-to-date Mission or Spanish Colonial Revival style. He also designed notable houses for Victor and Clara Keidel [33], Lawrence and Meta Krauskopf [134], and Walter and Helen Kolmeier [158]. After the Great Depression led to the closing of all banks in Fredericksburg, Edward and Joe were involved in the organization of the Fredericksburg National Bank, and Edward became its president. He also designed its building at 119 East Main Street [15] in 1936 as well as the Gillespie County Courthouse [3] in 1939. The courthouse project seems to have been his architectural swan song, as he subsequently focused all his efforts on banking. Edward and Minnie attended Bethany Lutheran Church, and Edward was consulting architect for its 1954 building.

PART 6

Gillespie County

165 Peter and Caroline Bonn House
356 Kuhlmann Road
Circa 1861–67

The land on Meusebach Creek south of town was settled by the Lochte family. Frederick and Dorette Lochte purchased 700 acres in 1854 and sometime after that built a two-story rock house on the property with a partial basement (extant but not visible from the road). On October 28, 1859, their son Fritz married Charlotte Rahe, and their daughter Caroline married Peter Bonn. Fritz and Charlotte eventually inherited the rock house; Peter and Caroline bought land nearby. Initially they lived in a log house, but sometime between 1860 and 1867 (when Frederick Lochte passed away), they built this story-and-a-half rock house. It had a large front room and a narrower back room, with usable space in the low half story above. The house resembles the Guenther house on Live Oak Creek as originally built in 1855 [167], but many more such houses were built after the war. Indeed, in 1869 the Bonns bought a very similar rock house in town [97], which had been built

quite recently. Like the Lochte house, the Bonn country rock house was later used as a barn; during this period, most of the woodwork was removed. The house has been rehabilitated and is being used as a bed-and-breakfast.

166 Meusebach Creek School
515 Kuhlmann Road
1930s

As with most rural schools in Gillespie County, this school has been housed successively in log, then rock, then frame buildings. There was a school in the Meusebach Creek community from shortly after the Civil War. Originally the school was a tiny log house, roughly nine by ten feet, on land donated by Frederick (Fritz) Lochte Jr. A new rock building was erected in the 1880s, also on Lochte property. This survives, in a ruinous state, on the Old Comfort Road. It was replaced by a frame structure, on land donated by Louis Bonn, son of Peter and Caroline (née Lochte) Bonn, who had a house across the road [165]. This served until the 1930s, when the present school was built. It was a framed structure with clapboards for siding and a hipped tin

roof. There was a cluster of six windows on the south side, providing abundant sunlight to the classroom. The door was at the northeast corner. Inside was a large classroom, plus a library and a cloakroom. An original teacher's desk remains in the classroom, as do a simple bench for students and several students' desks from Sears, Roebuck & Company. On the northwest corner of the structure was a cistern for drinking water; outhouses for girls and boys were a few yards to the north. An outdoor stage was off to the west. A frame house for the teacher was built a few yards to the south; this was later dismantled and sold to provide funds for the upkeep of the school. The new school building was used for a little more than two decades, until 1954, when the school was consolidated with the Fredericksburg schools.

167 Guenther-Lorenz-Hilker Complex
4222 State Highway 16 South, south of Live Oak Creek
1855, 1857, 1887

This complex was begun in the pioneering era and greatly enlarged in the late Victorian. Carl Hilmar Guenther purchased this property in 1851 because of its location near the point where Live Oak

Detail of *Guenther's Mill on Live Oak Creek*, by Hermann Lungkwitz. Oil on academy board, dated 1855. Photograph by the author; courtesy of C. H. Guenther & Son Inc., San Antonio.

Circa 1890. Courtesy of Institute of Texan Cultures, University of Texas at San Antonio, 071–0540.

Creek flows into the Pedernales River. When he purchased the land from Richard and Arthur Cloudts, two lieutenants from Hannover, there were already two log houses on the property. His first orders of business were to dig a mill race and to erect a mill. Then in 1855 he built a story-and-a-half rock house with a large front section, a lean-to

Measured floor plan by John Klein.

kitchen behind it, and a half story above. The front door entered directly in the *stube*, the larger room. A partition to the left of the front door created space for a small bedroom. The stair, essentially a built-in-place ladder, was at the south end of the back room. A limestone smokehouse was soon built behind the main residence.

In October 1855, his house complete, Guenther married Dorothea Pape, the daughter of a neighbor, Fritz Pape. In the 1850s the Live Oak Creek community included a son of a minister in Frankfurt, a son of a minister of war in Cologne, the landscape painter Hermann Lungkwitz from Halle and his brother Adolf, a tinsmith and silversmith, the portrait painter Richard Petri of Dresden, and several German farmers. A Lungkwitz painting of the mill and house soon after its completion in 1855 documents the original appearance of the house; this painting, titled

Guenther's Mill on Live Oak Creek, is still owned by the family and is proudly displayed at the Guenther House in San Antonio. Adolph later moved to town and built a shop and home on East Main Street [25].

In 1857 Guenther built another rock building, which he planned to use as a store. The building has one large room on the ground floor with a large raised hearth on the right side wall; against the left side wall opposite is a staircase leading to the half-story above. There is also a cellar underneath on the left side of the building, which was reached from the front porch. Immediately in front of this outbuilding is a rock-lined well of considerable antiquity. A limestone smokehouse was soon built behind the main house.

After several years of drought Carl Hilmar Guenther decided to move to San Antonio in 1859, where he built a very successful milling business that later became Pioneer Flour Mills. Though he initially sold the property to his father-in-law, the house came back into Guenther's possession, and on Christmas Day 1867 he sold the house and farm to Heinrich and Katherine Lorenz for $600. Heinrich and Katherine had been married in 1865, and by 1872 they had six children in the house. The Lorenz family built a one-story rock barn to the northwest of the main house, which is the back part of the present two-story barn. This barn was limestone with doors on all sides; in addition, the longer front and rear walls each had four slits to provide ventilation. Two of the floor joists are stamped "FROM Loomis and Christian, AUSTIN TEX," which strongly suggests a date in the 1870s.

Katherine Lorenz died in 1876, but the family continued to own the place for another ten years. In 1880 forty-six-year-old Heinrich was assisted in farming by his eldest son, Carl, while housekeeping was performed by daughters Frida and Emilia. In that year the household also included a hired hand, William McDougal, twenty-three, son of an Irish father and a Prussian mother, who probably lived in the room above the kitchen. Two years later McDougal married, and by 1900 he and his wife Frida had nine children.

In October 1886 the Lorenz family sold the farm to Carl Hilker, whose family kept it for many decades. The property valuation for tax purposes more than doubled between 1886 and 1887, indicating that great changes were made to the property. The Hilkers greatly enlarged the main house and the rock barn. The walls of the house were raised to an equal height on all sides, with two small windows in front and two larger windows on the sides of the upper floor and in the rear room downstairs. The higher walls necessitated a new roof, which was covered with standing-seam tin. The exterior of the house was plastered and then scored, which made the stones seem more regular and which also disguised the two phases of the building. The earliest known photograph of the enlarged house (probably taken between 1887 and 1892) shows all of these changes but not the front porch; a $50 increase in tax valuation for 1892 suggests that the Victorian-style porch was added in that year.

Southwest of Town

168 Henry and Bertha Basse House
1004 Bowie Street
1918–20

Henry Basse was the son of Adolf and Lina Basse and thus the grandson of Henry S. W. Basse, an early Lutheran minister and merchant, and his wife Charlotte [see 22]. The younger Henry Basse married

Bertha Fuhrmann in 1907 and worked as a stonemason before he and his brother Hugo founded the Basse Brothers Cement Yard in 1910. The company's concrete blocks (know as Basse blocks) were used extensively in local buildings over the next two decades, and its warehouse, also made of Basse blocks, still stands in the 300 block of North Adams Street. The idea for building houses out of concrete blocks did not originate with the Basse brothers: Sears, Roebuck & Company promoted such houses in its *Modern Homes* catalogues starting in 1909. Henry Basse's own house, built in 1918–20, used them as well, albeit in a much more elaborate house than those found in the Sears catalogues. The hipped roof and windows that are grouped in twos and threes echoed the recently popular Craftsman and Prairie styles, while the paired concrete columns on the front porch speak to the revival of Neoclassicism. Inside a central passage ran through the middle of the house, a feature avoided by earlier generations of Fredericksburg residents. This was the residence of Henry, Bertha, and their three children, Edna, Udo, and Adolph; there was also room for a sister-in-law, Ida Fuhrmann, and one of the Basse employees, a cement finisher.

169 Heinrich and Conradine Baethge House
430 Hayden Ranch Road
1868–69, 1889–90

This interesting farmhouse has three *fachwerk* rooms in front and a rock lean-to in the rear. Heinrich and Conradine Baethge arrived in Texas in 1854 and originally settled in Mason County. They bought twelve out-lots west of Fredericksburg in 1867 while still living in Mason County, but they had moved to Gillespie County by the time of 1870 census, presumably into the front part of this house.

The infill for the *fachwerk* portion of the house was adobe, which might have worked in drier climes but proved problematic in the Hill Country, at least in the absence of a plaster covering. The porch on the front and the south side of the house was certainly to provide a shady space for outdoor living, but it also was probably an attempt to delay the deterioration of the adobe. Both house and porch were originally shingled, but now the main roof is covered with tin.

Entry was into the middle room, which had a door in the middle of each wall. Most likely the center room was the *stube,* and the other rooms a kitchen and bedroom. Such three-room plans were unusual. The only other houses in Gillespie County to have three front rooms were the Kammlah house on Main Street [46] and the Welgehausen Ranch in the Crabapple community [181]. In New Braunfels the Heinrich Scholl house had a similar arrangement, originally with small rooms behind framing a small gallery. This was a plan familiar in Louisiana, and perhaps the builders of these houses passed through or even worked in the state.

Both Heinrich and Conradine died in 1888; they had already split their out-lots between sons Heinrich and Ferdinand, and the latter inherited the part with the house. Ferdinand had married Louise Eckert in 1884 and had shared the house with his parents and took care of them while they were alive. Ferdinand and Louise probably built the rock addition to add a more modern kitchen and more space. Ferdinand died in 1925, and Louise in 1935. Two years later the house was sold to August and Mathilde Behrend.

170 Cherry Mountain School
2866 Cherry Mountain Loop
1880s, 1890s, 1926, circa 1935–36

The buildings of this school complex neatly show the evolution of preferred building materials and technologies. The earliest building was
built of logs perhaps as early as 1883; about a decade later a second
room of rock was added to the rear. Big changes came in 1926, with the
construction of a new school building. The walls were concrete Basse
blocks, made in Fredericksburg, supplemented with a bank of eight
windows on both the north and south walls. The roof was hipped, and
the ends of the rafters were exposed, a typical feature of the bungalow
or Arts and Crafts style. The masonry work was done by Ed Roos, and
the carpentry by Fritz Rumler. The stage was added to the complex
around 1935–36. Just to the west on Cherry Mountain Loop is the Carl
and Emma Durst house, which started as a one-room log house in
the 1870s and was greatly enlarged with a rock house in 1896. Emma

was the daughter of John and Juliane Ruegner [see 5], a stonemason, and Carl also came from a family of masons. For the house of her twin sister, Bertha Ruegner Pfeil, in town, see 8.

171 Rode-Kothe House
1286 Cherry Spring Road, Cherry Spring
1879–80

This house is not accessible to the public but it is hard to ignore from a distance in just about any direction. The Rode-Kothe house in Cherry Spring, built 1879–80, is the most prominent house in northwestern Gillespie County. Built by Diedrich and Katherine Rode, it was later the residence of Willie and Hildegard Kothe. The main house is two and a half stories and built of native limestone, and an extensive array of outbuildings were built of rock as well. The house had a central passage twenty feet wide, which at that time was quite unusual in the Hill Country, with an encased stairway at the front. The first-floor rooms had eleven-foot ceilings and simple but attractive moldings for doors and built-in closets. The two front rooms were bedrooms; the back two were a kitchen and Diedrich's shop. Upstairs were two more bedrooms and a large room on the east side where Dietrich, a minister as well as a rancher, could hold Lutheran services. The outbuildings included a very substantial carriage house, a two-story building with a laundry and accommodations for servants and guests, a water tank,

Photo by Richard MacAllister, May 29, 1936, for Historic American Buildings Survey, Library of Congress.

a blacksmith shop, and a long rectangular sheep barn. Rode hired Fredericksburg men to haul sacks of wool to Austin. In the 1930s the Historic American Buildings Survey took several photographs of the house.

172 Christ Lutheran Church
1419 Cherry Spring Road, Cherry Spring
1906–7, 1928

In its limestone walls and extreme simplicity this small Gothic church looks back to St. John's Lutheran Church [182] in the Crabapple community, built in 1897. Completed in 1907, Christ Lutheran was given a new steeple in 1928, which seems to have been inspired by James Wahrenberger's Holy Ghost Church [77] in Fredericksburg of 1888–93, a design that led to a number of new steeples in Fredericksburg.

173 Cherry Spring School
5973 Ranch Road 2323, Cherry Spring
1905, 1935

This simple rock building with a gable roof was built in 1905. The entrance is in the west gable end, and there are windows in the north and south walls. The small rural school received a small allotment of funds from the state and the county, which in 1903 amounted to $190. The teacher was paid $30 to $35 a month for the six months or so that the school was in session; when it was not, he or she had to find other

work. In the years before World War I there would be some forty to fifty students of a wide variety of ages, all in one room. A pavilion was added in 1935, which was for end-of-the-year school closing programs. The stage also doubled as a second classroom; younger children studied here while older students—up to the ninth grade—were in the rock building. The school was consolidated with the Fredericksburg school district in 1962.

174 Lange's Mill
Lange's Mill Road, Doss
Circa 1872–75

The community of Doss is named for a family from Virginia. In 1860 both John and Thomas Doss were among the ten wealthiest individuals in Gillespie County. John identified himself on the census as a farmer, and his combined personal and real estate value of $21,000 put him second only to Felix van der Stucken. John's younger brother

Thomas was a miller, and his $8,800 in property made him ninth wealthiest individual in the county. Also living in his household was his father, William, who was a millwright. Pretty clearly the elder Doss built this mill on Threadgill Creek for his son.

The Doss brothers sold the mill to August Steiness in 1864, but Steiness died two years later. His widow sold the mill to Frederick William Lange. The dam attached to the mill was destroyed by a flood but was rebuilt in 1872–75. This stonework has been attributed to Philip Buchmeyer, a stonemason who settled in Loyal Valley in Mason County, just a few miles north of Cherry Spring. Lange died in 1877, and his son Julius took over the mill. Julius later ran a store and served as postmaster for the Lange community; he died in 1926 and is buried in the Lange Cemetery on Lange's Mill Road.

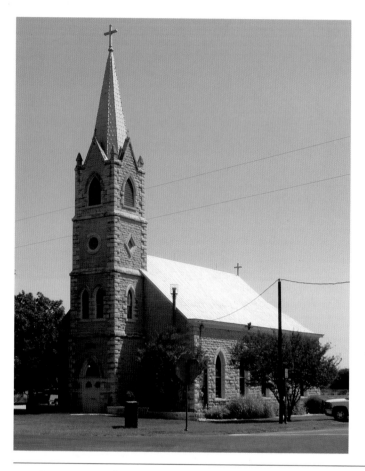

175 St. Peter Lutheran Church
14238 South Ranch Road 783, Doss
1912–13

This Gothic Revival church was built in 1912–13 of red sandstone walls with windows framed in white limestone. Four stonemasons from Fredericksburg were involved: William Klingelhoefer, L. Weber, O. Schmidt, and C. Feuge. Inside the benches were reused from the previous church until 1940, when the present ones were installed. The pastor of the congregation, D. H. Mayer, is remembered as having carved the altar, baptismal font, and pulpit, though the latter has been dramatically reduced in height to meet modern liturgical needs.

176 Old Doss School
177 New Doss School
11432 Ranch Road 648, Doss
1905, 1927

The first school in this area was built in 1884 a little over three miles south of its present location. The school moved north to Doss proper in 1894; the frame structure was replaced in 1905 by this two-room limestone schoolhouse. The limestone blocks are large and well cut; the window sills and lintels are heavily rusticated (that is, cut in a rough-hewn pattern); and in the east gable is a diamond-shaped piece of limestone into which is carved a five-pointed star. This structure, in turn, was replaced in 1927 by a larger, four-room school made of concrete blocks shaped like smoothly carved blocks of stone; the roof is hipped. Both the east and west walls have a generous grouping of windows. The entrance is set back behind the wall of the building and leads into a narrow central passage, with two classrooms on each side. Each classroom has five windows. The old school became the teacher's residence and later served as a fire station.

West of Town

178 Charles and Maranda Roberts House (McKee-Roberts-Baumann House)
287 North Ranch Road 783, Harper
1906–7

This house is a late example of a Victorian-style house, built by recent Anglo-Texan immigrants to Gillespie County, but later owned by a German Texan family. The house was originally built on the town's main street (what is now 23808 West US 290) and was given a Texas Historical Commission medallion in 1987, but it was moved to this more secluded location north of the Harper schools circa 1990. (Note that the marker refers to outbuildings that were at the original location but were not moved.)

Although the historical marker in front of the house says that it was built for W. T. McKee in 1902, county property tax records suggest that it was built for Charles A. Roberts in 1906–7 and then sold to Arthur Baumann in 1916. Roberts was a native of Illinois, a farmer, and was forty-three in 1906. In 1900 he and his wife Maranda had seven children; the oldest three were attending school. (Harper had a one-room schoolhouse from 1885, which expanded to two rooms in 1898; it burned in 1906 and was replaced with a stone building in 1908.) With a large family Maranda was probably very happy to have a

live-in servant, seventeen-year-old Minnie Johnson, and to move into this nice new house in 1907.

In 1916 the house was purchased by another farming family, Arthur Baumann and his wife, Selma (née Kaiser). Arthur and Selma were both native Texans; in 1910 Arthur was a farmer, but in 1940 he was a stonemason. For many years he operated the cotton gin that stood across the street from his house. In 1940 Texas was deep in the throes of the Great Depression: their daughter Martha Rose was working as a maid in a private home (the house of Father A. A. Gitter, longtime pastor of the Catholic church in Harper), and their son Max was a stonemason's helper—obviously working for his father. Son Fritz, fourteen, was in school, and Arthur, six, was about to start.

The wood-frame house uses the construction technique known as board-and-batten—that is, the walls consist of vertical boards butted up against one another, with the joints covered by strips of wood known as battens. Such houses could also be found in Fredericksburg in the decades around 1900, such as the Jenschke Sunday house [155]. The two gables on the front façade can also be found in Fredericksburg houses of this era, such as the Ellebracht house [130]. By this time, most folks in Fredericksburg had abandoned houses with two front doors, and this house also has a single front door. The front porch is quite simple, with six chamfered posts supporting the roof and a bit of gingerbread trim just under the eaves. Unlike the traditional Fredericksburg house with back rooms under a lean-to roof, the back wing of this house has a roof line perpendicular to that of the main roof.

The front door led into a central passage; on the left were the living room, dining room, and kitchen; on the right were two bedrooms and a bathroom; and straight ahead was the largest bedroom, which Baumann grandchildren remember as Grandma Selma's bedroom. Beyond this was a screened-in porch, accessible from the kitchen. The outbuildings included various buildings for storage, a laundry house, a smokehouse, a chicken coop, and a windmill. To the west of the house was a field where the Baumanns let their sheep graze, and to the east was a garden with a fish pond, stocked with goldfish. Arthur died in 1949, but Selma continued to live in the house until her death in 1980. In 1986 daughter Martha Rose and son Arthur (known as Junior) sold the house to Gene and Margaret Bode. The Bodes converted it into a tearoom and sandwich shop and later into a bed-and-breakfast (around which time the old white house was painted a dusky rose color), but neither of these projects was successful.

179 St. James Lutheran Church
23932 West US 290, Harper
1914

St. James Lutheran Church was organized in 1913, and this building was erected the next year. The foundation was limestone from the ranch of August Ernst Jr., four miles distant, with a date stone of red granite provided from the shop of the Nagel Brothers in Fredericksburg [6]. The lumber was hauled from Kerrville, which, having been connected to the railroad, had emerged as a rival town to Fredericksburg. The church was dedicated July 26, 1914, to the strains of "Now Thank We All Our God." The pointed arches atop each window recall the Gothic Revival style, as does the centered tower. Over the decades many changes have obscured the historic character of the building: the exterior is sheathed in modern synthetic siding, except for the limestone of the foundation and the tin on the roof of the steeple. Inside the pews are relatively recent, and the windows now have glass-block stained glass, giving it a very modern look. Only the small altar, pulpit, and baptismal font hint of the church's antiquity.

Nearby are Harper Presbyterian Church and St. Anthony's Catholic Church. The Presbyterian church was founded at Barnett Spring but moved to Harper in 1901. The church building retains its original shape, except for the installation of louvers in the formerly open belfry; the historic character is somewhat obscured by synthetic siding. St. Anthony's was founded in 1908, and a simple wood-frame structure was built soon thereafter. Julius Klingelhoefer did the masonry work, and Theodore Langerhans did the carpentry. Both men were Fredericksburg natives: Klingelhoefer lived in the *fachwerk* house

inherited from his parents [65], while Langerhans later built a bunga-low [144]. In 1924 a rectory and parish hall were added by the Kuen-emann Lumber Company [see 106]. A more modern and spacious structure has since replaced the original church building.

180 Pilot Knob School
Old Harper Road, Harper
Circa 1916

This rock school was built roughly halfway between Fredericksburg and Harper around 1916, but it was preceded by a number of previous structures dating back to 1880. The stone blocks are large and regular, an indication of its relatively late date. Earlier rock schoolhouses were built in Doss [176] and Cherry Spring [173]. Indeed, this seems to be the last rock schoolhouse built in the county. Atop the stone walls was a metal hipped roof. Inside was one large room that could be subdivided if there happened to be two teachers. The long shed that abuts the entry porch is said to have been built to provide a place for the children to play on rainy days. The school closed in 1963 after consolidation with the Fredericksburg school system.

181 Welgehausen Ranch
Ranch Road 965, Crabapple
Late 1850s, 1870s, 1890s

The Welgehausen Ranch is one of the best-preserved nineteenth-century ranches in the Hill Country. The ranch is private property, but the principal buildings are visible from Ranch Road 965 just north of Crabapple Creek.

Friedrich Welgehausen purchased this 640-acre spread in 1856. The family soon built a story-and-a-half house that utilized the German Texan construction technique of alternating logs with rows of mortared stone. An external staircase led to the loft above, saving precious space in the one room below. The little house accommodated Friedrich, his wife Juliane, and their four children. In 1862 their oldest, Conrad, married Margarethe Walter, who had grown up in Fredericksburg in the *fachwerk* house of her parents, Peter and Anna Margaret Walter [108] on West Creek Street. Conrad and Margarethe soon built their own one-room log and rock structure on the ranch; in the decades after the Civil War it would be enlarged to both sides, above, and to the rear.

In 1873 Friedrich and Juliane deeded their land, cattle, and furnishings to Conrad and moved into town. The first additions were probably begun soon after this. Conrad and Margarethe built a bedroom on the east and a kitchen on the west; both of these rooms had their own doors onto the front porch. It is likely that they also added a half story above all three rooms at this time. Later still, a lean-to addition to the rear created a new kitchen on the west and two other rooms; at this time the front part of the house was raised to a full two stories.

The ranch buildings also include a log and rock barn, the structure closest to the road, and another structure to the northwest of the main house, moved from the ranch of Margarethe's brother, Louis Walter; it which served as a laundry and smokehouse, separated by a dogtrot that was later enclosed.

---

182 St. John Lutheran Church
14689 Lower Crabapple Road, off Ranch Road 965, Crabapple
1897

This simple but substantial rock building features at one end a diminutive steeple, announcing that it was a church, and at the other end a chimney, announcing that it was heated. The rocks were all quarried locally and a lime kiln was built nearby; in addition to volunteer labor, this meant that the building cost the congregation only

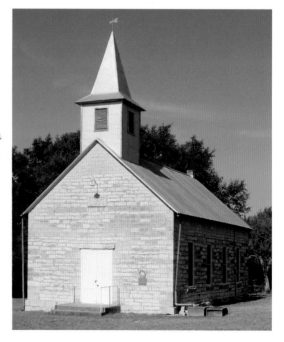

$600. The forty-five-by-twenty-five-foot structure was supervised by Julius Rusche. Double doors open into the single room, where the focal points were the altar, pulpit, and baptismal font, all made of wood and all painted white with touches of gold. Amidst the apparent simplicity the upper part of the altar has panels marked I–III and IV–X, alluding to the two panels of the Ten Commandments. On the altar table are carved the Alpha and the Omega, alluding to Jesus calling himself the beginning and the end.

183 Crabapple Teacherage
184 Crabapple School
14671 Lower Crabapple Road, Crabapple
1877–78, 1882

Across the way from the church are the Crabapple School and an adjacent house for the teacher, known as the teacherage. The land was donated in January 1877 by Matthias Schmidt, and the school opened in January 1878. Schmidt lived across Crabapple Creek and years before had been one of the stonemasons on Zion Lutheran Church

[61] in Fredericksburg. The first school for the Crabapple community was the building on the east side, which had two rooms, a large front room and a smaller back room under a lean-to, a fairly typical form for houses of the 1870s. The stonemasons for the older structure have been identified as Durst and Strackbein, probably John Durst, who years before had worked on the Methodist Church in Fredericksburg [86], and Christian Strackbein, who had recently built his own house [128] in town. The carpenter has been identified as Julius Rusche, who twenty years later supervised the construction of St. John's Lutheran Church [182] in Crabapple. The second building, a larger one-room limestone structure, was built in 1882 at a cost of $600. With the construction of this building, the original school became the teacherage. The school is still in use as a community center.

Northeast of Town

185 Willow City School
2501 Ranch Road 1323, Willow City
1905

The Willow City School was built in 1905, the third school building for children in the northeastern part of Gillespie County. This area was populated with Germans but also with Anglo-Southerners. The land was donated by J. W. Lindemann and J. C. Hardin. The school building's five bays, two stories, and hipped roof could have passed for

a New England academy building from a century before. Perhaps its form owes something to the Colonial Revival style, which was popular in the late nineteenth and early twentieth centuries. It sits on top of a rise like a Hill Country Acropolis. The stone is granite typical of nearby Llano County. There were two classrooms on the first floor and a large auditorium/classroom on the second floor. The building was remodeled in 1915, when a partition was installed in one of the first-floor classrooms to create a passageway. Only in 1920 was a well dug to supply water, and only in 1950 was a restroom built on the north side of the building. The school was consolidated with Fredericksburg in 1961, but the building is still in use as a community center.

186 James Calloway Hardin and Laura Hardin House (Hardin-Gold House)
207 Willow City Loop, Willow City
1905

Just northeast of the Willow City School is the impressive late Victorian house of James C. Hardin and his second wife, Laura May Hardin. Hardin was born in Knoxville, Tennessee, before the Civil War and was newly married to Mary Melissa Phillips and ranching in Blanco County by the time of the 1880 census. They lived in the northwest corner of Blanco County, little more than ten miles from Willow City as the crow flies. J. C.'s wife died in 1894, leaving a son and two daughters; around 1896 he married Laura May Wilson.

By 1905 they had purchased land in Willow City, donating some of it for the site of the new school. Their own house used the same materials as the school: Llano granite for the walls and Texas red granite for the window sills and lintels. The roof of the main block was hipped, but a central front room projects dramatically forward, while gables on the north and south provide usable room in the attic. There are L-shaped porches at the northeast, southeast, and southwest corners. There are doors on the north and south walls as well as very tall windows. The date 1905 is carved into the red granite lintel on the south door. The front room has a bay window to maximize light and ventilation. Some of the original Victorian trim remains in the gables and under the eaves. The house is unusual for Willow City, but it relates to the Christian and Francisca Stehling house in Fredericksburg, built in 1899 [79].

Inside the hall is T-shaped; the shorter part runs from the south door to the north; a door on the east leads into the parlor; the longer part of the hallway runs west. The door into the parlor is original and has a pane of etched glass, which provides some additional light to the hall. Under the main roof the longer part of the hall leads to four rooms, each with two windows. The two rooms on the south have fireplaces.

J. C. Hardin died in 1939, but Laura continued to ranch. At the time of the 1940 census she was living alone; the house was valued at $3,000, comparable to newer rock houses in town. She died in 1954 and was buried beside J.C. in the Willow City cemetery. Around 1960 the house was purchased by Vernon and Joyce Gold; it is still owned by their descendants. The only major changes to the house are the replacement of porch columns with cast iron from the mid-twentieth century and updates to the kitchen and bathroom.

187 Rheingold School
334 Rheingold School Road, Rheingold
1892, 1900

The Rheingold School is one of the more remote schools in the county, but it is well worth the trek. A founding date of 1873 is sometimes suggested, but the land on which the school sits was not donated by William Gold until December 18, 1891. A log house was quickly built; the front wall is plastered, and the side wall covered with board-and-battens. A second, frame room was added on the west, and later still two stone rooms on the north, each with a chimney. The construction of a new frame building in 1900 allowed the old structure to be converted into a teacherage. Later still a stage was added, making the

complex complete. The school closed in 1949 when it consolidated with the Fredericksburg school district.

188 Cave Creek School
470 Cave Creek Road, Cave Creek
1896, circa 1932

The residents of the Cave Creek community applied for permission to organize a school in 1890. The first building may be the one-room frame structure now attached to the stage. The larger one-room schoolhouse was built in 1896, according to the date on the chimney on the north wall. It has embossed tin siding and a tin roof. It is very unusual among Gillespie County schools in that there is not one door

centered on one gable end but two doors, one on each of the long sides. The teacher's desk, the blackboard, and the flue for the cast-iron stove were at the north end of the room. In the frame room attached to the stage is a fragment of a student desk—a "20th Century" model—from Sears, Roebuck & Company of Chicago. The stage received its tin roof and concrete floor in the early 1930s. Although the school was consolidated into the Fredericksburg school district in 1949, the building is used by the Cave Creek 4-H Club and other local groups.

189 St. Paul Lutheran Church
9732 Ranch Road 1631, Cave Creek
1884, 1890, 1928–29

St. Paul was the first church in Gillespie County built outside of Fredericksburg, though it took on much of its current appearance in

1928–29. In 1884 Conrad Herbort donated five acres for a church and cemetery at Cave Creek. The founding pastor was Michael Haag, who also served the area around Crabapple Creek. The church was built in 1884 and enlarged in 1890, but the exterior was covered in tin and the interior drywalled in the late 1920s; an altar niche was added at that time. The cemetery contains many interesting grave markers in marble, red granite, wrought iron, and cast iron. Terry Jordan considered the cast-iron grave markers of Wilhelm Herbort to be "perhaps the finest example of German metal funerary craftsmanship." Also noteworthy are the cast-iron fences around graves erected between 1895 and 1915; the fencing material was imported from cities such as St. Louis, Cincinnati, and New Orleans.

East and Southeast of Town

190 Fort Martin Scott
1606 East Main Street (US 290 east)
1848–53, 1980s

Fort Martin Scott was part of the first line of forts established by the US government to protect settlers from the harassment of Native Americans, especially the Comanche and Lipan. Initially called Camp Houston, it was renamed to honor an army officer who had died in the

Mexican-American War. The fort was in operation for five years—from December 1848 to December 1853—before the line of forts moved westward. It was never a large post: in 1850 it consisted of three commissioned officers, twelve noncommissioned officers, and seventy-six privates. Among the enlisted men forty had been born in Ireland, twelve in Germany, and four in Scotland. In addition there were twelve laundresses and one hospital matron.

As with most army installations, the grounds of the fort were not enclosed, and most of the buildings faced a rectangular parade ground. A house of four rooms on the west side of the parade served as quarters for the commanding officer. Other officers were each quartered in two rooms on the north side, and the enlisted men occupied two buildings on the south side. A guardhouse and prison were on the east side of the parade. The buildings were a hodgepodge of construction techniques—frame buildings with weatherboarding, log buildings, and several *jacales* and adobes, the latter two suggesting that Hispanic forms had been adapted for army use.

The land on which the fort was built was never army property; first Nathaniel Townsend of Austin owned it, then San Antonio banker and merchant John Twohig. In 1870 Twohig sold the 640 acres to Johan Wolfgang Braeutigam, who adapted the guardhouse for his residence and then built a store, saloon, and dance hall nearer to the highway. Many Fourth of July celebrations were held at Braeutigam's Gardens. The first Gillespie County Fair was held there in 1881, though in 1889 the fair was moved to town. Robbers murdered Braeutigam in 1884, and the saloon and store soon went out of business. However, his widow, Christine Kensing Braeutigam, remained on the homestead until her death in 1924, and the family retained the property until 1959.

Only one structure remains from the original fort, the stone structure on the east nearest to Baron's Creek. This three-room structure held the guardhouse, cells for prisoners, and a room for an officer that was repurposed as a magazine to store munitions. Later the Braeutigam family used these rooms as part of a larger frame house. In the 1970s the Braeutigam part of the building was demolished, and the rock rooms were restored to something like their 1850s appearance. In the 1980s an effort was made to reconstruct some of the buildings; on the north side are two officers quarters, built of adobe on the original foundations; across from this is a log barrack for enlisted men. While the reconstructions and the restored stone structure serve to give the modern visitor a sense of the size of the parade ground, the buildings themselves are rather speculative. The danger of attempting to reconstruct lost buildings with limited information becomes apparent when one looks closely at the log barrack. The reconstruction used the alternating rows of logs and a cemented layer of rocks, which a decade later became very characteristic of Germans in the Hill Country. However, using it in this context suggests either that the US Army relied on local and recently arrived German immigrants to build the fort *and* that they had already devised this system, which seems highly unlikely, or that this characteristic Hill Country type of log house was actually invented by army craftsmen. The inspector's report of August 1853 states only that the quarters are made of logs.

191 Grapetown Teacherage and School (Upper South Grape Creek School)

470 Grapetown Road, Grapetown
1888, circa 1910

The Grapetown School, originally known as Upper South Grape Creek School, is said to have been built of local stone between 1882 and 1884; the nearby one-room house for the schoolteacher was built in 1888, according to the date neatly carved into the lintel above the main door.

Given that the school has several early twentieth-century features—hipped roof, paired windows, and brick chimney—it may well be that the teacherage was the original school; a new one-room schoolhouse was built around 1910. The only other rural schools with hipped roofs are at Willow City (1905), Pilot Knob (circa 1916), White Oak (1920s), and Cherry Mountain (1926). The double-door entry of the newer structure was at the west, and the teacher's desk, blackboard, and cast-iron stove were directly opposite. Two sets of double windows were on the north and south walls. A well was dug, but the water tasted bad and was not used. In 1931 a cistern was installed at the southwest corner; the date may be seen on its concrete top of the pump.

192 Charles and Louise Enderlin House
3686 Grapetown Road, Grapetown
1872 and later

This rambling rural complex was originally two separate buildings that have been connected by a more recent owner. Charles Enderlin was a native of Karlsruhe, Baden, Germany. He lied about his age to fight in the Civil War—for the Union—and fought in the Battle of Fredericksburg (Virginia). He came to the Hill Country in 1867 and worked as a farmhand for Fritz Kneese and as a cowboy for Fritz

Kothmann in Llano. He married Louise Schaefer in 1870 and bought land along South Grape Creek in 1872. Charles and Louise had thirteen children. They started married life with a single room of log and rock; this expanded to include three rock rooms to the north, northeast, and east of the first room. The front door and a window faced south, where they placed a porch. This was unusual, as German Texans rarely placed their porches on the gable end. As their family grew, they added a separate story-and-a-half rock house that had a basement underneath. This strategy for expansion was not unlike that of the Kammlah family in town [see 46].

In 1892 Charles was one of the founders of the local post of the Grand Army of the Republic, an organization of veterans who had served in the Union army. In 1912 he and Louise bought the house of Emil and Bertha Riley on North Adams Street [162]. The next year they sold the ranch to their son, Charles Jr., and his wife Alwine, and moved into town. Eventually Charles was the last survivor of the charter members of the Fredericksburg GAR post. Charles died in 1931, and Alwine in 1934.

The Enderlin descendants sold the ranch to Harold and Libbie Grist in 1968. The Grists, working with local contractor Tyrus Cox, moved the front porch to the west and placed a large fireplace where the front door had been. They removed a partition to create one large room on the north side, with a large fireplace in the western wall. The stone house was connected to the main house by a sitting room, and a bathroom was added to the south, both of these being board-and-batten construction.

---

193 Luckenbach General Store
194 Luckenbach Dance Hall
412 Luckenbach Town Loop, Luckenbach
Circa 1910 (store), circa 1930 (dance hall)

The little community of Luckenbach was known as South Grape Creek for the first thirty years of its existence. Among the farmers who populated the area in the 1850s were three brothers, Albert Jacob, William, and August Luckenbach. Jacob and Justina were among the first settlers of Fredericksburg but moved twelve miles southeast of town in 1852. William and Catharine farmed, and William served as postmaster; youngest brother August and his wife Henriette farmed as well. During the Civil War Jacob joined a home guard organized by Engelbert Krauskopf, a unit organized by Confederates for Germans who refused to fight in the war. In 1862 August Luckenbach decided to join a group of German Texans who decided to flee to Mexico; they were caught near the border and gunned down in what became known as the Nueces Massacre.

South Grape Creek was renamed Luckenbach in 1886. In that decade Carl Albert Luckenbach, a son of Jacob Luckenbach and his wife Justina, married Wilhelmine Sophie "Minna" Engel, a native of New Braunfels in nearby Comal County. Her father, August W. Engel, was a schoolteacher, store owner, and preacher at Crane's Mill, seventeen miles northwest of New Braunfels. Minna's older brother, August Jr., also moved to Luckenbach, as did her brother William. Carl Albert and Minna had five children before her death in 1898. August Jr. had returned to Crane's Mill by 1900, but William put down roots in Luckenbach. He married Anna Schupp of Fredericksburg, and they had ten children.

The Engels family soon started a general store and later built a dance hall. The present general store had board-and-batten siding, a technique most popular in the Hill Country in the first decade of the twentieth century. The dance hall, known as Engel's Hall, was built at about the same time. It was rebuilt in the 1920s or 1930s, with a beautiful hardwood dance floor. Locals remember it as having the best dance floor in Gillespie County or even in Texas. The stage is at the north end, and on the south and west walls are large panels that are hinged at the top so that they can be pushed open from the inside. William and Anna's sons, Benno and Armin, allowed the Luckenbach School [204] to use the dance hall for the school closing, which was always a festive occasion, complete with a barbecue. The little rooms to the side of the stage were used by the students as dressing rooms. The performers for dances might play country and western music, oom-pah music (German polkas and waltzes), or a combination of the two. During dances young mothers would place their children on pallets in the room to the right of the stage and let them fall asleep to the music. There were a few tables around the edge of the dance floor. Benno and

---

Armin did not allow beer to be taken into the dance hall—that had to stay across the way at the saloon, which was also owned by the Engels.

Benno Engel sold the store and the dance hall—essentially, the whole town—to John Russell "Hondo" Crouch and his partners Kathy Morgan and Guich Koock in 1971. Crouch was a native of Hondo, Texas, west of San Antonio and had been a champion swimmer at the University of Texas at Austin, but had lived most of his life in nearby

Comfort. He declared himself the "Mayor" and the "Clown Prince" of the little town. Soon Hondo was joined by friends such as the singer-songwriter Jerry Jeff Walker, who so loved the atmosphere that he recorded an album there in August 1973, *Viva Terlingua*. The sessions culminated with a live recording concert in the dance hall on Saturday, August 18. Admission was $1. Hondo satirized the Texas White House [210], which was just a few miles to the northeast, and the 1976 Bicentennial celebration, which he rebranded as the Non-Buy Centennial Celebration. Sadly, Hondo died of a heart attack in September of 1976.

One year later Waylon Jennings recorded the song "Luckenbach, Texas (Back to the Basics of Love)," which became a national hit on country and pop radio stations. Though the songwriters, Chips Moman and Bobby Emmons, worked principally in Memphis and Nashville and had learned about Luckenbach from the Texas singer-songwriter Guy Clark, the song only enhanced the reputation of the town as a haven of simplicity and eccentricity. It was later the site of Willie Nelson's Fourth of July Picnic in 1995 and for the next four years. Live music can still be heard in the dance hall.

---

195 William and Anna Engel House
519 Luckenbach Town Loop, Luckenbach
Circa 1889–91, circa 1905–7, 1948

This house was built for William Engel and his family. William was brother-in-law of Carl Albert Luckenbach, who married William's sister Wilhelmina, known as Minna, in the 1880s. Family members recall that Minna ran the post office in the north front room of this house. William was in Luckenbach by 1890, and by 1900 he and his wife, the former Anna Schupp, had five children, all living at home. William described himself on the census of 1900 and 1910 as a merchant; by 1930 he was proprietor of a store and a cotton gin, the latter built down by the creek. Anna had passed away in 1929, and Sophia, the eldest daughter still at home, had taken over the housekeeping duties, and sons Benno, Arno, and Armin were working in the general store. William died in 1935; his sons Benno and Armin continued to operate the Luckenbach general store and the dance hall [193 and 194] until 1971.

The earliest part of the Engel house is on the north, a wooden frame covered with clapboards, originally one story, dating to the late 1880s or early 1890s. The floors were rough and the room was cold, which led to a remodeling in 1948, in which drywall, insulation, and new hardwood floors were installed. The southern part of the house, built of limestone, was added circa 1905–7. The new part of the house was one and a half stories tall, and the older part of the house had its roof raised to match. Windows on the front and south walls have heavy carved lintels but very thin sills. The front wall of the rock house has a door flanked by one window on each side, but the door is not centered; it is closer to the right window, indicating that entry is into the room on the right. The rock house has two rooms downstairs and up. The larger room downstairs was a parlor, and the smaller room on the south was the bedroom of William and Anna. The porch was originally two stories, with tawny brick piers and late Victorian gingerbread. At a later date the roof of the upper porch was removed, and metal awnings were installed on the front windows.

When the house was enlarged, a back porch was added, running nearly all the way across this elevation. At a later date this porch was enclosed. Originally, there were three back rooms, a kitchen in the center, a dining room, and another bedroom. In 1948 the kitchen was moved to the south. Kitchen cabinets and a kitchen sink were added for the first

time, and the woodburning stove was replaced by an electric range. The room was now heated by a butane stove at the southwest corner. Finally a bathroom was created at the north end of the former porch.

From the parking lot on the west side one can admire the limestone tank house, which originally had a wooden tank built atop it. The adjacent windmill from Aermotor Windmill Company of Chicago, which began producing windmills in 1888, pumped water into the tank. Beneath the tank house is a cellar, which provided a cool place for the storage of foodstuffs.

196 Luckenbach School
3566 Luckenbach Road, Luckenbach
1905, 1949

Education in Luckenbach began in a log cabin built around 1855. A limestone room was added to this structure in 1881. This building was replaced in 1905 by a new limestone structure. In 1949 another room was added, built of hollow tile. Restrooms and drinking fountains were not added until 1952. The earliest room of the adjacent teacherage is said to date to 1860; another room was added after 1907, using the stones from the earlier school building. There are now four rooms. As with all of Gillespie County's rural schoolhouses, this one was consolidated with the Fredericksburg school district in 1964.

197 Williams Creek (Albert) School
5501 South Ranch Road 1623, Albert
1897

The first school in this area was a log house situated beside Williams Creek. In 1897 the school was moved to its current site, and a one-room school was built with large blocks of limestone; the window sills and lintels were left rough-faced, which was quite fashionable at the time. The entry was on the west, and at the east end was a woodburning stove. One of the early teachers was Flora Eckert, who also taught at the Cherry Mountain School [170] and in the elementary grades at Fredericksburg's grammar school [151] while attending college in the summer. In 1920 and 1921 a twelve-year-old Lyndon Johnson attended this school. In 1922 a growing population of seventy students necessitated the hiring of a second teacher and led to the construction of another room across an open passageway, made with a wooden frame covered with tin. Typical of later schools, the new room had several windows clustered together. In 1950 the school merged with the Stonewall school.

198 Ferdinand and Augusta Mayer House
1364 Lower Albert Road, Albert
1899

The community of Albert was named for Carl Albert Luckenbach, son of the pioneering couple Jacob and Justina Luckenbach. The house of Ferdinand and Auguste Mayer is on the west side of the road and, seen from the north, appears to be a simple rock house with two rooms separated by a central passage; from the south, however, its L-shaped plan becomes clear. The lintels over the windows and doors are characteristic of Hill Country Victorian; the one over the front door announces, "F. MAYER. 1899." The stones are large and well fitted together. At each of the three gables there is a chimney; as there is a window under each of them, there are no fireplaces, and cast-iron stoves were used instead. The frame structure just to the west of the main house may well have been the original house. The Mayers had three children. In December 1907 the Mayer's eldest daughter, Emma, married Emil Beckmann, probably in the parlor of this house, and the couple moved to a log and rock house [207]; today it is on the premises of the Sauer-Beckmann Living History Farm, which is now part of LBJ State Park in nearby Stonewall. The Mayer house appears to be largely unaltered, though it has lost its original front porch with Victorian gingerbread decoration.

199 Lower South Grape Creek School
10273 East US 290
1901

Around 1871 a log structure was built near South Grape Creek to serve as a school. In 1889 it was renamed Lower South Grape Creek School to distinguish it from Upper Grape Creek School, now known as Grapetown School [191]. The first teacher was Theodore Hulsemann, who died in 1877. His probate inventory shows that he was not well remunerated. He owned a barn next to the school to house his old horse and a cast-iron cook stove, a clock, a daybed, a feather mattress, and a rocking chair. Associated with his teaching were a writing bureau (that is, a desk), three benches, an old flute, a telescope, a globe, and a German-English dictionary.

A new schoolhouse was built in 1901 a mile and a half north. Built of limestone, with a bell tower at one end and a chimney at the other, it closely resembled Williams Creek School [197] at Albert, built in 1897, albeit with one less window on each side. The entrance was on the east, and the teacher sat at the opposite end, against a windowless wall. As with Williams Creek School, it was later enlarged with another room at

the bell tower end, with embossed metal siding and a concrete floor; it did not, however, have an open passage between the two rooms, as was the case at Williams Creek. The school was closed in 1960, when it was consolidated with the Fredericksburg school district.

---

200 Heinrich and Johanne Lindig House
126 Elberta Street, Stonewall
1877, 1890, 1893

The house of Heinrich and Johanne Lindig, now the Stonewall Heritage Center, is another demonstration of the blending of Anglo-Texan and German Texan features. The two front rooms are separated by the Anglo-Southern dogtrot, with a ladder in the passage. Moreover, the logs are joined with V-notches, which Terry Jordan identified as a feature of upland south log houses that was taught to German immigrants to Texas. However, logs and rows of rock alternate in a German Texan manner not dreamt of in middle Tennessee. Like many other German pioneers, the Lindigs later added three rooms to the rear, built entirely of stone. This had the effect of closing off the dogtrot. Rather than placing the door flush with the front wall, as happened at the Klingelhoefer house in Fredericksburg [65], the Lindigs set it on the back wall, so that the two original rooms still open to the outside. The very tall side walls and large windows in the gables announced that this is a story-and-a-half house, with considerable room on the upper floor. When the rock rooms were added, two chimneys were built. From the outside these chimneys raise the expectation of open hearths inside, but they are both connected to flues.

Heinrich, Johanne, and their young children Carl and Wilhelmine came from Germany in 1868. Little Carl died later that year at age three. For several years Heinrich worked for his uncle, Conrad Bock, on his place at Cave Creek, where two other Lindig children, Auguste Marie and William Henry, were born in 1869 and 1871. Heinrich began to acquire horses and cattle in 1872–73, and around 1874 purchased 489 acres on the north side of the Pedernales River and built a one-room log house. This house had alternating rows of rocks and logs, which could not have been built before 1874, when Heinrich's cousin

---

Andreas built a kiln on the south side of the river [see 202]. The Lindigs also owned a horse and wagon and a dozen cattle. By 1880 they had five children, and four more were born in the next eight years. Around 1887–88 they built their new house with two more log rooms, but continued to use the original log house as the kitchen, as had so many German immigrants before them. The rock lean-to was in place by 1893.

Johanne died in 1921, and Heinrich in 1923. They are buried in the Stonewall Community Cemetery, one block south of US Highway 290. Their son Otto and his wife Amanda, who had married in 1904 and built a house nearby, inherited the part of the ranch that included his parents' house. Otto and Amanda had two sons, Reno, born in 1908, and Weigand, born in 1916. Weigand stayed on the land, and in 1966 he married Jean Black. In 1995, two years before she died, she donated the house to the Stonewall Heritage Society for relocation to this site. The log part was moved first, and the rock lean-to was moved in 2001, just before a tornado struck the area. The same tornado severely damaged the Weinheimer Dance Hall (built in 1935) in Stonewall, and flooring was salvaged to use in the back room of the Lindig house. The original 1874 log house, still on its original site, was damaged by the tornado, but Kay Huffman, a great-grand-daughter of Heinrich and Johanne, moved it to another property three miles north of Stonewall.

The appearance of the Lindig house prior to its move can be seen in the 1982 motion picture *Barbarosa*, starring Willie Nelson and Gary Busey. The house is first seen at 102:55, the very beginning of scene 16. It was used to portray a German Texan farmstead, although for interior scenes the crew built a more rustic open hearth fireplace rather than a more historically accurate cast-iron stove.

---

201 Heinrich and Anna Jacoby House
946 Ranch Road 1, Stonewall
1891

This house is an excellent example of how German Texan ways of building houses persisted into the last decade of the nineteenth century. Heinrich Jacoby (sometimes spelled Jacobi) was a native of Prussia who came with his family to Gillespie County in the first wave of immigrants. In the 1850 census his father, Nicolaus, forty-three, gave his occupation as laborer; ten years later he stated that he was a farmer. In 1868 Heinrich, then twenty-two, married Anna Otte, the nineteen-year-old daughter of a farm family from Hanover. They bought thirty-five acres in Stonewall in 1870, on which they lived. In 1880 they had four children, and the household also included a live-in servant, fourteen-year-old Clara Wertheim, who was born in Louisiana to German parents. On October 1, 1883, Heinrich and Anna bought another forty acres, a tract along the Pedernales River, from E. P. Hodges for $350. In the new location they built a small frame house with a porch on the north side facing the river. Around 1887 they sold their original thirty-five acres and began to build the front part of this house, which was completed by 1890.

The house was built of large blocks of limestone, with two rooms downstairs and one room upstairs. The house faced east with a two-story porch, which at various times has had a staircase to the upper floor. Underneath the staircase was a closet, precious storage space that was hard to come by in a house with eighteen-inch-thick limestone walls. The second story of the porch has a low roof, so low as to have limited head room and to obscure light into the two east-facing windows. The Victorian balusters were of a type popular in

Fredericksburg in the 1890s. Each room was heated by a cast-iron stove; flues tied into chimneys on the south and north walls. Both downstairs rooms had a front door, indicating that there was no central passage; another late example of a house with this feature is the Wunderlich rock house [117]. The Jacoby house has been attributed to Peter Nebgen, who in the mid-1890s built the Wilhelm and Wilhelmine Meier house, better known as the Texas White House [210].

Henry lived until 1919, and Anna until 1922. They are both buried in the Stonewall Community Cemetery. The Jacoby heirs sold the house to Walter and Ellie Pehl in 1950. They removed the staircase from the east porch and created an internal staircase in the north rock rooms. Their daughter Jeanette inherited the house from them, and she and her husband, Hubert Klein, remodeled the house around 1993. The interior staircase was removed, and a new staircase was built on the front porch. The upper-level balustrade was restored based on an early photograph. The western, one-story part of the house was enlarged to the north and south, providing an updated kitchen and bathroom while retaining the profile of the original wing. It is used it as a residence and as a bed-and-breakfast.

The road from Austin to Fredericksburg, designated as US

Highway 290 when it was completed in September 1924, originally ran along the Pedernales and thus through Stonewall. Gradually vehicular traffic (and speed) increased, and in 1957 it was decided to build a new State Highway 290 on the southern side of the settlement. As a result, most passersby see a side of Stonewall that postdates 1957 rather than the older structures. The old 290 was renamed the Old Austin Highway, but after Lyndon B. Johnson was elected president, it became Ranch Road 1.

202 Trinity Lutheran Church
4270 Ranch Road 1, Stonewall
1928

Andreas Lindig built a lime kiln in 1874 just south of the present church building, in what is now a small park. It was the first lime

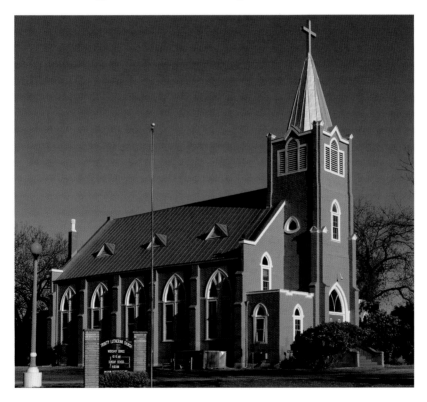

kiln in the eastern part of the county, though not as old as that of Julius Splittgerber in Fredericksburg. Christian Lindig, one of the sons of Andreas Lindig, sold the land to the Evangelical Lutheran congregation, which was established here in 1902. A large but simple frame building was erected two years later. Its original cornerstone rests beside the current church, though the original 1904 church was situated in the current location of the stone-veneered parsonage. Though now seemingly withdrawn from the busyness of Highway 290, from 1923 to 1957 this church was on the original Austin-to-Fredericksburg highway, now renamed Ranch Road 1.

The present structure was built in 1928. It is a catalogue of Gothic Revival features, especially the pointed arches in doors and windows and buttresses. It even had a chancel at the east end, a high-church feature that would have horrified earlier generations of Lutherans. Its most distinctive feature, however, is the pressed metal siding that covers its frame of wood, not unlike St. Paul's Lutheran Church at Cave Creek [189], which was remodeled in 1928–29. Inside Trinity Lutheran the floor slopes downward toward the altar and pulpit, allowing for good sight lines from the back. Trinity Cemetery, nearby on the west, was opened in 1904. Given that it opened at such a late date, it is not surprising that red granite and gray granite grave markers predominate. Among those buried here are Christian and Auguste Lindig, who sold the land to the congregation in the first place, Friedrich and Auguste Mayer, who lived nearby [see 198], and their daughter Emma and her husband Emil Beckmann, the farming couple whose house is now the centerpiece of the Sauer-Beckmann Living History Farm [207].

---

203 Emery and Mattie Hodges House
5530 Ranch Road 1, Stonewall
1903, 1907

After the Civil War families from the American South began to move into Gillespie County, especially the area around Stonewall, which had previously been a German community. William T. Hodges, an Alabama native who lived in neighboring Blanco County by the 1880s, owned

1,044 acres in Gillespie County by 1888 but did not build this house. Hodges and his wife Jemima had sold almost all of their land by 1897, but saved 100 acres that they gave to their son, David Emery Hodges. This was about the time of Emery's marriage to Martha Naomi Greer, known as Mattie, who had been born in Burnet County to the northeast. The property, which had been valued at $300 in 1896 and 1897, was soon valued at $350, suggesting the erection of a small log or frame house. The value shot up to $1,000 in 1903, when the front section of the present house was completed; the addition of the one-story wing in 1907 raised the value to $1500.

The front part of the house is made of large limestone blocks, said to have been quarried by Christian Lindig [see 202]. It has two stories above a basement, with a hipped roof. The front porch is one story across the entire front, with a second-story porch only on the center bay; this relates to the form of much more stylish versions of the Colonial Revival in other areas of Texas, though the upper banisters are gingerbread Gothic. The house was built with a central passage and two large rooms, though the stair was on the back porch. German Texans had little love of central passages, apparently considering them a waste of space. The house also had fireplaces instead of the cast-iron stoves beloved by German Texans. The west front room was a parlor, and the right front room was Emery and Mattie's bedroom. Their sons, Ernest, Alton, and Hiram, slept upstairs in one large room. The boys attended the Junction School [208] across the Pedernales, and Ernest was later interviewed about its original configuration when the school was being restored in 1972.

The rear wing of the Hodges house was added just a few years later. It, too, had a hipped roof but was built of concrete blocks, which were very

popular in Gillespie County in the first quarter of the twentieth century. Directly behind the living room was the dining room, and behind this was the kitchen. The porch was extended to create an L-shape on the east side of the new wing. A shed addition on the west side, also of concrete blocks, contained a pantry and a small porch, which led into the kitchen. Originally there were no bathrooms, but later one was placed in a space carved out of the central passage on the first floor. Another change was dividing the second floor into three rooms, with two large closets and a small bathroom worked in between.

Emery and Mattie lived the rest of their lives in this house; their sons farmed nearby. Emery died in 1949, but Mattie lived until 1971, which allowed her to witness the creation of the LBJ State Park and the LBJ National Historical Park. Her house and property were part of 399 acres that were acquired for the state park in 1965, more than doubling the original 245 acres. Though within the park boundaries, the house is not open to the public, as it now provides housing for the park superintendent.

---

204 Caspar and Dorothea Danz House
LBJ State Park, Stonewall
Circa 1861

This house blends Anglo-Southern and German customs: it is a double-pen log house with a dogtrot in between, about as Anglo-Southern as you could get, but the walls alternated logs with rows of rock, about as Hill Country German as you could get. The doors in both rooms open onto the dogtrot. The dichotomies continue on the inside: the west room has a fairly typical Anglo hearth, while the east room has a raised hearth, found in Fredericksburg homes such as the Kammlah House [46] and the Tatsch house [132].

Casper Danz, an early settler of Fredericksburg, and his second wife, Dorothea, purchased land along the Pedernales in 1860 and built a house soon thereafter. By 1880 Caspar and Dorothea were living in this house with nine children—six boys and three girls—which must have been somewhat crowded. Some additional space may have been utilized in a second dogtrot building a few yards to the north, but this

seems to have been largely a storage building, as there are no fireplaces
and no windows, only a small hatch in each end wall. There is no floor
between the door sills in the dogtrot, though the rooms themselves are
raised and reached by limestone steps. The raised floor allowed for a
shallow basement under the east room, which was accessed by a hatch
covering steps down. Caspar and Dorothea's son Arthur Danz married
Anna Maria Weinheimer, and they built a house [111] of Basse blocks
with Victorian trim just outside of Fredericksburg circa 1913–14. His
parents' house and outbuilding remain on their original site and are
now part of LBJ State Park, located west of the Visitor Center. The
most recent restoration was completed in 2010.

205 Heinrich Christian and Wilhelmina Behrens House
LBJ State Park, Stonewall
1872, 1972

At the eastern end of the Visitor Center at LBJ State Park is a strange
blend of pioneer rustic and suburban ranch house. Heinrich Christian and Wilhelmina Behrens were living on this site by the early
1870s. The limestone foundations of their one-room log house are

preserved at the northeast corner of the complex. A new house was built around 1872; like the Danz log houses [204], this house blended the Anglo-Southern dogtrot, with the German Texan technique of alternating logs with a row of rocks. One room was the kitchen, the other a parlor and bedroom, which the Germans called a *stube*. Neither room had a fireplace, as German Texans preferred cast-iron stoves for heating rooms and for cooking. By 1880 Heinrich and Wilhelmina were living in these two rooms with four children. When the Visitor Center was built in 1970, incorporating local limestone but with a more modern look, the two rooms and the dogtrot were preserved, given a broad wrap-around porch unlike anything in the Hill Country, and connected to the other buildings with a covered porch. While the impulse to preserve was praiseworthy, the result is rather jarring.

206 Friedrich and Christine Sauer House
LBJ State Park, Stonewall
Circa 1869 and after

This house puts the "Sauer" in the Sauer-Beckmann Living History Farm. It is a great example of a pioneering German Texan log and rock house being given multiple rock additions. Johann Friedrich Sauer

married Christine Strackbein in 1865, and they lived in Fredericksburg for the first four years of their marriage. In 1869 they moved
to the Pedernales settlement and built a one-room house using the
typical German Texan method of alternating a log with a row of rocks
mortared in place. This method was at once more airtight and more
permanent. Their fourth child was born that year, five more had come
along by 1880, and one more was born after that. The first room had
front and back doors and a window on the west.

Friedrich and Christine added three limestone rooms over time.
The second room, a kitchen with a cast-iron stove, had its own front
door, with a window on the front and another on the west side; its
porch projects several feet forward from the earlier porch. The two
back rooms have one small casement window apiece; as a result, they
are rather dark. This may not have made a pleasant habitation, but it
was a nice cool place for food storage. Only the northwest room has a
fireplace, and it was one of the later rooms.

The Sauers also built a number of support structures. A tank house
made of limestone stands in front of the house; above its rock first
floor is a large wooden cistern to hold rainwater. Behind the house is
another limestone building, this one nearly two stories tall. It is said
to have been a smokehouse, though this seems unlikely given the half
story above. Just to the west of this structure is a hen house and yard
for the chickens. And at some point another rock room was built to the

east of the house: this was a new kitchen with better ventilation, having doors on the south and east and windows on the north and west.

In 1887 the family bought land in Doss, at the opposite end of the county, and their sons settled there. In 1900 the Sauers sold the farm to Herman Beckmann and joined their sons in Doss, building a two-room frame house and living there the rest of their lives. One of their daughters, Auguste Sauer, married Christian Lindig, and stayed in the area; she was a midwife at the birth of the son of Sam Ealy Johnson and Rebekah Baines Johnson, Lyndon.

207 Emil and Emma Beckmann House
LBJ State Park, Stonewall
Circa 1915

Emil and Emma Beckmann were a young farming couple, and this was their dream house. Herman Beckmann bought the Sauer place [206] for his sons, Emil and Otto, in 1900. It is said that Emil occupied the old house, and Otto the newer rock kitchen to the east. Emil eventually was able to buy his brother's share of the farm. In 1907 Emil married Emma Mayer, daughter of Friedrich and Auguste Mayer, who had

built a Victorian rock house a decade before [198]. Emil and Emma
made their home on Emil's farm. A year of high prices for cotton in
1915 allowed them to build a new Victorian house, a frame addition
on the south side of the rock kitchen, and a new barn to the southwest.
The new house was covered with pressed tin siding and had attractive
Victorian ornament on the front and back porches and on the ridge of
the roof.

Its L-shaped plan contained three rooms and a central hallway.
From the front porch one could enter the hall or go into Emil and
Emma's bedroom to the left. There had been virtually no central halls
in the first twenty-five years of settlement in Gillespie County, apparently having been considered a profligate waste of space. They were
still not that common in 1915; Emma and Emil may have seen the idea
in a magazine or a book. The hall opened into a parlor on the east and
into the children's bedroom on the west. A door on the west wall of the
children's bedroom led onto a breezeway and then into the kitchen.
This breezeway was perhaps still called a dogtrot in 1915, but perhaps
not. The three rooms in the main house were all heated by cast-iron
stoves. All doors in the house had transoms above to insure some circulation of air even when the doors were closed.

Both Emil and Emma lived into their seventies. He died in 1951,
she in 1961, and they are buried together in Trinity Lutheran Cemetery
[see 202]. Their daughter Emma sold the farm to the State of Texas
in 1966, and the Sauer-Beckmann Living History Farm was opened in
1975.

---

208 Junction School
US 290, LBJ National Park (LBJ Ranch District), Stonewall
1910

There was a school in this vicinity from 1881; the present one-room
schoolhouse was opened November 21, 1910, and has been restored to
its early appearance. The building is wood-framed but with embossed
metal siding pressed into the shape of stonework. There were doors at
the south and north; usually the teacher's desk was situated in front
of the north door. The interior was heated by a wood-burning stove

in the center of the room. This one-room school served generations
of students from 1910 to 1947, when it was consolidated with the
Stonewall school district. Its most famous student, however, was an
early enrollee: four-year old Lyndon Johnson, who attended school
here for several months in 1912. His family moved to Johnson City the
next year. On April 11, 1965, President Johnson returned to the school
to sign the Elementary and Secondary Education Act, one of the key
features of his Great Society agenda. At his side was his first teacher,
Katie Deadrich. The building, which remains on its original site, was
purchased by the National Park Service in 1972 to become part of the
LBJ National Park. It was restored in the 1980s: later partitions and
an indoor bathroom were removed, returning it to its original form as
a school with one room.

209 Reconstructed LBJ Birthplace
US 290, LBJ National Park (LBJ Ranch District), Stonewall
1964

In 1964 President Lyndon B. Johnson hired Austin architect J. Roy
White, who had long been in charge of architectural changes at the
LBJ Ranch, to reconstruct his birthplace, which had stood just to the

Circa 1893–97. LBJ Library, Johnson Family Collection, B10144.

west of the main house before being demolished in the 1940s. White was able to use an 1897 photograph showing the family of Sam Ealy Johnson Sr. standing in front of the house as well as surviving foundations for chimneys. The house, built in 1889, had a classic Anglo-Texan floor plan: a dogtrot separated the two front rooms, and behind on the left was a combination dining room and kitchen. The exterior walls were covered with the board-and-batten technique—that is, tall vertical boards butted against one another, with the joint covered by thin strips of wood called battens. Very soon after construction, if not originally, the west end of the front porch was enclosed to make another room. Sam Ealy Johnson Jr. brought his new bride, Rebekah Baines, to live in the house in 1907. The future president was born in the west parlor the next year. He (and later his two sisters) slept in the nursery, the room enclosed from the front porch, until the family moved to Johnson City in 1913. From 1964 to 1966 the reconstructed cottage was used as a guest cottage for overflow guests at the main ranch house, known as the Texas White House. For that reason the house was given electricity and modern plumbing, but not central air or heat.

210 LBJ Ranch House (Texas White House)
US 290, LBJ National Park (LBJ Ranch District), Stonewall
Circa 1894, 1912, 1952, 1956, 1961, 1967–68

This ranch house, which began in great simplicity, served as the Texas home of US senator Lyndon Baines Johnson and his wife, Lady Bird Johnson, and then as the Texas White House. It was both a peaceful haven for LBJ and his family and a facility where he could entertain foreign leaders and other dignitaries in a colorful Texas style.

German immigrants Wilhelm and Wilhelmina Meier bought the land in 1882, and that fall they built a one-room log house. Sometime between 1892 and 1896 they contracted for a rock house to be built by Peter Nebgen, John Siebel, and Max Schoenewolf. Nebgen was a stonemason who built a number of other rock houses in the Stonewall area; Siebel was a carpenter who was working in San Antonio at the time of the 1880 census. The house originally faced west, with two rooms in front—a parlor and a kitchen—and another behind. Two bedrooms were on the upper floor. The two gables on the front façade allowed more headroom in the upstairs rooms and gave a hint of the Victorian style, which was just now finding its way into vernacular houses of the Hill Country.

Wilhelmina Meier died in 1908, and the next year Wilhelm sold the house to Clarence Martin, an attorney and later a judge, and his wife,

Frank. Clarence and Frank were also uncle and aunt to Lyndon B. Johnson, who was born on the family farm nearby. The Martins enlarged the house in 1912 with a frame addition to the east. Directly east of the rock house they built a room with a staircase, known by the Johnsons as the den, behind which was the kitchen. To the east of the den, two rooms served as music room and parlor. These rooms projected parallel to the rock house, though it was a full two stories and thus taller. The center rooms were set back, and there was a two-story porch in front of it, supported by two columns. The most notable change to the older part of the house was the creation of a raised hearth in the living room; this and other stonework was done by Lawrence Klein Sr., a son-in-law of original stonemason, Peter Nebgen.

Newlyweds Lyndon and Lady Bird Johnson visited his Uncle Clarence and Aunt Frank in 1934. However, it was not until 1951 that they purchased the ranch, which consisted of 243 acres. By then LBJ had become a member of that very exclusive club known as the United States Senate and felt the need to acquire an estate comparable to those of his fellow senators. Uncle Clarence had passed in 1936, and though Aunt Frank continued to live there, the ranch house slowly began to deteriorate. When Aunt Frank moved to Stonewall, LBJ and Lady Bird entrusted the renovation of the house to their friend Max Brooks, of the Austin architectural firm Kuehne, Brooks and Barr. Brooks assigned the design work to J. Roy White, who went on to be responsible for virtually all of the design changes made to the property in LBJ's lifetime.

The renovation was carried out in 1952, and every room was redone to some degree or another. The contractor was Marcus Burg, a Stonewall builder; his construction foreman was Lawrence Klein Jr., whose father and grandfather had also worked on the house. The kitchen and bathrooms were completely modernized, although Lady Bird later regretted the removal of the old claw-footed tub and pedestal sinks. The music room became the master bedroom, and the parlor behind it a guest bedroom for Rebekah Baines Johnson, LBJ's mother. In the den the fireplace in the west wall was rebuilt and surrounded with panels of knotty pine. Three televisions were placed against the south wall of the living room, so that LBJ could see all

Photo by Robert Knudson, June 16, 1968. LBJ Library, White House Photo Office Collection, D599–11A.

three network news programs from his place at the north end of the dining room table. In 1953 they threw their first barbecue, the principal form of entertainment at the ranch.

After LBJ had a major heart attack in 1955, a pool and cabana were built to provide LBJ with a pleasant means of exercise. In addition, an office was built on the west side of the house. It had its own porch facing south; the south and north walls had wooden siding, and the west wall was of solid limestone, tying in with the older part of the house. Inside, the center of this wall had a floor-to-ceiling limestone fireplace, flanked by paneled walls of knotty pine with storage closets behind. LBJ's desk was in the northeast corner, facing toward the fireplace, the desks of two secretaries, and a television that was built in above the north closet.

While LBJ was vice president, the guest bedrooms upstairs were improved and given separate bathrooms in response to the increased number of foreign dignitaries who were entertained at the ranch. In 1967 and 1968 additional changes were made in anticipation of the family returning to the ranch full-time after LBJ completed his term in office. The master bedroom became an enlarged dressing room and bathroom for LBJ, and similar accommodations for Lady Bird were built in the room to the north; bedrooms for LBJ and Lady Bird were built in a one-story addition to the east. Lady Bird's had ample bookshelves, while LBJ's had another three televisions and direct access to the cabana and pool.

The Johnsons donated the ranch, the reconstructed birthplace, and the boyhood home in Johnson City to the people of the United States in 1969; in December of that year Congress authorized the creation of the Lyndon B. Johnson National Historic Site. After he left the White House, LBJ was able to enjoy life on the ranch for only a few years; he died in 1973. Lady Bird continued to live there until her death in 2007. They are buried side by side in the well-kept family cemetery on the grounds. Their gravestones are of the Texas red granite that is so characteristic of the Hill Country. Since then, the National Park Service has worked to restore the house to the period of LBJ's residence, opening first the public rooms and LBJ's office, and more recently the bedroom suites of the president and first lady. In addition to the LBJ Ranch District near Stonewall, the LBJ National Historical Park also include the Johnson City District in Blanco County, which includes LBJ's boyhood home.

Acknowledgments

Any book is a long journey. This particular trip was part of a longer work that will be published shortly.

I have accumulated debts of gratitude from many folks in Fredericksburg and farther afield.

I very much appreciate the openness and helpfulness of the staff of the Pioneer Museum Complex of the Gillespie County Historical Society. My thanks go to Paul Camfield, Carol Schreider, Stephen Vollmer, and Dr. James Lindley, who all served as director of the organization. Thanks as well to Evelyn Weinheimer, the knowledgeable photo archivist.

When I was a consultant on an interpretive plan for the Kammlah house, I enjoyed working with Laurie Zapalac; while that project was under way, a parallel historic structures report was being prepared by Volz and Associates of Austin (now Volz, O'Connell, Hutson): John Volz, Candace Volz, and Tere O'Connell.

Also of great assistance were staff members of other local museums and historic sites, especially Joe Cavanaugh, Richard Koone, and Reagan Grau at the National Museum of the Pacific War, Bernice Weinheimer of the Stonewall Heritage Center, Iris Neffendorf, park superintendent of the LBJ State Park and Historic Site, and Stephanie Loden, curator at the Texas Parks and Wildlife Department headquarters in Austin.

I very much appreciate the dedication of the staff and the depth of the collection at the Texas Collection at Baylor University, my home away from home. I am indebted as well to the Briscoe Center for American History and the Alexander Architectural Archive at the University of Texas at Austin, my former home away from home.

The Pioneer Memorial Library in Fredericksburg has a friendly and efficient staff and a wonderful Texas Room, a little oasis of cool and calm in a sometimes hot and hectic tourist town. The staff at the Institute of Texan Cultures in San Antonio and the LBJ Library in Austin have been very helpful in providing historic illustrations.

Owing to the large number of historic houses that have been converted into bed-and-breakfast operations, I have had a chance to stay in quite a few historic homes. Thanks to First Class Bed and Breakfast, Main Street Bed and Breakfast, Absolute Charm Bed and Breakfast, and especially Gastehaus Schmidt.

Individual owners have also been kind enough to show me their properties: Bernice and Vernon Fluett of Clear Springs Log Cabin, Paul Hamilton of Kuenemann House, Barbara Heinen of the Keidel Inn, Jon Morse of A Place in Time, Linda Nevels of Commander's Place, and Claude Saunders of Magnolia House, all in Fredericksburg, and Jeanette Pehl Klein of Heimplatz am Fluss in Stonewall.

Realtors have also been kind enough to show me buildings that are on the market. Among these are Keith Kramer, who took me through the Weirich house on Main Street, and Dennis Kusenberger, who showed me the Fisher house and the Jung house.

The owners of homes and buildings have also been exceedingly kind. I must mention Beverlyn Allen, Bill Borron (and his late wife Jan), Liz Brookshire, Phyllis Ann Keidel Burkett, Dale and Vicky Dittmar, Jean and Beverly Dubose, Mike Gold, Cris Graham, Dr. Fred Grimes, Lindy Haley, Sharon Hanna, John Hill, John Hollimon, Penny Perry Hughes, Sharon Joseph, Linda Langerhans, Atlee Lochte, F. C. Lochte, the late Philip O'B. Montgomery III, Jordan Muraglia, Don Nagel, David Sawtelle, Tina Shilkun, and Jody and Mike Tomforde. David Ross and Brent Waldoch provided access to several of the historic properties owned by Dian Stai, which are always a treat to visit.

I have also benefited from conversations and emails with Janine Briley, Bernadine Dittmar, Benno Engel Jr., Joe Kammlah, Susan Koch, Ora Ann Knopp, Megan MacDaniel, Amanda Ochse, and Della Pohler.

Fredericksburg historian Glen Treibs kindly reviewed the manuscript and thereby saved me from a number of errors. Fredericksburg architect John Klein has been helpful throughout the process, but especially so at the end by producing measured floor plans of several buildings. Helen "Shatzie" Crouch has welcomed me into her home and her place of business and shared her knowledge of Gillespie County history and decorative arts.

Among my Fredericksburg friends Karen Haschke truly stands out. I met her ten years ago, as I started my larger project on German Texan material culture, and she has opened the doors of the Klingelhoefer house to me and to my students many times over the years, and also opened the door to many another historic building by introducing me to the owners.

I have also had assistance from scholars who are somewhat farther afield, particularly Richard Cleary of the University of Texas at Austin and Donald Linebaugh of the University of Maryland at College Park. Both Richard and Don have read through various chapters of both manuscripts, and Don went the extra mile by creating a measured drawing of the Klingelhoefer floor plan. Their support and help are much appreciated.

The crew at Texas A&M University Press has been extremely supportive throughout this process. I trust that their enthusiasm and support for this project has been justified by the results.

My wife Kim has shared many a Schnitzelburger with me and has wandered through many an old house and has listened to my rambling stories about people long dead and buildings long lost. My thanks to her for her patience and her love.

Sources

Sources for the historical information used in the text are listed, by site, on the following pages. Frequently cited sources have been shortened, as indicated below:

Biggers, *German Pioneers*	Don H. Biggers. *German Pioneers in Texas.* Fredericksburg: Fredericksburg Publishing Co., 1925
Gerlach, *Commemorative Volume*	Henry Gerlach. *Commemorative Volume for the 75th Year Jubilee of St. Mary's Parish of Fredericksburg, Texas.* Translated by Stephen E. Montgomery Jr. Fredericksburg: Stephen E. Montgomery Jr., 1995. Originally published as *Fest Schrift zum 75 jährigen Jubiläum der St. Marien Gemeinde zu Friedrichsburg, Texas* (San Antonio: Standard Printing Co., 1921).
HABS	Historic American Buildings Survey. Library of Congress Prints and Photographs Division, Washington, DC; available at http://www.loc.gov/pictures/collection/hh/.
Jordan, *Texas Graveyards*	Terry Jordan. *Texas Graveyards: A Cultural Legacy.* Austin: University of Texas Press, 1982.
Kirchen-Buch	*Kirchen-Buch: Church Record Book of the Vereins-Kirche, 1849–1870.* Translated by Ella A. Gold. Fredericksburg: Gillespie County Historical Society, 1986.
Kowert, *Historic Homes*	Elise Kowert. *Historic Homes in and around Fredericksburg.* Rev. ed. Fredericksburg: Fredericksburg Publishing Co., 1990.
Kowert, *Old Homes*	Elise Kowert. *Old Homes and Buildings of Fredericksburg.* Fredericksburg: Fredericksburg Publishing Co., 1977.
Limestone and Log	J. Roy White and Joe B. Frantz. *Limestone and Log: A Hill Country Sketchbook.* Austin: Encino Press, 1968.
Mechanics Lien Record	Gillespie County Mechanics Lien Record, Gillespie County Clerk, Gillespie County Courthouse.

Penniger, *Fredericks-burg*	Robert Penniger. *Fredericksburg, Texas—The First Fifty Years: A Translation of Penniger's Fiftieth Anniversary Festival Edition.* Translated by Charles L. Wisseman Sr. Fredericksburg: Fredericksburg Publishing Co., 1971. Originally published as *Fest-ausgabe zum 50-jährigen Jubiläum der Gründung der Stadt Friedrichsburg* (Fredericksburg, 1896).
Pioneers I	Gillespie County Historical Society. *Pioneers in God's Hills: A History of Fredericksburg and Gillespie County—People and Events.* Austin: Von Boeckmann-Jones, 1960.
Pioneers II	Gillespie County Historical Society. *Pioneers in God's Hills, Volume Two: A History of Fredericksburg and Gillespie County—People and Events.* Fredericksburg: Gillespie County Historical Society, 1974.
Property Tax Records	Gillespie County Property Tax Rolls, 1848–1910. Microfilm reels: 108601 (1848–92), 108602 (1892–1901), and 108603 (1901–10). Texas State Library and Archives, Austin.
Sanborn	Sanborn Fire Insurance Maps for Fredericksburg, Texas. June 1896, February 1902, July 1910, September 1915, October 1924, and January 1938. Sanborn Fire Insurance Map Collection, Briscoe Center for American History, University of Texas at Austin.
School Histories	Gillespie County Program Building Committee, *Gillespie County School Histories.* Fredericksburg: Dietel & Son Printing, 1983.
US Census	US Census, Gillespie County, Texas. 1850–1940.
UT-AAA	Alexander Architectural Archive, University of Texas Libraries. University of Texas at Austin.
UTSA-ITC	Institute of Texan Cultures, University of Texas at San Antonio.

Part 1. All around the Marktplatz and Courthouse Square

1 VEREINS-KIRCHE REPLICA

Penniger, *Fredericksburg*, 59–60, 86. Marvin Eickenroht, "The Kaffee-Kirche at Fredericksburg, Texas, 1846," *Journal of the Society of Architectural Historians* 25, no. 1 (March 1966): 60–63. Kowert, *Old Homes*, 132–35.

2 PIONEER MEMORIAL LIBRARY

Penniger, *Fredericksburg*, 55, 90. Sanborn, 1915, sheet 3. Kowert, *Old Homes*, 135–37. "1892 and 1939 Gillespie County Courthouses, Fredericksburg, Texas," report prepared by Wagner and Klein, Inc., July 3, 2000; copy courtesy of Sharon Joseph.

3 AND 4 GILLESPIE COUNTY COURTHOUSE; OLD UNITED STATES POST OFFICE

Pioneers II, 135–37 (Stein). "1892 and 1939 Gillespie County Courthouses, Fredericksburg, Texas," report prepared by Wagner and Klein, Inc., July 3, 2000; copy courtesy of Sharon Joseph. HABS, "First Courthouse, Main & Crockett Streets, Fredericksburg, Gillespie County, TX."

5 JOHANNES AND JULIANE RUEGNER HOUSE

US Census, 1870. Property Tax Records, 1853–74. *Kirchen-Buch*, 44. Sanborn, 1915, sheet 6. Kowert, *Old Homes*, 1–2.

6 NAGEL BROTHERS MONUMENTAL WORKS

Sanborn, 1915, sheet 6.

7 GILLESPIE COUNTY JAIL

Sanborn, 1915, sheet 6. Penniger, *Fredericksburg*, 51–55. Kowert, *Old Homes*, 12–14.

8 ADOLPH AND BERTHA PFEIL HOUSE

US Census, 1880. Sanborn, 1915, sheet 6. HABS, "Pfeil House, 125 West San Antonio Street, Fredericksburg, Gillespie County, TX." Kowert, *Old Homes*, 152–54. Personal communication, Sharon Joseph, May 28, 2014.

9 FRIEDRICH AND CAROLINE WEIHMILLER HOUSE

US Census, 1860, 1870, 1880, 1900, 1910, 1920, 1930. Sanborn, July 1910, sheet 3. Historic photograph by David R. Williams, in David Reicherd Williams (1890–1962) Photographs, Negatives, and Archival Records, UT-AAA. David R. Williams, "Toward a Southwestern Architecture," *Southwest Review* 16 (April 1931): 301–13. Kowert, *Old Homes*, 54–56. *Limestone and Log*, 66–68. John J. Leffler, "A Hill Country Icon: The Life and Legend of the Nimitz Hotel, Fredericksburg, Texas," study submitted to the Texas Parks and Wildlife Department, July 2005, 20–21.

10 FELIX AND CHRISTINE VAN DER STUCKEN HOUSE

Sanborn, 1896, sheet 2; 1902, sheet 2. Kowert, *Old Homes*, 98–99.

11 ALFRED AND CORNELIA VAN DER STUCKEN HOUSE

US Census, 1910. Kowert, *Historic Homes*, 161–65.

12 F. W. ARHELGER WHEELWRIGHT SHOP

Sanborn, 1896, sheet 2; 1902, sheet 2. Kowert, *Historic Homes*, 68–71.

13 AUGUST AND SEDONIE SEMBRITZKY HOUSE

August and Sedonie Sembritzky to F. Stein, January 7, 1905, Mechanics Lien Record, vol. 1, 7–8. Sanborn, 1910, sheet 2; 1915, sheet 2.

Part 2. Main Street, East of the Marktplatz and Courthouse Square

14 MAIER BUILDING

Kowert, *Old Homes*, 114–16. Sanborn, 1896, sheet 2; 1902, sheet 2; 1910, sheet 2; 1915, sheet 2. On Bridgman, see *The American Contractor*, vol. 31 (August 13, 1910): 51.

15 FREDERICKSBURG NATIONAL BANK

Pioneers II, 135–37 (Stein).

16 BANK OF FREDERICKSBURG

Kowert, *Old Homes*, 109–11. *San Antonio Daily Express*, April 18, 1898; Sanborn, 1902, sheet 2; 1910, sheet 2; 1915, sheet 2.

17 CENTRAL DRUG STORE

Kowert, *Historic Homes*, 118–21. Mechanics Lien Record, vol. 1, 5–7. Sanborn, 1902, sheet 2; 1910, sheet 2; 1915, sheet 2.

18 LOUIS PRIESS STORE AND HOUSE

Kowert, *Historic Homes*, 34–37.

19 SCHANDUA BUILDING

Kowert, *Historic Homes*, 44–46. Sanborn, 1910, sheet 2; 1915, sheet 2.

20 LOUIS KOTT BUILDING

Pioneers II, 64–66.

21 WHITE ELEPHANT SALOON

Kowert, *Old Homes*, 106–8. *Pioneers* II, 108–10.

22 BASSE-HENKE HOUSE

Kowert, *Old Homes*, 30–31. Sanborn, 1896, sheet 2; 1902, sheet 2; 1910, sheet 2; 1915, sheet 2.

23 KEIDEL DRUG STORE

Kowert, *Old Homes*, 104–5. Sanborn, 1910, sheet 2.

24 ALBERT AND MATHILDE KEIDEL HOUSE

Kowert, *Old Homes*, 104–5. *Pioneers* I, 79–81. Sanborn, 1896, sheet 2; 1902, sheet 2; 1915, sheet 2.

25 ADOLF LUNGKWITZ SHOP AND HOUSE

Kowert, *Old Homes*, 102–3. Sanborn, 1896, sheet 2; 1902, sheet 2; 1910, sheet 2; 1915, sheet 2.

26 CHARLES PRIESS STORE AND HOUSE

Kowert, *Old Homes*, 99–101. "Keidel Hospital Stands as Tribute to Pioneers," *Fredericksburg Standard Centennial Edition*, May 1, 1946, 4. Sanborn, 1896, sheet 2; 1902, sheet 2; 1910, sheet 2; 1915, sheet 2.

27 AND 28 OTTO KOLMEIER STORE; OTTO AND DOROTHEA KOLMEIER HOUSE

Date on lintel over front door. US Census, 1900, 1910, 1920. Sanborn, 1902, sheet 2; 1910, sheet 1; 1915, sheet 1. Kowert, *Old Homes*, 44–45 (Crenwelge).

29 ROBERT AND SELMA STRIEGLER HOUSE

Kowert, *Historic Homes*, 135–37. Sanborn, 1910, sheet 1; 1915, sheet 1.

30 GEORGE AND ELIZA WAHRMUND SHOP AND RESIDENCE

Kowert, *Old Homes*, 80–82. Sanborn, 1896, sheet 2; 1902, sheet 2; 1910, sheet 1; 1915, sheet 1. Historic photo, "Mrs. George Wahrmund's Millinery and Dressmaking Shop, Fredericksburg, Tex.," ITC-UTSA.

31 MAIER-STOFFER HOUSE

Kowert, *Old Homes*, 66–67. Sanborn, 1896, sheet 2; 1902, sheet 2; 1910, sheet 1; 1915, sheet 1.

32 NIMITZ HOTEL

Kowert, *Old Homes*, 196–99. *Pioneers* I, 148–49. John J. Leffler, "A Hill Country Icon: The Life and Legend of the Nimitz Hotel, Fredericksburg, Texas," study submitted to the Texas Parks and Wildlife Department, July 2005. Sanborn, 1896, sheet 2; 1902, sheet 2; 1910, sheet 1; 1915, sheet 1.

33 VICTOR AND CLARA KEIDEL HOUSE

Margaret Miller, "Schmidt Home Is Spanish classic," *Fredericksburg Post*, June 27, 1984, 15B. *Pioneers* I, 86–89 (Keidel). *Pioneers* II, 135–37 (Stein). Sanborn, 1896, sheet 2; 1902, sheet 2; 1910, sheet 1; 1915, sheet 1 (old Keidel house); 1924, sheet 2; 1938, sheet 2.

34 FRIEDRICH AND MARIA KIEHNE HOUSE

Kowert, *Old Homes*, 41–43. Penniger, *Fredericksburg*, 34. *Pioneers* I, 92–93. Property Tax Records, 1849–65. US Census, 1860, 1880. Sanborn, 1896, sheet 2; 1902, sheet 2; 1910, sheet 1; 1924 and 1938. Historic photograph by David R. Williams, in David Reicherd Williams (1890-1962) Photographs, Negatives, and Archival Records, UT-AAA. HABS, "Kiehne-Forster House, 405 East Main Street, Fredericksburg, Gillespie County, TX" (photographs only).

35 CARL AND MARGARETHE WEYRICH HOUSE

Kowert, *Old Homes*, 76–78. Property Tax Records, 1848–75. Sanborn, 1924, sheet 2.

36 AFRICAN METHODIST EPISCOPAL CHURCH

US Census, 1880. Kowert, *Historic Homes*, xiv.

37 HEINRICH AND ELISE OCHS HOUSE

Property Tax Records, 1868–78. Sanborn, 1896, sheet 1; 1902, sheet 1; 1910, sheet 3.
Kowert, *Old Homes,* 84–86 and 112–13.

38 WILLIAM AND ELISE WAHRMUND HOUSE

Kowert, *Historic Homes,* 80–82. Sanborn, 1896, sheet 1; 1902, sheet 1; 1910, sheet 3.

39 SCHWARZ BUILDING

Kowert, *Historic Homes,* 55–58. Mechanics Lien Record, vol. 1, 34–36.

40 SCHMIDT HOTEL

Kowert, *Old Homes,* 112–13. Sanborn, 1896, sheet 1; 1902, sheet 1; 1910, sheet 3. Historic
photo, "Louis Dietz's Central Hotel, Fredericksburg Texas," ITC-UTSA.

41 A. L. PATTON BUILDING

Kowert, *Old Homes,* 112–13.

42 HOERSTER-BLUM BUILDING

Kowert, *Historic Homes,* 22–30.

43 A. L. AND EMMA PATTON HOUSE

Kowert, *Old Homes,* 181–82. *Pioneers* II, 104–7. Sanborn, 1910, sheet 3.

44 WISSEMAN-GENTEMANN-HANISCH HOUSE

Kowert, *Old Homes,* 58–60. Property Tax Records, 1848–62. Sanborn, 1896, sheet 1;
1902, sheet 1; 1910, sheet 4; 1915, sheet 4.

45 MECKEL HOUSE / HANUS SANITARIUM / SISTERS OF DIVINE
PROVIDENCE CONVENT

Kowert, *Old Homes,* 118–20. Sanborn, 1896, sheet 1; 1902, sheet 1; 1910, sheet 4.

46 HEINRICH AND AUGUSTE KAMMLAH HOUSE

Sanborn, 1896, sheet 1; 1902, sheet 1; 1910, sheet 4; 1915, sheet 4; 1924, sheet 5.
Property Tax Records, 1848–74. HABS, "Heinrich Kammlah House, 309 West Main
Street, Fredericksburg, Gillespie County, TX" (photos and data pages only). Historic
photo, Daughters of the Republic of Texas Library, San Antonio. *Pioneers* I, 72–73.
Kowert, *Old Homes,* 6–8. Volz & Associates, Inc., "Kammlah House Historic Struc-
tures Report," Austin, 2007.

47 MATTHIAS AND MARIA FASSEL HOUSE

Property Tax Records, 1876–80. Sanborn, 1896, sheet 1; 1902, sheet 1; 1910, sheet 4;
1915, sheet 4; 1924, sheet 5. Kowert, *Old Homes,* 8–10.

48 AUGUST AND ALWINA WEBER SUNDAY HOUSE

Pioneers II, 151–54. Kowert, *Old Homes,* 11–12.

49 WHITE OAK SCHOOL

School Histories, 138–42.

50 ANNA BESIER HOUSE

Property Tax Records, 1876–92. Kowert, *Old Homes,* 28–29.

51 OSCAR KRAUSKOPF BUILDING

Sanborn, 1915, sheet 4. Kowert, *Old Homes,* 18–20.

52 ITZ HOTEL, SALOON, AND RESIDENCE

Property Tax Records, 1866–75. Sanborn, 1896, sheet 1; 1910, sheet 4; 1915, sheet 4. US
Census, 1880, 1900. Kowert, *Old Homes,* 21–23. Kowert, *Historic Homes,* 104–9.

53 AUGUST ITZ STORE

Sanborn, 1896, sheet 1; 1910, sheet 4; 1915, sheet 4. US Census, 1880, 1900, 1910, 1920,
1930, 1940.

54 LUDWIG AND PAULINA EVERS STORE AND RESIDENCE

Sanborn, 1896, sheet 1; 1910, sheet 4; 1915, sheet 4. Kowert, *Old Homes,* 24–25.

55 WILLIAM C. AND EMMA HENKE HOUSE

Sanborn, 1896, sheet 1; 1902, sheet 1; 1910, sheet 4. Kowert, *Old Homes,* 26–27.

56 GEORGE WILHELM AND SOPHIE CRENWELGE HOUSE

Sanborn, 1896, sheet 1; 1902, sheet 1; 1910, sheet 4; 1915, sheet 4; 1924, sheet 5. Kowert,
Old Homes, 44–45.

57 CRENWELGE RENT HOUSE

Sanborn, 1896, sheet 1; 1902, sheet 1; 1910, sheet 4; 1915, sheet 4; 1924, sheet 5. Kowert,
Old Homes, 46–47.

58 JOHANN AND SOPHIE SCHLAUDT HOUSE

US Census, 1920, 1940. Sanborn, 1896, sheet 1; 1902, sheet 1; 1910, sheet 4; 1915, sheet
4; 1924, sheet 5. Kowert, *Old Homes,* 47–49.

59 KRAUS BUILDING

US Census, 1880, 1900, 1910, 1920, 1930, 1940. Sanborn, 1896, sheet 1; 1902, sheet 1;
1910, sheet 4; 1915, sheet 4; 1924, sheet 5. Kowert, *Old Homes,* 50–53.

60 AND 61 ZION LUTHERAN PARSONAGE; ZION LUTHERAN CHURCH

Sanborn, 1896, sheet 1 (old church and old parsonage); 1902, sheet 1 (old church and
old parsonage); 1910, sheet 4 (new church and old parsonage); 1938, sheet 5 (new
parsonage). Penniger, *Fredericksburg,* 63, 91. *Pioneers* I, 8–10.

62 LOEFFLER-WEBER HOUSE

Property Tax Records, 1858–75. Kowert, *Old Homes,* 122–25.

63 HENRY AND AMALIA KAMMLAH RENT HOUSE

Kowert, *Old Homes,* 15–16. Property Tax Records, 1868–74. *Pioneers* II, 190.

64 GEORG AND CLARA PETER HOUSE

Property Tax Records, 1867–75. Kowert, *Old Homes,* 94–95.

65 JOHANN JOST AND ELISABETH KLINGELHOEFER HOUSE

Property Tax Records, 1848–75. Sanborn, 1924, sheet 6. *Pioneers* I, 94–95. Kowert, *Old
Homes,* 38–39.

66 FREDERICK AND HULDA WALTER HOUSE

US Census, 1880, 1910. Sanborn, 1924, sheet 6. Property Tax Records, 1893–1910.

67 LUDWIG AND CATHERINE SCHNEIDER HOUSE

Sanborn, 1915, sheet 5. Kowert, *Old Homes,* 36–37.

68 EMIL AND ALMA GOLD HOUSE

US Census, 1900, 1910, 1920, 1930. Mechanics Lien Record, vol. 1, 1–2. Kowert, *Historic Homes,* 48–50.

69 EMIL AND MATHILDA WEBER HOUSE

US Census, 1910, 1920, 1930, 1940. Texas Historical Commission marker.

Part 4. South of Main Street

70 MUELLER-PETMECKY HOUSE

Kirchen-Buch, 8, 15, 22, 28, 37, 48, 56, 72, 120. *Pioneers* II, 4–5 (Arhelger), 108–10 (Petmecky).

71 WILLIAM AND OLGA RAUSCH HOUSE

US Census, 1880, 1900, 1940; US Census, Bexar County, Texas, 1920. Property Tax Records, 1900–1910. Sanborn, 1902, sheet 2 (partial of Lungkwitz house); 1910, sheet 1; 1915, sheet 1; 1924, sheet 1 (all partial). Kowert, *Old Buildings,* 168–69.

72 SCHMIDT-GOLD HOUSE

US Census, 1870. Property Tax Records, 1866–75. *Pioneers* II, 238. Kowert, *Old Buildings,* 126–27

73 HEINRICH AND LOUISE MOELLERING HOUSE

Property Tax Records, 1877–80. *Pioneers* II, 225–26, 238. Kowert, *Old Buildings,* 128–29.

74 AUGUST AND WILHELMINE SCHMIDT HOUSE

US Census, 1870. Property Tax Records, 1850–69. Sanborn, 1924, sheet 6. Elise Kowert, "Architects Turn Old Home into 'Rehabilitated' Beauty," *Fredericksburg Standard-Radio Post,* October 22, 1986. Kowert, *Historic Homes,* 1–2.

75 STOFFERS-LOCHTE HOUSE

Kowert, *Historic Homes,* 82–84. Sanborn, 1910, sheet 2; 1915, sheet 2; 1924, sheet 2.

76 AND 77 HOLY GHOST LUTHERAN CHURCH PARSONAGE; HOLY GHOST LUTHERAN CHURCH

Penniger, *Fredericksburg,* 64–65. Sanborn, 1915, sheet 3. *Holy Ghost Lutheran Church* (dedication program, September 25, 1949), church archives.

78 AUGUST WILHELM AND CAROLINE JORDAN HOUSE

US Census, 1860. Property Tax Records, 1866–87. Sanborn, 1924, sheet 10.

79 CHRISTIAN AND FRANCISCA STEHLING HOUSE

Kowert, *Historic Homes,* 84–86.

80 AUGUST AND CAROLINE JORDAN HOUSE

Property Tax Records, 1885–87. *Pioneers* II, 209. Kowert, *Old Homes,* 30–32.

81 WILLIAM AND CAROLINA JORDAN HOUSE

Property Tax Records, 1868–75. Kowert, *Historic Homes,* 30–32.

82 ST. JOSEPH'S HALL

Sanborn, 1910, sheet 3; 1915, sheet 3. Gerlach, *Commemorative Volume,* 39. Kowert,
  Historic Homes, 143–45.

83 ST. MARY'S SCHOOL

School Histories, 47–45, 122–24. Sanborn, 1910, sheet 3; 1915, sheet 3 (Dangers house,
  nuns' house).

84 OLD ST. MARY'S CATHOLIC CHURCH

Sanborn, 1910, sheet 4. Gerlach, *Commemorative Volume,* 16, 19, 30–31. HABS, "Old St.
  Mary's Catholic Church, San Antonio Street, Fredericksburg, Gillespie County, TX."
  Kowert, *Historic Homes,* 19–21. *Building St. Mary's Parish, 1846–2012* (Fredericks-
  burg: St. Mary's Catholic Church, n.d.), 85–104.

85 ST. MARY'S CATHOLIC CHURCH

Sanborn, 1910, sheet 4. Gerlach, *Commemorative Volume,* 39–43. Ralph Edward New-
  lan, "Leo M. J. Dielmann: Ecclesiology and the Continuation of a German Gothic
  Architectural Tradition in Twentieth-Century Texas" (master's thesis, University of
  Texas at Austin, 1988), 80–86. *School Histories,* 122–24. Willard B. Robinson, "To
  the Glory of God: Texas Churches Designed by Leo M. J. Dielmann," *Journal of Texas
  Catholic History and Culture* 2 (March 1991): 26–53. *Building St. Mary's Parish,
  1846–2012* (Fredericksburg: St. Mary's Catholic Church, n.d.), 48, 64–66, 107–19.

86 METHODIST EPISCOPAL CHURCH

Sanborn, 1910, sheet 4. Biggers, *German Pioneers,* 187–88. Kowert, *Historic Homes,*
  17–18.

87 FRIEDRICH AND MARGARETHE GENTEMANN HOUSE

Property Tax Records, 1884–86. *Limestone and Log,* 68–69. Kowert, *Historic Homes,*
  2–3.

88 JOHN AND MATHILDA METZGER SUNDAY HOUSE

Sanborn, 1910, sheet 4; 1915, sheet 4; 1924, sheet 5. Property Tax Records, 1898–1909.
  Pioneers I, 132–34.

89 JOHN AND ANNA SPEIER HOUSE

Sanborn, 1910, sheet 4; 1915, sheet 4; 1924, sheet 5. Kowert, *Historic Homes,* 64–65.

90 JOHANN AND MARGARETHE WEIDENFELLER HOUSE

US Census, 1870, 1880, 1900, 1910. Sanborn, 1924, sheet 6.

91 HEINRICH AND ELIZA OCHS HOUSE

Kowert, *Old Homes,* 53–54.

92 METHODIST EPISCOPAL CHURCH, NORTH

Sanborn, 1915, sheet 5 (old church). *Pioneers* II, 61–63 (Kneese).

93 JOHANN AND LOUISE HOFFMANN HOUSE

US Census, 1880. Sanborn, 1924, sheet 6. Kowert, *Historic Homes,* 8–10.

94 CATHARINA LOTH HOUSE

Property Tax Records, 1854–88. Kowert, *Old Homes,* 144–46.

95 JOSEPH AND CATHERINE KOLLETT HOUSE

Gillespie County Miscellaneous Records, vol. A, part 1, 54–55. Kowert, *Old Homes,*
169–71.

96 MARTIN AND MARIA HEINEMANN HOUSE

US Census, 1870, 1880. Kowert, *Old Homes,* 183–85.

97 AND 98 PETER AND CAROLINE BONN HOUSE; ADOLF AND AUGUSTE
BONN HOUSE

US Census, 1860, 1870, 1880, 1900, 1910. Property Tax Records, 1868–75. *Pioneers* I,
269, 277. *Pioneers* II, 7–8, 191, 236. Kowert, *Old Homes,* 88–90.

99 JOHANN NIKOLAUS AND CAROLINE TATSCH HOUSE

Property Tax Records, 1853–75. Sanborn 1924, sheet 8. *Pioneers* II, 246. Kowert,
Historic Homes, 14–15.

100 EMIL NAGEL HOUSE

Property Tax Records, 1906–8. US Census, 1910, 1920, 1930, 1940 Sanborn, 1924, sheet
8. Cemetery Records, Der Stadt Friedhof, Fredericksburg.

101 PETER AND ELISABETH WUNDERLICH HOUSE

Property Tax Records, 1866–87. Sanborn, 1924, sheet 8. Kowert, *Old Buildings,* 154–56.

102 JOHN AND MARGARETHE RAULZ HOUSE

US Census, 1880. Property Tax Records, 1852–69. Sanborn 1924, sheet 8. Kowert, *Old
Buildings,* 172–73. Seth Eastman, *A Seth Eastman Sketchbook, 1848–49* (Austin:
University of Texas Press, 1961), 53, 55, 56.

103 GOEBEL-MECKEL-ROOS-WISSMER-STAUDT-JENSCHKE HOUSE

US Census 1860, 1870, 1880, 1900, 1910, 1920, 1940. Sanborn, 1924, sheet 8. Kowert,
Historic Homes, 5–6.

104 CHARLES AND IDA HOTOPP HOUSE

U.S. Census 1900, 1930, 1940. Sanborn 1924, sheet 8.

105 SOPHIE SPAETH HOUSE

Mechanics Lien Record, vol. 1, 42–43 (Joseph and Meta Klein house). Kowert, *Historic
Homes,* 6–8.

106 HENRY AND ELIZABETH KUENEMANN HOUSE

Property Tax Records, 1851–1910. US Census, 1860, 1870, 1880, 1910. Sanborn, 1910,
sheet 3; 1915, sheet 3; 1924, sheet 4. Texas State Historical Marker.

107 ADAM AND EVA KRIEGER HOUSE

HABS, "Staudt Sunday House, 512 West Creek Street, Fredericksburg, Gillespie County,
TX." Kowert, *Old Homes,* 154–56.

108 PETER AND ANNA MARGARET WALTER HOUSE

Property Tax Records, 1848–75. *Pioneers* II, 148–50. Kowert, *Old Homes,* 92–94.

109 FRIEDRICH AND SOPHIE BEHR HOUSE

Sanborn, 1938, sheet 6. Kowert, *Historic Homes,* 50–52.

110 AND 111 ANTON AND ANNA MARIA WEINHEIMER HOUSE; ARTHUR
AND ANNA DANZ HOUSE

US Census, 1920, 1930 (Danz). *Pioneers* II, 155–58. Kowert, *Historic Homes,* 25–27.

112 RUDOLPH AND HELENE MUELLER HOUSE

Kowert, *Historic Homes,* 13–14.

113 AND 114 KURT AND MARGARETA KEIDEL HOUSE; FELIX AND HATTIE
KEIDEL HOUSE

US Census, 1920, 1930, 1940. *Pioneers* I, 79–81, 90–91. *Pioneers* II, 53–54.

115 HEINRICH AND MARIE LEHNE HOUSE

Kowert, *Historic Homes,* 52–53.

116 AND 117 ADOLPH AND MARTHA WUNDERLICH LOG HOUSE; ADOLPH
AND MARTHA WUNDERLICH ROCK HOUSE

Property Tax Records, 1881–92. Kowert, *Old Homes,* 174–75.

118 RUDOLPH AND LOUISE ECKERT HOUSE

US Census, 1860, 1880, 1900, 1910, 1920. Kowert, *Historic Homes,* 76–79.

119 WILLIAM AND MARIA KLINGELHOEFER HOUSE

Historic photograph, "William Klingelhoefer House, Fredericksburg, Texas," ITC-UTSA.
Kowert, *Old Homes,* 131–32.

Part 5. North of Main Street

120 PETER AND THERESE SCHMITZ HOUSE

Kowert, *Old Buildings,* 34–36.

121 JOHN J. AND WILHELMINE WALCH HOUSE

Property Tax Records, 1849–74. Sanborn, 1924, sheet 11. Historic photograph, "Walch
House, Fredericksburg, Texas," ITC-UTSA. Kowert, *Old Homes,* 156–58.

122 JULIUS AND MINA BROCKMANN HOUSE

Property Tax Records, 1871–74. US Census, 1880. Sanborn, 1924, sheet 3. Kowert, *Historic Homes,* 3–5.

123 JOHN AND BERTHA SCHANDUA HOUSE

Kowert, *Old Homes,* 74–75.

124 FRIEDRICH WILHELM AND ANNA MARIE ELIZABETH SCHUMACHER
HOUSE

Limestone and Log, 64–65. Kowert, *Old Homes,* 90–92.

125 HEINRICH AND WILHELMINE CORDES HOUSE

US Census, 1860, 1880, 1900, 1920. Kowert, *Old Homes,* 129–30 (Cordes), 92 (Schumacher). Sanborn, 1924. Measured floor plan, "Unidentified House, Town Creek &

Crockett Street," 1971, University of Texas at Austin, School of Architecture, Texas Architecture Archive, UT-AAA.

126 HEINRICH AND MARGARETE BIERSCHWALE HOUSE

Sanborn, 1910, sheet 3. *Pioneers* I, 3–4. Kowert, *Old Homes*, 140–42. H. Bierschwale account book (private collection of Bierschwale family).

127 JOHN AND MARIA WALTER HOUSE

Property Tax Records, 1867–75. US Census, 1880. Kowert, *Historic Homes*, 21–23.

128 CHRISTIAN AND KATHERINA STRACKBEIN HOUSE

Property Tax Records, 1872–82. Julius E. DeVos, *The Eckert's Golden Opportunity* (Mason: J. E. DeVos, 1977), 38–41. Kowert, *Historic Homes,* 75–76.

129 ELISE VOGEL SUNDAY HOUSE

Kowert, *Historic Homes,* 102–4. Property Tax Records 1887–1910. US Census, 1860 (Vogel and Weber), 1880, 1910.

130 HENRY AND SOPHIE ELLEBRACHT HOUSE

Property Tax Records, 1867–1910. US Census, 1880. Kowert, *Old Homes,* 195–99.

131 H. E. AND AUGUSTA WAHRMUND HOUSE

US Census, 1910, 1920, 1940. Gravestones, Greenwood Cemetery, Fredericksburg.

132 JOHN PETER AND MARIA ELIZABETH TATSCH HOUSE

HABS, "John Peter Tatsch House, 210 North Bowie Street, Fredericksburg, Gillespie County, TX." Historic photos, "Exterior of Peter Tatsch House, Fredericksburg, Texas" and "John Tatsch and Daughter, Caroline Tatsch, in Front of His Stone House, Fredericksburg, Tex." ITC-UTSA. Sanborn, 1924, sheet 7. Biggers, *German Pioneers,* 96–98. Kowert, *Old Homes,* 5–6.

133 MAX AND LYDIA BIERSCHWALE HOUSE

US Census, 1920, 1930. *Pioneers* I, 3–4. Personal communication, Sharon Joseph, May 28, 2014.

134 LAWRENCE H. AND META KRAUSKOPF HOUSE

Pioneers I, 107–8.

135 ANTON AND CATHARINA KUNZ HOUSE

Property Tax Records, 1872–75. Kowert, *Historic Homes,* 33–34.

136 WILLIAM AND LINA BIERSCHWALE HOUSE

US Census, 1880. *Pioneers* I, 3–4. Mary Carolyn Hollers George, *Alfred Giles: An English Architect in Texas and Mexico* (San Antonio: Trinity University Press, 1972), 38–39. Kowert, *Old Homes,* 116–18.

137 WILLIAM AND ANNA KUNZ HOUSE

Kowert, *Historic Homes,* 132–34.

138 A. W. AND HENRIETTA MOURSUND HOUSE

Property Tax Records, 1888–1909. Kowert, *Old Homes,* 176–78. Associated Press, "Commission Quietly Doubles Size of LBJ Park," *Austin American,* January 1965 (photocopy), Texas Parks and Wildlife Department archives, Austin.

139 ST. MARY CATHOLIC CEMETERY

Jordan, *Texas Graveyards*, 89–122, esp. 96, 115, 123. *Building St. Mary's Parish, 1846-2012* (Fredericksburg: St. Mary's Catholic Church, n.d.), 177–83.

140 DER STADT FRIEDHOF

Plan von Friedrichsburg, 1846, in Penniger, *Fredericksburg*, 109. Jordan, *Texas Graveyards*, 89–122. *Cemetery Records of Der Stadt Friedhof, Fredericksburg, Texas: A Texas State Historical Cemetery, 1846-2002* (Fredericksburg: City Cemetery Association, 2002).

141 HAHN-BURGDORF HOUSE

US Census, 1860, 1870, 1880, 1900, 1910, 1920. *Kirchen-Buch*, 110. Property Tax Records, 1869–1900. Sanborn, 1924, sheet 11. Kowert, *Historic Homes*, 73–74 (Burgdorf) and 46–48 (Hahne). *Pioneers* II, 198 (Eckert) and 203 (Hahn).

142 JOHANN FRIEDRICH AND DOROTHEA KNEESE HOUSE

Property Tax Records, 1875, 1882. *Pioneers* II, 61. Kowert, *Historic Homes*, 86–89.

143 CHARLES AND ANNA JUNG HOUSE

Kowert, *Old Homes*, 185–88.

144 THEODORE AND MATHILDE LANGERHANS HOUSE

Kowert, *Historic Homes*, 189–91. Kowert, *Historic Homes*, xiv.

145 GOTTLOB AND CHRISTIANE FISCHER HOUSE

Property Tax Records, 1867–74. Kowert, *Old Homes*, 190–92.

146 JULIUS AND SOPHIE SPLITTGERBER HOUSE

Property Tax Records, 1851–69. Sanborn, 1924, sheet 9. Kowert, *Historic Homes*, 11–12.

147 CHRISTIAN AND ELIZABETH CRENWELGE HOUSE

Historic photographs, "Christian Crenwelge House, Fredericksburg, Texas," ITC-UTSA. Kowert, *Old Homes*, 162–92.

148 JOHANN JOSEPH AND KATHARINA KNOPP HOUSE

Property Tax Records, 1872–75. Historic photographs, "Johann Joseph Knopp House, Fredericksburg, Texas," ITC-UTSA and UT-AAA. Kowert, *Old Homes*, 159–62.

149 ADOLPH AND AUGUSTE GOLD HOUSE

US Census, 1900. Sanborn, 1924, sheet 11.

150 SCHMITT-HENKE HOUSE

Kowert, *Old Homes*, 146–47.

151 AND 152 METHODIST COLLEGE / PUBLIC SCHOOL / OLD GRAMMAR SCHOOL; OLD HIGH SCHOOL

Sanborn, 1915, sheet 1, 1938, sheet 9. US Census, 1880. Penniger, *Fredericksburg*, 58, 93. Kowert, *Old Homes*, 1, 45.

153 FRANZ AND AGNES STEIN HOUSE

Sanborn, 1902, sheet 1; 1910, sheet 1. *Pioneers* I, 199–202. *Pioneers* II, 135–37. "1882 and 1939 Gillespie County Courthouses, Fredericksburg, Texas," report prepared by Wagner and Klein, Inc., July 3, 2000; copy courtesy of Sharon Joseph. Personal communication, Sharon Joseph, May 28, 2014.

154 JOSEPH AND ELLA STEIN HOUSE

Pioneers I, 199–202.

155 ROBERT AND MARIA JENSCHKE SUNDAY HOUSE

Property Tax Records, 1900–1909. Kowert, *Historic Homes,* 42–43.

156 WILLIAM AND CORA HABENICHT HOUSE

US Census, 1940. *Pioneers* II, 37, 147. Personal communication, Elizabeth Brookshire,
    June 10, 2014.

157 GOLD-GROBE HOUSE

US Census, 1910, 1940. Sanborn, 1924, sheet 11. Texas Historical Commission marker.

158 WALTER H. AND HELEN KOLMEIER HOUSE

US Census, 1930, 1940. Gillespie County Historical Society, *Gillespie County* (Mount
    Pleasant, SC: Arcadia Publishing, 2013), 62.

159 OUR LADY OF GUADALUPE CATHOLIC CHURCH

Gerlach, *Commemorative Volume,* 43–44. *Building St. Mary's Parish, 1846–2012,* 121–
    23. St. Mary's Catholic Church, "Our Lady of Guadalupe Catholic Church," http://
    church.stmarysfbg.com/about-stmarys/olg.cfm, accessed March 2, 2012.

160 JOSEPH WILSON AND RUTH HUFFMAN BAINES HOUSE

US Census, 1870, 1900. Property Tax Records, 1905–8. Rebekah Baines Johnson, *A
    Family Album,* ed. John S. Moursund (New York: McGraw-Hill, 1965). Texas Histor-
    ical Commission marker. David Minor, "Baines, Joseph Wilson," *Handbook of Texas
    Online,* http://www.tshaonline.org/handbook/online/articles/fba15, accessed August
    27, 2014.

161 WALTER AND LILLIE BIERSCHWALE HOUSE

US Census, 1920, 1930. *Pioneers* I, 3–4. Personal communication, Sharon Joseph, May
    28, 2014.

162 EMIL AND BERTHA RILEY HOUSE

Mechanics Lien Record, vol. 1, 3–5.

163 MORITZ-HITZFELD-JACOBY HOUSE

US Census, 1910, 1920, 1930, 1940. Sanborn, 1938, sheet 7. Texas State Historical Marker.

164 EDWARD AND MINNIE STEIN HOUSE

Construction blueprints by Edward Stein, collection of Claude and Lisa Saunders.
    Pioneers II, 135–37.

Part 6. *Gillespie County*

165 PETER AND CAROLINE BONN HOUSE

US Census, 1860. Kowert, *Historic Homes,* 149–52. Kowert, *Old Homes,* 88–90.
    Kirchen-Buch, 109.

166 MEUSEBACH CREEK SCHOOL

School Histories, 61–74.

167 GUENTHER-LORENZ-HILKER COMPLEX

Property Tax Records, 1853–1900. US Census, 1880. [Elise Kowert], "Major Mill Grew
from Home on Live Oak," *Fredericksburg Standard*, March 13, 1957, sec 2, pp. 1, 6, 7.
Carl Hilmar Guenther, *An Immigrant Miller Picks Texas: The Letters of Carl Hilmar
Guenther*, trans. Regina Beckmann Hurst and Walter D. Kamphoefner (San Antonio:
Maverick Publishing Company, 2001), 37–68.

168 HENRY AND BERTHA BASSE HOUSE

Pioneers I, 8–10. US Census, 1910, 1920, 1930. Gravestone, Der Stadt Friedhof,
Fredericksburg.

169 HEINRICH AND CONRADINE BAETHGE HOUSE

Kowert, *Historic Homes*, 129–31.

170 CHERRY MOUNTAIN SCHOOL

School Histories, 18–24. *Kirchen-Buch*, 44 (Emma Ruegner's date of birth). "Durst
House," Texas Historical Commission marker.

171 RODE-KOTHE HOUSE

Pioneers II, 71–76, 115–17. HABS, "Rode-Kothe House, East of U.S. 87 at Cherry Spring,
Cherry Spring, Gillespie County, TX." Kowert, *Historic Homes*, 170–79.

172 CHRIST LUTHERAN CHURCH

F. A. Bracher, "Evangelical Lutheran Christ Church, Cherry Spring," in Biggers, *German
Pioneers*, 207–8, 225.

173 CHERRY SPRING SCHOOL

School Histories, 25–29.

174 LANGE'S MILL

Drury Blakeley Alexander and Todd Webb, *Texas Homes of the Nineteenth Century*
(Austin: University of Texas Press, 1966), 241 and plate 50. *Pioneers* I, 197. Martin
Donnell Kohout, "Doss, TX (Gillespie County)," *Handbook of Texas Online*, http://
www.tshaonline.org/handbook/online/articles/hnd34, accessed January 22, 2014.
Vivian Elizabeth Smyrl, "Lange's Mill, TX," *Handbook of Texas Online*, http://www.
tshaonline.org/handbook/online/articles/hvl94, accessed January 22, 2014.

75 ST. PETER LUTHERAN CHURCH

Die Heilsgeschichte: The Story of St. Peter Lutheran Church (Fredericksburg: Dietel &
Son, 1996), 29–35. F. A. Bracher, "Evangelical Lutheran St. Peters Church, Doss," in
Biggers, *German Pioneers*, 206–7.

176 AND 177 OLD DOSS SCHOOL; NEW DOSS SCHOOL

School Histories, 38–41, 54–56.

178 CHARLES AND MARANDA ROBERTS HOUSE

US Census, 1900, 1910, 1940. Property Tax Records, 1900–1910. *School Histories*,

54–55. Recorded Texas Historic Landmark historical marker. "Oldest Harper House Revived," *Kerrville Daily Times*, November 30, 1986, Hill Country and TV Listings section, pp. 1–3 and 31; Reverend A. A. Gitter, "The Baumann House," typescript of presentation at dedication of historical marker, September 12, 1987, collection of Susan (Baumann) Koch. "1st Historic Marker in Harper Presented to Baumann House," *Harper Herald*, September 18, 1987, 1. Personal communication, Susan (Baumann) Koch, August 30 and August 31, 2014.

179 ST. JAMES LUTHERAN CHURCH
F. A. Bracher, "Evangelical Lutheran St. James Church, Harper," in Biggers, *German Pioneers*, 210–11, 225. Gerlach, *Commemorative Volume*, 61, 63–64 (St. Anthony Catholic Church).

180 PILOT KNOB SCHOOL
School Histories, 107–10.

181 WELGEHAUSEN RANCH
Kowert, *Historic Homes*, 58–64.

182 ST. JOHN LUTHERAN CHURCH
F. A. Bracher, "Evangelical Lutheran St. John's Church, Crab Apple," in Biggers, *German Pioneers*, 203–4.

183 AND 184 CRABAPPLE TEACHERAGE; CRABAPPLE SCHOOL
School Histories, 30–37.

185 WILLOW CITY SCHOOL
School Histories, 143–46.

186 JAMES CALLOWAY HARDIN AND LAURA HARDIN HOUSE
US Census, 1880, 1910, 1930, 1940. Personal communication, Mike Gold, June 28, 2014, and August 9, 2014.

187 RHEINGOLD SCHOOL
School Histories, 111–16.

188 CAVE CREEK SCHOOL
School Histories, 10–17.

189 ST. PAUL LUTHERAN CHURCH
Jordan, *Texas Graveyards*, 108–9.

190 FORT MARTIN SCOTT
Kowert, *Historic Homes*, 179–88. Kowert, *Historic Homes*, xiii–xiv. *Pioneers* II, 9–11. US Census, 1850.

191 GRAPETOWN TEACHERAGE AND SCHOOL
School Histories, 51–53.

192 CHARLES AND LOUISE ENDERLIN HOUSE
Kowert, *Historic Homes*, 121–25.

193 AND 194 LUCKENBACH GENERAL STORE; LUCKENBACH DANCE HALL
Property Tax Records, 1886–1910. *Limestone and Log*, 58–59. Jerry Jeff Walker, *Viva*

Terlingua (MCA Records, 1973), album cover and liner notes. Jan Reid, *The Improbable Rise of Redneck Rock* (Austin: Heidelberg Publishers, 1974), 93–118. Becky Crouch Patterson, *Hondo, My Father* (Austin: Shoal Creek Publishers, 1979). Glen E. Lich and Brandy Schnautz, "Luckenbach, TX," *Handbook of Texas Online*, http://www.tshaonline.org/handbook/online/articles/hnl48, accessed March 2, 2014. Personal communication, Ora Ann Knopp, April 21, 2014.

195 WILLIAM AND ANNA ENGEL HOUSE

Property Tax Records, 1886–1910. Texas Historical Commission marker. Personal communication, Benno W. Engel Jr., April 25, 2014. Personal communication, Della Pohler, May 9, 2014.

196 LUCKENBACH SCHOOL

School Histories, 77–79.

197 WILLIAMS CREEK (ALBERT) SCHOOL

Texas Historical Commission marker. *Limestone and Log*, 42–43. Rebekah Baines Johnson to Miss Flora Eckert, July 11, 1992, in *Letters from the Hill Country: The Correspondence Between Rebekah and Lyndon Baines Johnson*, ed. Philip R. Rulon (Austin: Thorp Springs Press, 1982), 15. *Pioneers* II, 18–19.

198 FERDINAND AND AUGUSTA MAYER HOUSE

Marian L. Martinello, *The Search for Emma's Story* (Fort Worth: Texas Christian University Press, 1987), 29–31.

199 LOWER SOUTH GRAPE CREEK SCHOOL

Texas Historical Commission marker.

200 HEINRICH AND JOHANNE LINDIG HOUSE

Personal communication, Bernice Weinheimer, April 2014. *Kirchen-Buch*, 155. Kay K. Huffman, "Descendants of Christian Heinrich Peter Lindig," http://familytreemaker. genealogy.com/users/h/u/f/Kay-K-Huffman/GENE1-0001.html, accessed May 20, 2014.

201 HEINRICH AND ANNA JACOBY HOUSE

Property Tax Records, 1870–1910. US Census, 1880, 1900. *Limestone and Log*, 50–51.

202 TRINITY LUTHERAN CHURCH

HABS, "Evangelical Lutheran Church, Congregation of the Trinity, Ranch Road 1 at Lower Albert Road, Stonewall, Gillespie County, TX." Marian L. Martinello, *The Search for Emma's Story* (Fort Worth: Texas Christian University Press, 1987), 26–29.

203 EMERY AND MATTIE HODGES HOUSE

US Census, 1900, 1920, 1930. Property Tax Records, 1885–1909. Associated Press, "Commission Quietly Doubles Size of LBJ Park," *Austin American*, January 1965 (photocopy), Texas Parks and Wildlife Department archives, Austin. Personal communication, Iris Neffendorf, Park Superintendent, Lyndon B. Johnson State Park and Historic Site, April 21, 2014. Measured drawings of the Hodges Home, October

17, 1975, Texas Parks and Wildlife Department archives, Austin. Personal communication, Stephanie Loden, Curator, Texas Parks and Wildlife Department, April 17, 2014 and April 23, 2014. *Limestone and Log*, 30–33. *School Histories*, 64–65.

204, 205, 206, AND 207 CASPAR AND DOROTHEA DANZ HOUSE; HEINRICH CHRISTIAN AND WILHELMINA BEHRENS HOUSE; FRIEDRICH AND CHRISTINE SAUER HOUSE; EMIL AND EMMA BECKMANN HOUSE

Limestone and Log, 34–37. Marian L. Martinello, *The Search for Emma's Story* (Fort Worth: Texas Christian University Press, 1987). Kowert, *Historic Homes*, 99–101. *Pioneers* II, 120–21.

208 JUNCTION SCHOOL

HABS, "Lyndon B. Johnson Ranch, Junction School, Ranch Road 49 at Reagan Road, Stonewall, Gillespie County, TX." *School Histories*, 61–74.

209 AND 210 RECONSTRUCTED LBJ BIRTHPLACE; LBJ RANCH HOUSE

HABS, "Lyndon B. Johnson Ranch, House, Park Road 49, Stonewall, Gillespie County, TX." Edwin C. Bearss, "Historic Structure Report: The Texas White House, Lyndon B. Johnson National Historical Park, Texas" (Santa Fe: National Park Service, 1986). Kowert, *Historic Homes*, 89–99. Hal K. Rothman, *LBJ's Texas White House: "Our Heart's Home"* (College Station: Texas A&M University Press, 2001).

Index